Praise for this book

"When America's early history was written, the West was ignored. Most of the West was either under France or Mexico or unknown. After the Louisiana Purchase and the Mexican War, many historians still overlooked the West while many Americans were migrating there for adventure, seeking fortune or to breathe. Robert Baron masterfully corrects this neglect in *The Light Shines from the West*. He weaves the history of the First Peoples and the role women, politics, migration, and the economy have played in this dynamic, vital half of our country. A MUST read!"

—Patricia Schroeder
Former Congresswoman, Colorado (1973-1997)
Former CEO, Association of American Publishers (1997-2008)

"I wish this important and magnificent book had existed sixty years ago when I first arrived in the West. Although I have always been interested in cultural history, I had not come across a book about the western region's unique history and influence on American thought that Baron's book provides. It is the insightful overview that I had long hoped to find. Segments of it were awesome, wonderful surprises; especially astonishing is the chapter, "Women the West". I predict the book will be popular and have a very strong positive effect over time.

—Huey D. Johnson
Founder, Resource Renewal Institute

"Robert Baron and his contributors have created a lively and fascinating book that explores the centrality of the West in the intellectual, cultural, and political life of the nation. Beyond creating the physical attributes of the United States, the exploration and settlement of the West has infused our collective imagination, and helped define what it means to be American."

James David Moran
Vice President for Programs and Outreach
American Antiquarian Society

"A powerful scholar and storyteller fits the American West into the American mosaic."

—Dick Lamm
Former Governor of Colorado
Author of *Brave New World of Health Care*

"*The Light Shines from the West* paints the wonderfully complex, historic story of the American West by integrating social, economic, cultural, environmental and political perspectives into a fascinating and needed understanding of everyone's West. I greatly enjoyed the read, and the various approaches to the American West."

—John L. Gray
Director, Smithsonian American History Museum.

"The section on the 'Women of the West' highlights how little recognition is given to these trail-blazing women who were the backbone of the family and their communities. They developed many important institutions such as hospitals, civil rights organizations and churches. Hard work unimaginable to most people today was the unifying experience for women in the vast open spaces of the American West. As a result, there is a formidable list of firsts, such as the first female Supreme Court Justice, Sandra Day O'Connor, and the first woman in space, Sally Rice. The unifying strength of all the women who lived in the American West was fierce fortitude and independence of spirit augmented by a backdrop of immense possibility. They were indeed trailblazers."

—Lee Everding
Director, Denver Eclectics

"*The Light Shines from the West* is one of the most interesting and thorough accounts of the westward development of the American nation that it has ever been my pleasure to read. With clear, well documented, and often poetic prose, it tells not only the well-known part of this epic story, but also the small, significant personal stories that are usually neglected. It is a history book that is as fascinating as a well-constructed novel. While it's strong throughout, as a person of native ancestry I found the third chapter on Native Americans written by Daniel Wildcat particularly gratifying. I believe it to be the best summary of what Western expansion really meant—and still means—to the original people of this continent. I hope this book will find its way not only into every library but also into our high school and college classrooms. There has never been a time in our history when a book such as this has been more needed."

—Dr. Joseph Bruchac
Author of *Our Stories Remember*

"A MUST read for anyone interested in understanding the enduring impact of the west on the American experience, *The Light Shines form the West: A Western Perspective on the Growth of America* by Robert C. Baron is an intelligent, comprehensive, interpretive collection of the numerous diversely penetrating influences of the region on the history and future of the United States. It is destined to become major source material about the American West and our country in general."

—Bobby Bridger
Songwriter, playwright
Author of *Buffalo Bill and Sitting Bull: Inventing the Wild West*

"The breathtaking landscape of the North American West is so powerful that it has led to the development of a unique human culture that transcends national boundaries and is deeply attached to place. The fascinating essays in this volume shine a light of understanding on the West and the people, both indigenous and immigrant, who have called it home for a long time."

—Harvey Locke
Founder, Yellowstone to Yukon Coalition
Co-Founder, Nature Needs Half Movement

"*The Light Shines from the West* offers a multi-authored overview of the history of the United States from the perspective of the West. Its publication coincides with renewed academic interest in national history from a western perspective, and this book offers a text for students and lay readers with a broad chronological span and a novel approach which will stimulate a very different appreciation of the American story."

—Andrew O'Shaunessey
Vice President, Thomas Jefferson Foundation
Author of *The Men Who Lost America*

"At a time when the President is withdrawing protection from two Utah National Monuments, including sacred tribal sites, and Congress is turning the Arctic National Wildlife Refuge over for unnecessary oil exploitation, *The Light Shines from the West: A Western Perspective on the Growth of America* reminds us of the unique legacy of the American West and its people."

—Larry J. Schweiger
Former President, National Wildlife Federation
Author of *Last Chance*

The *Light Shines from the West* presents western history like light through a prism that casts western history, its people and events with different understanding. Jefferson's view of the potential of the West, while competing elements of Spanish French, English and Russian interests were growing at the same time, foreshadows the future of the United States with opportunity not seen through traditional studies of Jefferson's Louisiana Purchase.

This prism casts the western migrating people wanting to go west for farmland, gold, and new lives. Railroads are born of the need for transportation drawn by a growth in the west to bring supplies and needed resources, both material and human. It speaks to the different view of women's work and roles in settling the west versus their counterparts whom they left behind in the east. This prism views the Native American Indians as First People and the white man as the immigrant, changing and abandoning their traditions and ways of life.

This prism shines a different light on women's rights emerging in the west, political thought and the country's economic future being influenced by the hardy people who dared to take on new challenges. Through the prism we see our western history as a fundamental element of the future of this country.

—Ed Nichols
Former CEO, History Colorado
State Historic Preservation Office

"This is a transformative book: one which will likely cause readers to take another, deeper, look at this most special, vast and beautiful, region we call home. There is out there a most special region which we call the West, a unique place. It is something different, perhaps most specially in the innate outlook and approach to life. This book persuasively tells us how these special qualities evolved among those who became Westerners, especially in periodic waves of new ideas—new thinking about social justice, greater protection for our lands, expansion of women's rights, all of which have been passed on to and shared with the whole nation.

This book is a must read for anyone who seriously hopes to gain a better understanding about just what is this whole entity we call the West? Having read it, I know that I will never think about the West the same way ever again."

Brock Evans
President, Endangered Species Coalition

The
Light Shines
from the
West

By Robert C. Baron

Books
Wilderness in America (screenplay)
Heaven and Nature Sing: Land, Wilderness, and Writers
Conversations on Conservation – 106 Video Interviews
Four Children from Baden
Journey to the Mountaintop: On Living and Meaning
Pioneers and Plodders: The American Entrepreneurial Spirit
Hudson: The Story of a River
What Was It Like Orville? Observations on the Early Space Program
Footprints on the Sands of Time
Twentieth Century America: Key Events in History
20th Century America: One Hundred Influential People
Colorado Rockies: The Inaugural Season
Digital Logic and Computer Operations
Microelektronik 1, 2, and 3
Micropower Electronics

Editor with Contributing Essay
*The Libraries, Leadership, and Legacy of John Adams
and Thomas Jefferson*
Thomas Jefferson: In His Own Words
John Adams: In His Own Words
Thomas Hornsby Ferril and the American West
Thoreau's World and Ours: A Natural Legacy
Soul of America: Documenting Our Past, Volume I: 1492–1974
Soul of America: Documenting Our Past, Volume 2: 1858–1993
The Mountains of California
The Garden and Farm Books of Thomas Jefferson
*Of Discovery and Destiny: An Anthology of America's Writers
and the American Land*
America: One Land, One People – Noted Historians Look at America

The

Light Shines

from the

West

A Western Perspective
on the
Growth of America

Robert C. Baron

Fulcrum Publishing
Golden, Colorado

Library of Congress Cataloging-in-Publication Data

Names: Baron, Robert C., author.
Title: The light shines from the West : a Western perspective on the growth of America / Robert C. Baron.
Other titles: Western perspective on the growth of America
Description: Golden, CO : Fulcrum Publishing, [2018] | Includes bibliographical references and index.
Identifiers: LCCN 2017061864 | ISBN 9781682751640
Subjects: LCSH: West (U.S.)--History. | West (U.S.)--Civilization. | West (U.S.)--Discovery and exploration. | United States--Territorial expansion.
Classification: LCC F591 .B265 2018 | DDC 978--dc23
LC record available at https://lccn.loc.gov/2017061864

Printed in the United States of America
0 9 8 7 6 5 4 3 2 1

Fulcrum Publishing
4690 Table Mountain Dr., Ste. 100
Golden, CO 80403
800-992-2908 • 303-277-1623
fulcrum.bookstore.ipgbook.com

Contents

Preface

by Peter, Newell, Gertie, Pat, and Melanie Grant

The Light Shines from the West is a new and thoughtful slant on the history of America. Our nation's past provides fertile ground for different perspectives, opposing views, and continuing reinterpretations, and *The Light* helps us to understand the issues and conflicts that beset all of us in the twenty-first century.

We have been asked to write the preface to this ambitious and wholly illuminating treatise about the American West. Certain themes present common threads that have guided our family—and indeed many westerners—through the years: try to do what is right, work hard, provide for family, be honest, respect our fellow beings, and work to better our communities. In the truest sense, however, the Grants have persevered and overcome our challenges—our family history represents a microcosm of the migration, hardships, and ongoing development of the West to this day in many of its myriad dimensions, whether in mining, the law, medicine, railroads, finance, politics, or public service.

Judge James Grant was of signature stature and achievement in many professional and business activities for his time. His community activities, political leadership, and family support give guidance to all of us even today. Born in North Carolina in 1812, he moved to Chicago to escape the ravages of slavery and build a new life; he then migrated to Davenport, Iowa. The judge remains a symbol of the social and cultural convolution around the issue of slavery besetting the country: the early to mid- and late-nineteenth century migration west, and its growing industrialization. Judge Grant proved to be brilliant in the practice of railroad law and was involved in the formation of the Rock Island Railroad and its building tracks to the frontier, and he was equally well regarded for helping write the Iowa Constitution and bill of rights. Becoming an Iowa district court judge was only one of his roles.

After the Civil War, the judge and his wife cared for and educated some seventeen nephews and nieces from the Deep South; he sent them—both nephews and nieces—wherever they could get an education and start a new life. One became governor of Colorado, another a surgeon general of Colorado, and still another the first US attorney for the Territory of Alaska. Later, on a visit west to Colorado, Judge Grant helped his nephew, James, start and finance a smelter in Leadville, Colorado, then overcome a devastating fire, and ultimately relocate to Denver to continue serving the burgeoning mining industry in the early years of Colorado's statehood. James Grant became the first Democratic governor of Colorado.

In Judge Grant alone are captured many shared challenges and successes of men and women who overcame their own hardships in migrating to the western frontier; his business achievements are illustrative, however, of the West's flourishing growth. We are part of his legacy, if not by bloodline, then through impact and emphasis on the lasting value of education for the next generations of American citizenry.

His legacy also includes Dr. William West Grant who, in the field of medicine, performed the first appendectomy in the Rocky Mountain West and thereby manifests innovative steps in improving the health of early day pioneers. In turn his son, William West Grant Jr., known as Will "Pop" Grant, became a respected lawyer in the law firm of Grant, Shafroth, and Toll. A strong and vocal opponent of the Ku Klux Klan in the 1920s, he also ran for mayor of Denver in 1934, albeit unsuccessfully. In the late 1930s, isolationist sentiment against further involvement in European conflicts and the pending war was sweeping the country; Pop Grant took the unpopular stand of actively supporting Great Britain and its preparation for war, for which he was awarded the Order of the British Empire by Great Britain.

Will Grant's wife was the statuesque Gertrude Hendrie, the only daughter of one of Colorado's most successful manufacturing entrepreneurs of the early twentieth century, Edwin B. Hendre. Their children were Ned Grant, Bill Grant, and Melanie Grant Lambert. Melanie married an Englishman and their offspring are making names for themselves in England to this very day. Ned and Bill and their wives and children have perpetuated the theme of leadership in a wide array of involvements, including television and radio, banking, cattle ranching, real estate development, neighborhood and community service, art, finance, and preservation of our western way of life, including open lands.

Growing recognition and appreciation for the role of women in shouldering the vicissitudes of the migration west and addressing the inequalities of opportunity characterize twentieth and twenty-first century western America. The Grant family reflects this cultural shift as well: women in the Grant family have become seriously committed and known in their own chosen career or profession or volunteer fields. The Grant family women have succeeded admirably. They mirror an ongoing social/economic trend showing active participation and leadership in many endeavors.

We are taken by the vision and the theme in this enlightening book. We hope this will lead to more understanding of the dynamics of our western history and make us better citizens for it.

Introduction

by Robert C. Baron

Eastward I go only by force, but westward I go free.
—**Henry David Thoreau**[1]

Why did we become what we are and not something else? Or, as a smaller question, why did the American political experiment establish the shape it has maintained? Or, as a much smaller one, why does the United States consist of just the land area the map now shows: why are there not two or more nations in that area, why does it not include parts or all of Canada or Mexico?
—**Bernard DeVoto**[2]

Much of world history is written east to west—from Greece to Rome to France and England, then across the ocean to Massachusetts, Pennsylvania, and Virginia, and quickly over the plains and mountains to the promised land of Southern California. Minnesota, Wisconsin, Iowa, Idaho, Nebraska, Kansas, Colorado, and Utah are merely footnotes in this northeastern view of American history.

Yet history could be written north and south. The Canadian Maritimes share much with New England. British Columbia has much in common with the state of Washington, as does Montana with Saskatchewan. They are closer in history, climate, the movement of people, and values than either to the distant east. Mexico shares a common history and people with the American Southwest—with Texas, New Mexico, Arizona, and Southern California. History could be told from this vantage point as well.

For the past century, the story of America should be told west to east. Most innovation, growth, and ideas have come from the west. The ocean of commerce is now the Pacific and not the Atlantic. America has far more riding on developments in the Pacific Rim than back in England, France, Germany, and Greece.

Why this East Coast and Eurocentric view of American history? It is partially because the sliver of America between Massachusetts and Virginia has been home to many historians. Western history, like women's history, has been judged less important than colonial history or Civil War history. It is also because publishers, residing in Manhattan and Boston, have assumed that nothing of importance occurred beyond the Alleghenies. Some still believe that the river dividing America in two is the Hudson and not the Mississippi.

The East has frequently believed that the West only exists for its economic and environmental benefit. But does it?

An alternative view of America is one reason for this book. The American story could be told in two chapters: 1607 to 1829, and 1820 to 2018. The first part is eastern centered—settlement for a century and then increased power for the next 100 years. Independence was won by the eastern colonies, and all presidents from 1789 until 1829 were from Virginia and Massachusetts. The period from 1820 until today, however, is western oriented, with a century of settlements followed by western political and economic leadership. This book addresses that story.

A second reason for this book is to build on Bernard DeVoto's essay "West: A Plundered Province" first published in *Harper's Magazine* in August 1934, and three important books: DeVoto's *Across the Wide Missouri*, Richard Lamm and Michael McCarthy's *The Angry West*, and Patty Limerick's *The Legacy of Conquest*.

When traveling to Europe or Asia, most people do not consider the history or current status of Philadelphia, Cleveland, Detroit, or Baltimore very important. After all, these cities are pale imitations of London, Paris, or Rome. Europeans think of America as the American West—the vast distances, mountains and plains, national parks and forests, independent people, cowboys and Indians, and other real and imaginary parts of the American scene.

For the past century, and especially after World War II, the American West has been the locus of growth—in jobs, innovation, and the American story. So, what is the West? What is different about its people? Who are some of its major figures? Why have women had a greater role in the West, in suffrage, in medicine, in education, in ranching, and in leadership? Why have so many political ideas originated in the West? What is special about the history and geography of the West, its people, and its character?

In his essay Bernard DeVoto wrote, "The West begins where the average annual rainfall drops below twenty inches. When you reach that line which marks that drop—for convenience, the one hundredth meridian—you have reached the West."

I would like to enlarge that definition to include two more features: (1) areas west of or on the Mississippi River that divides the country in two and (2) the states that entered the union after 1818, two centuries after Jamestown and the settlement of Massachusetts by the people on the *Mayflower*. In 1821, the land of the Louisiana Purchase had been mostly explored, and Missouri entered the union, the first state west of the Mississippi River. By 1859, California and Oregon were states, and the United States was continent-wide.

Twenty-three states are included by this definition: Arizona, Arkansas, California, Colorado, Idaho, Illinois, Iowa, Kansas, Minnesota, Missouri, Montana, Nebraska, Nevada, New Mexico, North Dakota, Oklahoma, Oregon, South Dakota, Texas, Utah, Washington, Wisconsin, and Wyoming. Eleven of these states entered the Union before the Civil War, and the remaining dozen states entered the Union before 1912. Alaska and Hawaii are not included in this book as they each have their own special history.

Table 1.1 lists the twenty-three states, the date of the first European settlements, when statehood occurred, and what percentage of the state is public lands—that is, owned by us, the people of the United States. It also shows the growth in state population over two centuries.

From independence onward, America moved west. In 1820, there were few European settlers living in the West. In the census of 1850, the western region had about 11 percent of the American population. By 1870, it was up to 24.5 percent, and by 2010, these twenty-three states had more than 45 percent of the population. And western growth has not only been in population but also in job creation, innovation, education, and opportunities.

***

To tell this story, as with many others, one has to start with Thomas Jefferson. Jefferson had been interested in exploration of the American continent as a young man, as secretary of state under George Washington, and as vice president under John Adams.

The election of 1800 was one of four presidential elections that did not have a clear winner, and its conclusion was the most important

TABLE 1.1

States admitted after 1818, west of or on the Mississippi[3]

State	First Settlers	Became State	% Public Lands	Population K							
				1820	1850	1870	1900	1940	1970	2000	2010
Arizona	1776	1912	38.7%	—	—	10	123	499	1775	4798	6392
Arkansas	1786	1836	12.6%	—	210	484	1312	1949	1923	2631	2916
California	1769	1850	45.9%	—	93	560	1485	6907	19971	32521	37254
Colorado	1858	1876	35.9%	—	—	40	540	1123	2210	4168	5029
Idaho	1842	1890	61.6%	—	—	15	162	525	713	1347	1568
Illinois	1680	1818	1.1%	55	851	2540	4822	7897	11427	12419	12830
Iowa	1788	1846	0.3%	—	192	1194	2231	2538	2825	2900	3046
Kansas	1727	1861	0.5%	—	—	364	1470	1801	2249	2668	2853
Minnesota	1805	1858	6.8%	—	6	440	1751	2792	3806	4830	5304
Missouri	1735	1821	3.7%	87	682	1721	3106	3785	4678	5540	5989
Montana	1809	1889	29.0%	—	—	21	243	559	694	950	989
Nebraska	1839	1867	1.1%	—	—	123	1066	1315	1570	1705	1826
Nevada	1849	1864	79.6%	—	—	42	42	110	488	1871	2701
New Mexico	1605	1912	35.4%	—	62	92	195	532	1017	1860	2059
N. Dakota	1812	1889	3.9%	—	—	2	319	642	618	662	673

TABLE 1.1 *continued*

States admitted after 1818, west of or on the Mississippi[3]

State	First Settlers	Became State	% Public Lands	Population K							
				1820	1850	1870	1900	1940	1970	2000	2010
Oklahoma	1889	1907	1.6%	—	—	—	790	2336	2559	3373	3751
Oregon	1811	1859	53.0%	—	12	91	414	1090	2092	3397	3831
S. Dakota	1859	1889	5.4%	—	—	12	402	643	666	777	814
Texas	1642	1845	1.8%	—	213	819	3048	6415	11199	20119	25146
Utah	1847	1896	63.1%	—	11	87	277	550	1059	2207	2764
Washington	1811	1889	28.6%	—	1	24	518	1736	3413	5848	6725
Wisconsin	1766	1848	5.1%	—	305	1055	2068	3138	4418	5364	5686
Wyoming	1834	1890	48.4%	—	—	9	93	251	332	525	564
Total West				142	2638	9745	28664	49133	81703	12480	140701
Total US			27.4%	9636	23192	39818	76212	132165	203302	281424	308745
% West				0.1%	11.4%	24.5%	37.6%	37.2%	40.2%	43.5%	45.6%

It took all of the original thirteen colonies 170 years (from 1620 to 1790) to reach a populat on of a few hundred thousand. By 1790, only Pennsylvania and Virginia had more than 400,000 people. Growth in the West was far more rapid.

in American history. The House of Representatives, after more than thirty-five ballots, finally selected Jefferson as president over Aaron Burr. The importance of this decision was embedded in the fact that, had either John Adams or Aaron Burr been chosen, neither would have bought Louisiana. Jefferson did. And without the Louisiana Purchase, the continent might instead have developed into several independent countries similar to the dozen in South America. We, in the West, might be speaking Spanish, French, Russian, or even proper English.

Chapter 1 begins with westward expansion under President Thomas Jefferson. When he became president, Jefferson purchased the Louisiana Territory and sent explorers westward. On June 20, 1803, he wrote instructions to his personal secretary and explorer Meriwether Lewis, informing him of what to look for and record on his exploration. Subjects were to include geography, climate, geology, botany, biology, zoology, meteorology, mineralogy, medicine, and Indian nations. These instructions were also followed later by Zebulon Pike, Stephen Long, and, in the 1840s, by the teams evaluating paths to the Pacific for the transcontinental railroad. By the mid-nineteenth century, the West was largely mapped and documented.

Settlement followed exploration, and the story starts in Chapter 2. Within fifty years, much of the West was inhabited by farmers, ranchers, and miners, and in 1890, the Census Bureau said that there was no longer a frontier; the country was settled. By 1912, the last western states had entered the union and the West began to accumulate power.

This story begins with Native Americans, who have been here for millennia. There were very few Europeans west of the Mississippi when Jefferson was elected president. Native Americans occupied the West, and various attempts were made by the United States to solve the "Indian Problem." Chapter 3 tells the story of Native Americans during the past two centuries.

Next is a description of our northern and southern neighbors. One has to recognize French Canadians in the Louisiana Territory and Hispanics who settled Santa Fe before the Pilgrims reached Plymouth Rock and who have been here for more than four centuries. In addition, Spanish, French, and English exploration of the North American continent are described. These stories are told in Chapter 4, as US boundaries were established.

There was something special about the European Americans who went west, and they went for many reasons: hunger, financial opportunities, land ownership, personal or religious freedom, curiosity, a new start, or in some cases, because they didn't fit in back East. They were independent, and measured each other based on who they were—not who their ancestors were. Chapters 5 and 6 are the story of the westward migration before and after the Civil War. In 1862, President Abraham Lincoln signed the Homestead Act and the Morrill Act and that had influence on western development.

Women's roles were different in the West than they were back East. In 1900, women had the vote in four states—all of them western. By the time the Nineteenth Amendment granting women the right to vote was passed on August 18, 1920, women had the vote in twenty-three states—twenty-two of them were midwestern and western states. The first women to serve as a congressperson, senator, governor, and Supreme Court justice were westerners. Chapter 7 introduces that history.

Since the election in 1928 of Herbert Hoover, an Iowan, to the presidency, two-thirds of American presidents have been born or raised in the West. Political ideas have come from the West, whether from the right with Hoover, Barry Goldwater, and Ronald Reagan, or the left with William Jennings Bryan, Robert La Follette, Humphrey, George McGovern, and Eugene McCarthy. In the last half century, political leadership has shifted westward, and that story is discussed in Chapter 8.

Chapter 9 describes the rural West. Although the growth of western cities since 1940 has been considerable (Utah and Nevada are now 90 percent urban), most of the land in the West remains rural. How does the rural land affect the character of the West?

Chapter 10 introduces the history of the western land and its people, their education, and their economic situations. How has the West developed over the past century in education, medicine, and job creation? Much of the West has public lands owned collectively by the people of the United States—what was the policy of public lands promoted by Theodore Roosevelt and its influence on the West?

Over time, economic power has shifted westward. Silicon Valley, Salt Lake City, Denver, and Austin have succeeded Detroit, Philadelphia, Cleveland, and Baltimore as centers of job creation. Young people continue moving west for economic reasons as well as for the quality of life. Mexico, western Canada, and the Pacific Rim have added to the strength of the US economy, and the major beneficiaries of the North American Free Trade Agreement (NAFTA) are the western states.

The shift of political and economic power westward is a part of twentieth-century history that is not completely understood and even less reported in the eastern press and by eastern historians. Much has occurred in the West that deserves attention in its own right.

Chapter 11 introduces the literary and artistic West and the many stories found there, told in both fact and fiction, in writing and the arts. The West has provided fertile ground for both the mind and spirit across the creative spectrum.

Finally, Chapter 12 deals with the characteristics of the West and westerners. How is a westerner different from a New Englander, a citizen of the Deep South, or a resident of metropolitan New York City area? The chapter describes the relationship between the East and the West in the United States, and it contains some observations about the role and future of the American West in the twenty-first century.

There is an extensive bibliography for the reader who wishes to read more about a particular subject.

This book, which examines the past two centuries of American history and the development and character of the West, might open further studies in women's studies, Native American studies, western history, biography, literature, and art.

CHAPTER 1

Thomas Jefferson and the West

by Robert C. Baron

During four decades, while the future of the Trans-Mississippi West was being decided, Jefferson was the most towering westerner of them all. In the 1780s and 1790s, when American possession of the West seemed incredibly far in the future, he taught himself more about the plains and the Rockies than anyone else, as if preparing unconsciously to govern these vast spaces one day. During his presidency in 1801–1809, he responded brilliantly to unexpected events in foreign affairs, using his knowledge and insight to protect vital explorations and organize the newly acquired territory of Louisiana. Then as a senior statesman until his death in 1826, he was the counselor of men whose hope for the future of the West were Jeffersonian in essence. The western policies of Madison, Monroe and John Quincy Adams were a part of his legacy.

> —**Donald Jackson**, *Thomas Jefferson and the Stony Mountains: Exploring the West from Monticello*[1]

The View from Virginia

Thomas Jefferson was born in Shadwell, Albemarle County, Virginia on April 13, 1743, at the edge of the western settlements. To the west one could see the Blue Ridge Mountains; little was known about what was beyond that ridge, and it was a barrier to westward migration. There were gaps in the mountains, but few settlers were interested in the passage. The people of Virginia, like those of the other colonies, clung to land near the Atlantic Ocean.

Jefferson's father, Peter Jefferson, was one of the first settlers in that part of Virginia. Peter was a farmer, surveyor, and mapmaker, and in 1746, he was one of a group that explored the western part of Virginia that was wilderness. In 1751, he and Joshua Fry produced their *Map of the Most Inhabited Part of Virginia*. Peter was a large landowner, a justice of the peace, a sheriff, and for two terms, a member of the House of Burgesses. The father influenced the son, and Thomas Jefferson became interested in western lands, exploration, and measurement.

In his autobiography, Jefferson wrote about his father: "He was chosen with Joshua Fry, Professor of Mathematics of W&M College to

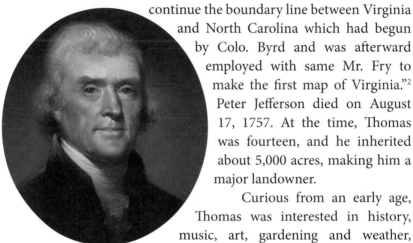

continue the boundary line between Virginia and North Carolina which had begun by Colo. Byrd and was afterward employed with same Mr. Fry to make the first map of Virginia."[2] Peter Jefferson died on August 17, 1757. At the time, Thomas was fourteen, and he inherited about 5,000 acres, making him a major landowner.

Curious from an early age, Thomas was interested in history, music, art, gardening and weather, moral philosophy, natural history, botany, agriculture, mathematics, zoology,

Thomas Jefferson

as well as the classics, and he began collecting books.

In February 1770, when he was a young lawyer practicing in Williamsburg, there was a fire at Shadwell, and Thomas's library of 400 to 500 volumes was destroyed, valued at around £200. He immediately started a new library and added books throughout his life.

In 1769, Jefferson began work on Monticello, a project that continued for forty years. He read extensively on architecture, landscaping, and gardening, and would go on to cultivate plants from around the world and domesticate many wild plants of North America. An avid gardener, he started his *Garden Book* in March 1766 and continued it for sixty years. His *Farm Book* was started in 1774. Jefferson kept records of every aspect of his life.

On January 1, 1772, Jefferson married Martha Wayles Skelton, a twenty-three-year-old widow, and brought her to the unfinished Monticello. The following year, he inherited 11,000 acres upon the death of his father-in-law, John Wayles.

Dreams of the West

On July 20, 1775, Jefferson arrived at Philadelphia for the Continental Congress. On July 4, 1776, the Declaration of Independence was adopted. Jefferson's *Memorandum Book* for that date has an entry: "Paid [John] Sparhawk for a thermometer." He noted the temperature four times that day.

For the remainder of his life, Jefferson documented the temperature twice per day: "as early as possible in the morning," and between three and four in the afternoon. Weather was important to a farmer and gardener. On April 11, 1818, in a letter to Jacob Bigelow on climate and the seasons at Monticello, Thomas Jefferson, based on his records, noted the high and low temperatures, the monthly average temperature and rainfall, the earliest and latest frosts and how many days of frost, wind direction and strength, the schedule of plants blooming and ripening, and the migration dates of some birds.

As a man of science, Jefferson referred to meteorology as a "department of science." In 1779, his findings, made with Bishop James Madison, were published in the *Transactions of the American Philosophical Society*. The following year, both he and Bishop Madison were nominated for membership in the society. Jefferson tried to organize weather networks throughout the colonies and later the states to collect data. So this work was important to him not only as a farmer but also as a part of his scientific studies. On January 21, 1780, Jefferson became a member of the American Philosophical Society in Philadelphia, where Benjamin Franklin was the president. Later, Jefferson himself became the society's president, a position he held for eighteen years. Most of his discussions on exploration were done privately through the society until he became president of the United States.

From an early age, Jefferson knew not only much of his own Virginia's geography but also the continent's. In *Notes on the State of Virginia*, his only book published in 1785, he wrote about the rivers of the West, including the Illinois, Ohio, Tainasae (Tennessee), and Cumberland (Shawnee) rivers:

> The Mississippi will be one of the principal channels of future commerce for the country westward of the Alleghaney. From the mouth of this River to where it receives the Ohio, is 1000 miles by water, but only 500 by land, passing through

the Chickasaw country. From the mouth of Ohio to that of the Missouri, is 230 miles by water, and 140 by land.... The Missouri is, in fact, the principal river, contributing more to the common stream than does the Mississippi, even after its junction with the Illinois. It is remarkably cold, muddy, and rapid. Its overflowings are considerable. They happen during the months of June and July.[3]

At the time of the Constitution, each state transferred its claims of western lands to the federal government. On March 1, 1784, Jefferson prepared a report for the government of the western territories, which covered all territories between the Allegheny Mountains and the Mississippi River. It described how to establish territories and how these areas could become states on the same basis as the original thirteen. Slavery was forbidden in the Trans-Appalachian West. "After the year 1800, there shall be neither slavery nor involuntary servitude in any of said states."[4]

Vermont becomes a state in 1791, Kentucky (originally part of Virginia) in 1792, and Tennessee (part of North Carolina) in 1796.

As secretary of state (1790–1793), Jefferson had been interested in pacification of the western lands on the eastern side of the

The Mississippi a few miles above La Crosse, Wisconsin.

Mississippi and the ability to get crops and other items on the Ohio, Illinois, and other rivers down the Mississippi to ships waiting in New Orleans.

Meanwhile, land across the continent was claimed by many countries. Spain had land to the west and south, England to the west, French Canadians to the northwest, and all three of these countries plus Russia on the Pacific Coast. Who would own the boundless land of the North American continent?

On December 4, 1783, Jefferson wrote to George Rogers Clark:

> I find they have subscribed a very large sum of money in England for exploring the country from the Mississippi to California. They pretend it is only to promote knowledge. I am afraid they have thoughts of colonizing into that quarter. Some of us have been talking here in a feeble way of making the attempt to search the country; but I doubt whether we have enough of that kind of spirit to raise the money. How would you like to lead such a party?[5]

George Rogers Clark, who had conquered the Ohio Valley during the Revolutionary War, declined the honor of exploring the West. Two decades later, his younger brother, William Clark, went on the trip to explore the continent.

Jefferson's Library and the West

On August 3, 1771, Jefferson sent a letter to his friend Robert Skipwith with a list of books for *A Gentleman's Library*, and on September 1, 1785, he sent James Madison a list of books for *A Diplomat's Library*. While in Europe, Jefferson's interests in book collecting expanded.

In his years in France as minister (1785–1789), Jefferson began a major library of books on American geography from both English and other European booksellers—especially French and Spanish. He was fluent in these languages and could read them for their content, and he noted that he was especially interested in the original Spanish writers on American history.

> While I was in Europe, I had purchased everything I could lay my hands on which related to any part of America, and particularly

had a pretty full collection of the English, French & Spanish authors on the subject of Louisiana. The information I got from these was entirely satisfactory and I threw it into a shape which would easily take the form of a memorial.

—**Letter to William Dunbar**, March 13, 1804[6]

Jefferson's *Memorandum Books* from his time in France and travels through England, Italy, Holland, and the Rhineland have 199 entries for the purchase of books. There are also many other entries for the purchase of maps and for book binding. Although the English and the French were, at that time, exploring the Pacific Coast of North America, Jefferson's major attention was on Louisiana and its boundaries.

Jefferson had a library that was unequaled in America. He continued to add volumes after he returned to Virginia and was in touch with European booksellers throughout his life.

After the British burned down Washington in 1814, Jefferson sold his books to the Library of Congress. There were 175 titles on American geography and another 125 on the geography of Europe, Asia, and Africa in the library that Thomas Jefferson sent to Washington.

A complete list of Jefferson's books on American geography and exploration occupies 197 pages of Millicent Sowerby's annotated catalog.[7] Among his purchases were books by Jean Chappe d'Auteroche, William Bartram, Mark Catesby, Diaz del Castillo, Samuel de Champlain, Pierre François Xavier de Charlevoix, Marquis de Chastellux, Daniel Coxe, Richard Hakluyt, Louis Hennepin, Thomas Hutchins, Baron de Lahontan, Sieur de La Salle, Antoine-François de Laval, Antoine Le Page du Pratz, Robert Rogers, and Amerigo Vespucci.

Westward Exploration

The French were exploring the West for the fur trade. Ships were also looking for a Northwest Passage across the continent. Spain, France, England, and Russia were establishing or considering settlements on the Pacific Coast.

In March 1780, James Cook explored Oregon looking for a Northwest Passage. On the Cook voyage was an American from Connecticut named John Ledyard, whom Jefferson later met in France.

He was the first American to set foot in the Pacific Northwest, and he wrote a book called *A Journal of Captain Cook's Last Voyage to the Pacific Ocean … in the Years 1776, 1777, 1778, and 1779.*

Ledyard hoped to walk across Russia, cross the Bering Sea from Siberia to Alaska by ship, and then walk across the North American continent. Jefferson participated in this plan by requesting permission for the American Ledyard to cross Russia; however, after he'd gotten to Siberia, the Empress Catherine denied permission and he had to return to Moscow.

> I have this moment received a letter from Ledyard, dated Cairo November the 15th. He therein says, "I am doing up my baggage, and most curious baggage it is, and I leave Cairo in two or three days. I travel from hence southwest, about three hundred leagues, to a black King; there my present conductors leave me to my fate. Beyond, I suppose, I go alone. I expect to hit the continent across, between the parallels of twelve and twenty degrees north latitude. I shall, if possible, write you from the kingdom of this black gentleman." This seems to contradict the story of his having died at Cairo in January, as he was then, probably, in the interior parts of Africa.
> —**Letter to Thomas Paine**, May 21, 1789[8]

The Canadian explorer Alexander MacKenzie made an overland trip to the Pacific Ocean in 1793 that was documented in his book *MacKenzie's Voyages … through the Continent of North America to the … Pacific Oceans….* This and other books provided background information to Jefferson before Lewis and Clark's trip.

The Presidency: 1801–1809

It was as president that Jefferson accomplished the greatest amount for the West, when he both purchased Louisiana and sent Lewis and Clark and other explorers west.

French and Spanish Explorers

In Colonial America, the British colonists cleared wilderness and built settlements and farms within a hundred miles of the Atlantic Ocean. The French traveled throughout the wilderness of North America, bringing trade and religion to the Indians, and explored the North American continent. There were few French towns, and the land remained wild except for a few trading posts and Jesuit missions. Some men explored for wealth; some explored for God.

French explorer Samuel de Champlain and his men explored the St. Lawrence River and visited Lakes Huron, Ontario, Michigan, and Superior. René-Robert Cavelier Sieur de LaSalle, Hernando de Soto, Louis Jolliet, Father Jacques Marquette, and other Frenchmen explored the Mississippi River Basin; the land in the Mississippi Valley was named Louisiana after King Louis XIV of France. French explorers, traders, and trappers traveled through all of Louisiana over the Great Plains and to the Rocky Mountains. LaSalle came down from Canada and traveled down the Mississippi River. A colony was established at the mouth of the Mississippi River in 1689, with the Louisiana Territory extending north and northwest from New Orleans. Maps are shown in Chapter 4.

The French had thought about building a connection between New Orleans up the Mississippi River to the Great Lakes and then to Quebec. Forts would act as barriers to exclude Britain from the Mississippi Valley and hold back the westward movement of the colonies, but Britain blocked that plan. Louisiana continued under French control for two centuries until France lost the French and Indian War (1754–1763), after which Louisiana was ceded to Spain, and Canada was surrendered to England.

Spain looked at Louisiana as a buffer zone between the United States and the Spanish Southwest. There had been Spanish weakness in North America, but there was steady development of New Orleans during the last decades of the eighteenth century. At times, Spain threatened to refuse to open Louisiana to American trade. The Treaty of San Lorenzo in 1795 allowed frontier goods through New Orleans and provided free access down the Mississippi to the ocean. This was very important to the western states, which shipped their goods on the Ohio and other rivers down the Mississippi where American goods could then be deposited in New Orleans for transfer to ocean-going ships. Westerners wanted free navigation of the Mississippi River.

When talk of returning control of Louisiana to France reached Thomas Jefferson, now secretary of state, in February 1793, he let it be known that the United States was concerned.

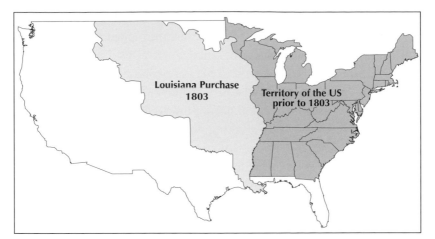

Louisiana Purchase
1803

Territory of the US
prior to 1803

The Louisiana Purchase doubled the size of the United States.

France was upset that they had lost Canada and their land in the Mississippi Valley. And when Napoleon Bonaparte became emperor of France in 1799, he wanted to regain Louisiana and reestablish a French Empire in the Indies and the heartland of North America.

The second Treaty of San Ildefonso on October 1, 1800, returned Louisiana from Spain to France. In 1801, Jefferson learned that the Louisiana Territory had been secretly ceded to France; a closing of the Mississippi River and the port of New Orleans could lead to war with France.

To prevent this from happening, a revolt in Hispaniola, an important trading source of sugar and other products for France, had to be first quashed. Napoleon sent 34,000 troops to the island of Hispaniola (now Haiti and Santa Domingo), before sending several thousand additional troops to Louisiana.

But within a few months, 24,000 Frenchmen were dead of yellow fever and 8,000 were in the hospital. In time, 60,000 French troops were dead, and Napoleon's dream of a colonial empire in the Caribbean and North America was dead as well.

President Jefferson sent Robert Livingston, the minister to France, to attempt to negotiate the purchase of New Orleans for the United States. He had approval to spend $2 million to negotiate buying the lower Mississippi area. In a letter to Livingston on April 18, 1802, Jefferson pointed out that "there is on the Globe, one single spot, the possessor of which is our natural and habitual enemy. It is New Orleans through which the produce of three-eighths of our territory must pass."[9] If France closed the Mississippi River to American trade, Jefferson implied that the United States might join England against France.

In 1803, James Monroe, the governor of Virginia and now special envoy to France, joined Livingston. Secretary of State James Madison had been informed by Jefferson of the importance of the mission and that "St. Domingo delays their taking possession of Louisiana and they are in the last distress of money for current purposes."[10]

When Livingston met with Talleyrand, the French secretary, Talleyrand refused to discuss the sale of New Orleans and asked instead what the United States would pay for all of Louisiana. After much discussion and various prices, France offered to sell all of Louisiana for $15 million. This was 828,000 square miles for a purchase price of four cents per acre. The purchase was financed with twenty-year bonds by Barings Bank of London and Hope and Company of Amsterdam. The United States put up no cash. The purchase effectively doubled the size of United States, as the country moved across the Mississippi River and up to the Rocky Mountains.

Why did Napoleon sell Louisiana? Napoleon got cash, which he needed. His dream of building a Caribbean empire now over, he turned his attention to Europe and other conquests. He also wanted to keep America neutral in his upcoming war with England.

On April 30, 1803, France sold Louisiana to the United States. The purchase seemed in violation of the Constitution, or at least could be considered unconstitutional, as there were no references in the Constitution to the federal government buying land. Jefferson did consider and write a possible amendment to the Constitution but never submitted it to Congress.

There was some opposition to the purchase, generally on a regional basis. New England was against it since they could see their future influence declining. Why should they give money, of which they had so little, for land, of which they had so much? Support elsewhere was positive, however—especially in the West and South.

The Louisiana Purchase was written as a treaty that had to go before Congress. The Constitution requires a two-thirds vote for the ratification of a treaty, and on October 19, 1803, the Senate approved the Louisiana Treaty and Purchase by a vote of 24 to 7.

But what did it include? When French diplomat Talleyrand was asked about the boundaries of Louisiana, he replied: "I can give you no direction. You have made a noble bargain for yourself and I suppose you will make the most of it."[11]

So it was up to Thomas Jefferson to explore Louisiana—what it contained and what its boundaries were. And so he did.

Lewis and Clark Expedition: 1804–1806

Thomas Jefferson had a vast collection of maps and books on Louisiana. He had been interested in exploring the West for years—as we've seen, with George Rogers Clark in 1783, John Ledyard, and Moses Marshall, as well as with the French botanist Andre Michaux in 1793, and J. Marshall. But these were private possible explorations, organized and funded through the American Philosophical Society; now that Jefferson was president, he could use the government to explore.

On January 18, 1803, before the Louisiana sale was finalized, Thomas Jefferson sent a message to Congress requesting $2,500 for a Western expedition. While he intended in time to research the Louisiana Territory (the boundaries of Louisiana from the Mississippi River to the Rocky Mountains), his ideas were broader—what was to the west of Louisiana, and was there a method of reaching the Pacific Ocean through America? He selected his secretary, Meriwether Lewis, to lead the expedition with a dozen chosen accomplices. Lewis was joined by William Clark as co-leader of the expedition. The place to start the expedition was the Missouri River north of St. Louis and heading west, perhaps with a single short portage over the mountains.

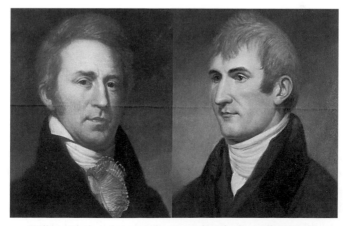

William Clark and Meriwether Lewis by Charles Willson Peale.

The object of your mission is to explore the Missouri River and such principal stream of it, as by its source and communication with the waters of the Pacific Ocean, whether the Columbia, Oregon, Colorado, or any other river, may offer the most direct and practicable water communication across this continent for the purposes of commerce.

Beginning at the mouth of the Missouri, you will take observations of latitude and longitude at all remarkable points on the river, and especially at the mouths of rivers, at rapids, at islands, and other places and objects distinguished by such natural marks and characters of a durable kind, as that they may with certainty be recognized hereafter. The courses of the river between these points of observation may be supplied by the compass, the logline, and by the time, corrected by the observations themselves. The variations of the compass, too, in different places should be noticed.

—**Instructions to Captain Meriwether Lewis**, June 20, 1803

Thomas Jefferson was interested in all phases of natural history, and so he added orders requiring studies of astronomy, biology, botany, geography, geology, horticulture, meteorology, mineralogy, and zoology. He instructed Lewis to spend time during the spring of 1803 in Philadelphia studying natural history, medicine, and navigation with Benjamin Smith Barton and others. That was a lot of information for a young man to absorb, and yet Jefferson's instructions to Lewis were later followed by Zebulon Pike, Stephen Long, and other explorers up to the middle of the nineteenth century.

Other objects worthy of notice will be the soil and face of the country, its growth and vegetable productions, especially those not of the United States; the animals of the country generally, and especially those not known in the United States; the remains and accounts of any which may be deemed rare or extinct; the mineral productions of every kind, but more particularly metals, limestone, pit coal, and saltpeter; salines and mineral waters, noting the temperature of the last and such circumstances as may indicate their character; volcanic appearances; climate as characterized by the thermometer, by the proportion of rainy, cloudy, and clear days, by lightning, hail, snow, ice, by the access and recess of frost, by the winds, prevailing at different seasons; the dates at which particular

plants put forth or lose their flowers, or leaf; times of appearance
of particular birds, reptiles, or insects.
—**Instructions to Captain Meriwether Lewis**, June 20, 1803[13]

In addition, Jefferson had been interested from a young age in
the Indians of North America, their beliefs, their history, and their language. He wanted to know about the various tribes of the West. He
went on to describe how the Natives were to be treated—as friends:
"Make them acquainted with the position, extent, character, peaceable
and commercial dispositions of the United States" and invited some of
them to come to Washington.

> You will therefore endeavor to make yourself acquainted, as far as
> a diligent pursuit of your journey shall admit, with the names of the
> nations and their numbers; the extent and limits of their possessions;
> their relations with other tribes or nations; their language, traditions,
> monuments; their ordinary occupations in agriculture, fishing, hunt-
> ing, war, arts, and the implements for these; their food, clothing,
> and domestic accommodations; the diseases prevalent among them
> and the remedies they use; moral and physical circumstance which
> distinguish them from the tribes they know.
> —**Instructions to Captain Meriwether Lewis**, June 20, 1803[14]

Lewis and Clark departed St. Louis on May 11, 1804. A shipment sent by Lewis and Clark in April 1805 when they left their
winter base in what is now North Dakota had reached the president's
house in Washington on August 12—this was his last communication until they returned in 1806. For two years, Jefferson wondered
where they were, whether they were still alive, and what they had
discovered. They returned to St. Louis on September 23, 1806. As
their story of exploration is well known and documented, it won't be
recounted here.

On reaching St. Louis on September 23, Lewis immediately
wrote to Jefferson:

> "It is with pleasure that I announce to you the safe arrival of myself
> and party at 12 OClk with our papers and baggage…. With respect
> to the exertions and services rendered by that estimable man Capt.
> William Clark in the course of the late voyage, I cannot say too much,

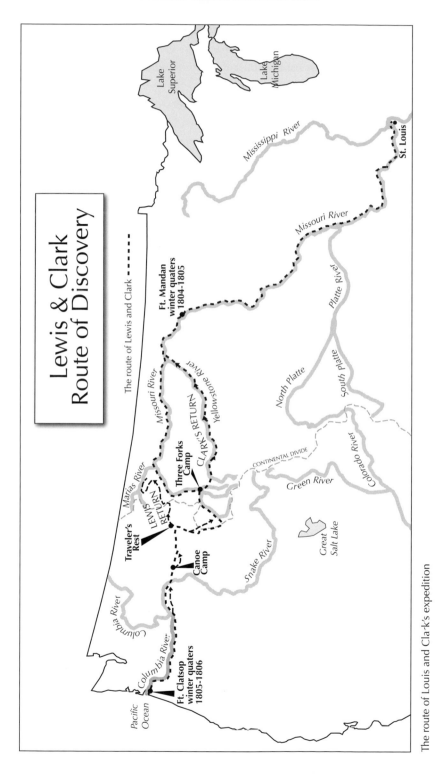

Lewis & Clark
Route of Discovery

The route of Lewis and Clark ------

Lake Superior

Lake Michigan

Mississippi River

St. Louis

Missouri River

Platte River

Ft. Mandan
winter quaters
1804-1805

Missouri River

Yellowstone River

CLARK'S RETURN

Three Forks
Camp

North Platte

South Platte

CONTINENTAL DIVIDE

Colorado River

Green River

Marias River

LEWIS
RETURN

Traveler's
Rest

Canoe
Camp

Snake River

Great
Salt Lake

Columbia River

Columbia River

Ft. Clatsop
winter quaters
1805-1806

Pacific
Ocean

The route of Louis and Clark's expedition

if sir any credit be due for the success of that arduous enterprise in which we have been mutually engaged, he is equally with myself entitled to your consideration and that of our common country."[15]

In his Sixth Annual Message to Congress on December 2, 1806, Thomas Jefferson sent this report:

The expedition of Messrs. Lewis and Clarke, for exploring the river Missouri, and the best communication from that to the Pacific Ocean, had all the success which could have been expected. They have traced the Missouri nearly to its source, descended the Columbia to the Pacific Ocean, ascertained with accuracy the geography of that interesting communication across our continent, learned the character of the country, of its commerce, and inhabitants; and it is but justice to say that Messrs. Lewis and Clarke, and their brave companions, have by this arduous service deserved well of their country.[16]

While Jefferson was president, the country added its seventeenth state: Ohio, in 1803.

Senior Statesman: 1809–1826

When he returned to Monticello in 1809, Thomas Jefferson saw America move westward. Louisiana was admitted to the union in 1812, Indiana in 1816, Mississippi in 1817, Illinois in 1818, and Alabama in 1819. In 1820, Maine (which had been part of Massachusetts), was admitted to the union. As part of that legislation, Missouri was admitted in 1821—the first state west of the Mississippi River.

Jefferson was, however, concerned with the admission of Missouri as an additional slave state. It seemed to him that slavery was becoming a much greater problem than when he had written his report for the government of the Western Territory. There were regional conflicts, possible secession of southern or western states, and the first discussions of general emancipation. The clouds that would lead to the Civil War were forming.

Jefferson's garden continued to grow, due in part to seeds brought back by Lewis and Clark and other explorers. Agriculture knew no political boundaries, and Jefferson corresponded with friends around the world on gardening.

Jefferson continued to stay aware of geographic exploration in the West. He added to his library the books *Lewis and Clark: Expedition to the Pacific Ocean,* Zebulon Pike's *An Account of Expeditions to the Source of the Mississippi and Through the Western Parts of Louisiana…,* and Humboldt's *Political Essay on New Spain.*

In a letter to Lucy Lewis on April 19, 1808, President Jefferson had even written: "I have never ceased to wish to descend the Ohio & Mississippi to New Orleans, and when I shall have put my house in order, I shall have the leisure, and so far I have health also, to myself in seeing what I have not yet seen."[17] But he never did.

Jefferson also provided counsel to his successors James Madison, James Monroe, and John Quincy Adams relative to the desires of European powers to continue settlement of the New World. Although he did not write it, his thoughts are in the Monroe Doctrine, written December 2, 1823. To the end, Jefferson wished to continue the policy of keeping America out of European quarrels and allowing the New World to develop in its own direction. The fact that America is one country stretching from sea to sea is a credit to the vision and accomplishments of Thomas Jefferson.

Jefferson had laid a foundation in government and provided land to the West. But how was it to develop? Would there be one or many countries? How long would it take to be settled? And what would happen to the Native Americans currently inhabiting that land?

CHAPTER 2

The Land

by Robert C. Baron

*Quomodo lucem diemque omnibus hominibus, ita omnes
terras fortibus viris natura aperuit.*

As light and the day are free to all men, so nature
has left all lands open to brave men.
—**Tacitus**[1]

A country is its land—its geography; its mountain ranges and plains; forests and deserts; rivers and lakes; location on the planet; boundaries and neighbors; weather and climate; prevailing winds; the amount of land that can be cultivated; its soils, fertility, and natural resources; and the animals and plants that inhabit it.

While people matter and are important parts of a story, their history and current situation, both economically and politically, are dependent in large part on the land. Before looking at the United States and especially the western United States, let's examine a few other places.

Egypt is on the Nile, whose annual floods fertilized the land and fed the country for millennia. The vastness of Russia and China had a major influence on both of their histories, cultures, and isolation. Most of Europe, while having fertile land, had few secure borders, and each country could be conquered and absorbed by other peoples. The separation of

Britain, across the channel from Europe, led to its development as a trading nation with no invasion for a thousand years.

Australia is a country almost the size of the continental United States. But Australia has few rivers. As a result, it has grown around the ocean, with few people in the interior. The United States has a network of rivers, with the Mississippi River as a spine, and other rivers—the Ohio, the Illinois, the Missouri, the Arkansas, the Jefferson, the Red River, and many others—feeding into the Mississippi. America grew inland in the Mississippi Valley. The outlet for the products of these settlers was New Orleans, where their goods could be shipped around the world.

Some countries, because of climate and location, have productive agricultural lands, while other countries have to struggle to feed their people or have them immigrate to other countries. Frigid places, high heat, deserts, or flooded landscapes affect the history of a country. There have been many key examples of climate and geography influencing a nation.

A country, in short, is inextricably related to its land. Perhaps a review of the land of the United States in three periods—Colonial times, the independent nation that Jefferson saw in his lifetime, and the American West as it developed during the nineteenth century might be of interest.

The United States became the fourth largest country in the world, with Russia being almost twice as large and Canada and China slightly larger. The land that became the United States was large, about 3,000 miles east and west and 1,000 miles north and south. (For reference, the distance between London and Moscow is 1,550 miles.)

The Land: Colonial America through the Nineteenth Century

In this section, we'll look at the English settlements; French and Spanish settlements are covered in Chapter 4.

With the first European settlements in the early seventeenth century, the British colonies and their people lived along the Atlantic Ocean. Eastern rivers are short and only flow small distances west to east. The two exceptions, the Hudson and the Connecticut, flow north to south, and do not connect to other major rivers.

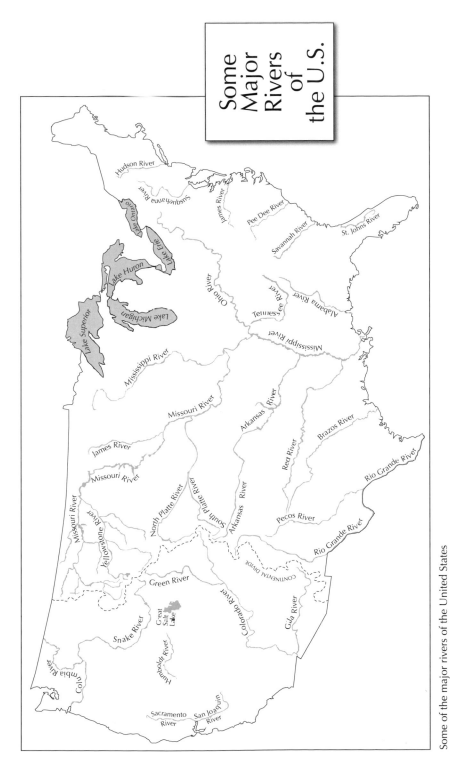

Some of the major rivers of the United States

In Colonial times, agricultural lands were plentiful in the East, and most people earned their livelihood from farming. The climate was acceptable, neither as cold as Canada and Russia nor as hot as the Caribbean or Mexico. Rainfall was plentiful, with between forty and fifty-five inches of moisture per year in the eastern cities and towns. The people settled along the Atlantic Ocean, with wilderness to their backs and protection in front provided by distance and the British Navy. The colonies produced raw materials that were sent to England, with manufactured goods being shipped to the colonies in return. Communication between the colonies was mainly by ship.

There was plentiful wood, coal, and iron in the eastern states. Distances were short, at least as measured by today's standards. The Appalachian Mountains were about 100 miles from the Atlantic Ocean; the distance across Massachusetts 125 miles; and from Boston to Charleston, the most northern and southern large cities in the colonies, was less than 950 miles.

By the time the first Federal Census was taken in 1790, the thirteen original colonies and most of the 3.9 million people were huddled within 100 miles of the Atlantic Ocean. The center of population was 23 miles to the east of Baltimore. To the west were 3,000 miles of wilderness.

After the Revolution, and between 1779 and 1812, the federal government took major steps to control the lands to the West. It requested the states to transfer all unsettled lands between the Appalachian Mountains and the Mississippi River to the federal government, created the General Land Office, and began to sell lands to settlers while keeping some to be owned by the nation.

The lands in the Ohio Valley and the Northwest Territory were fertile. Settlers went west to good land with excellent climate and rainfall. The problem was how to get their crops to market and provide goods to purchase. (The land that became the Midwest is covered in Chapter 5.)

America has two major mountain ranges: the Allegheny Mountains are close to the Atlantic Ocean; the Rocky Mountains are a thousand miles from the Pacific Ocean. Between them is a rich land six times the size of France.

> The Mississippi Valley is, all in all, the most magnificent
> dwelling that God has ever prepared for the habitation of

man, and nonetheless one can see that it still forms only a vast Wilderness.

—**Alexis De Tocqueville**[2]

Thomas Jefferson and other colonial leaders thought about the land of this continent. Spain controlled territory to the south and southwest of the original thirteen states. England managed land to the north and northwest. France was interested in recovering its lost territories in North America. On the Pacific Coast, Spain, France, England, and Russia were making claims. And the western territories might choose to establish their own governments and not enter the union.

Without Jefferson and the Louisiana Purchase, the American West might have evolved into several countries, similar to the dozen countries of South America or the almost fifty in Europe. As we saw in Chapter 1, the Louisiana Purchase doubled the size of country, and the Lewis and Clark expedition opened the eyes of Americans to what lay to the west. Jefferson believed that Louisiana gave the United States enough land for a thousand years, a logical conclusion since in the 170 years between 1620 and 1790, Americans had moved barely 100 miles from the coast.

A storm rolls in across the plains of eastern Colorado in the Pawnee Buttes National Grassland.

Yosemite Fall

What was learned about the land of the American West in the first decades after the Louisiana Purchase? In the first place, the West had a variety of landscapes, climates, and degrees of fertility. There were mountains and deserts, extensive prairies and grasslands, rivers and lakes, forests and wetlands. Thick forests were often short distances from sagebrush deserts, depending on moisture and altitude. There were seasonal and annual variations in rain, snow, and sleet. Heat waves and cold winters affected flora and fauna.

The explorers were overwhelmed by the extent of the American West—its grasslands, forests, mountains, deserts, rivers, and animals. (For some of their writings, see the beginning of Chapter 11.) The

French explorers in the eighteenth century and the American explorers and mountain men in the nineteenth were amazed by what they saw. There were plains, mountains, and very special wild places such as the Grand Canyon, Yellowstone, and Yosemite. The mountain men traveled over the western land as fur trappers, in search of beaver and trading opportunities. Leaving from St. Louis and rendezvousing at Green River, Wyoming, and other places, they saw the country long before European settlements. The names and exploits of some of the mountain men are known today—John Colter, Jim Bridger, Thomas Fitzpatrick, Joseph Walker, George Drouillard, Warren Ferris, Jedediah Smith, Jim Clyman, and Kit Carson.

> It is the time of fulfillment, the fullness of time, the moment lived for itself alone. The mountain men were a tough race, as many selective breeds of Americans have had to be; their courage, skill, and mastery of the conditions of their chosen life were absolute or they would not have been here. Nor would they have been here if they had not responded to the loveliness of the country and found ... something precious beyond safety, gain, comfort, and family life.
>
> **—Bernard DeVoto**[3]

Buffaloes at Rest by Louis Kurz, lithographer, 1911.

Mesquite Flats Sand Dunes, Death Valley.

There were grasses that ranged in height between a few feet to taller than a man and his horse. Centuries of selection had resulted in grasses that might have roots four to six feet deep and could survive in limited rainfall. Grasses seeded themselves naturally; the bison and other grazing animals lived off the grasses. The soil would not erode until settlers plowed these fields.

There were large bison herds, estimated conservatively at somewhere between 50 and 80 million animals, migrating between the Mississippi River and the Rockies and between Texas and Canada. Some estimates were even higher. In 1866, General Philip Sheridan believed there were as many as 100 million bison in the region between the Indian Territory and Kansas. There were grizzly bears, wolves, coyotes, elk, antelope, prairie dogs, hawks and eagles, and a variety of other animals throughout the West.

Land fertility in the West varied. The terrain in what would become Illinois, Iowa, Kansas, Missouri, Nebraska, and Wisconsin provided for good farming with adequate moisture. As one traveled toward the Rocky Mountains, however, soil became less productive.

The land was poorer, and moisture in some places was inadequate for farming.

There were differences between the American East and West. In the East, three things were required: land, rain, and wood. Land for settlement, rain for growing crops, and wood for building homes and tools.

At one time, most items were made of wood—barrels, baskets, wagons, carts, wheels, rakes, plows, hoes, looms, nails, fences, clocks, shovels, hammers, axes, saws, and other tools. Specialized woodworking machinery—saws, planes, and machines for shaping, boring, and mortising—were valuable in a country with a vast abundance of forest products.

As settlers went across the Mississippi, however, two of the three factors for settlement were missing. While Wisconsin, Minnesota, and the Pacific Coast regions had forests, there were few trees in Kansas, North Dakota, Iowa, or most of the West, and rainfall amounts were lower. Table 2.1 shows average annual moisture for a dozen eastern and western cities today. From the averages, it is obvious that there is far less moisture in the West than in the East, and that affects its history. For example, Connecticut currently receives three times as much rain

TABLE 2.1

Average Annual Rainfall in a Dozen Eastern and Western Cities[5]

East Precipitation	Inches	West Precipitation	Inches
Atlanta, GA	49	Albuquerque, NM	9.5
Atlantic City, NJ	40	Billings, MT	14.8
Baltimore, MD	42	Boise, ID	12.2
Boston, MA	44	Denver, CO	16.5
Cape Hatteras, NC	56	El Paso, TX	9.4
Charleston, SC	47	Las Vegas, NV	4.5
Charlottesville, VA	46	Los Angeles, CA	15.1
New Haven, CT	46	Phoenix, AZ	8.3
New York, NY	44	Rapid City, SD	16.6
Philadelphia, PA	41	Salt Lake City, UT	16.5
Providence, RI	45	San Francisco, CA	22.3
Wilmington, DE	41	Yakima, WA	8.3

Grazing land near Laramie, Wyoming ca. 1941.

as Colorado; New Jersey four times as much as New Mexico; Virginia three times as much as Utah. (Of course, in any given year, a city's moisture can vary. In 2013, New York City had 66.3 inches of moisture, 50 percent above its normal annual rainfall. Los Angeles, in a drought year, had 3.65 inches of rain, 75 percent less than its average.)

Dr. Edwin James, the recorder of Stephen Long's 1820 expedition to the Rocky Mountains, referred to the West as the Great American Desert, "a dreary plain, wholly unfit for cultivation, and of course uninhabitable by a people depending upon agriculture for their subsistence." He hoped the area with his native grasses might "forever remain the unmolested haunt of the native hunter, the bison and the jackal."[4] History has proven him correct about rainfall. There was the devastating Dust Bowl of the 1930s, and much of the West experiences severe droughts to this day.

The geography and geology of the West are indeed different from its eastern counterparts. There are few navigable rivers in the Rocky Mountain region, and temperatures throughout much of the area can be extreme. If rainfall, climate, fertile soil, and access to rivers to get crops to market were important, then the history of the American West was to be different from that of the East. Ranching, taking advantage of the large areas and lower rainfall, could replace farming, which would be less successful.

In contrast, the land in the East is flat, with few mountains. The land in Massachusetts and Connecticut average 500 feet in elevation, and much of the Midwest is about 1,000 feet in elevation. Colorado, Wyoming, and New Mexico average between 5,700 and 6,800 feet above sea level.

Mariposa Grove in California

Early explorers and the mountain men recognized that the Rocky Mountains were quite different from the Appalachians. The mountains in the East were not very high (2,500 to 6,000 feet), and there were many passes through them. The Rockies were much higher, with peaks between 10,000 to 14,000 feet, and there were few passes. And while some explorers did get over the Rocky Mountains, Jefferson's hope for a short portage over turned out to be impossible.

It eventually became apparent that there was no Northwest Passage across the continent. If settlers wished to get to coastal Oregon with its fertile valleys and fifty inches of moisture, or to Northern California with its thirty inches of moisture, most would have to go north on the Oregon Trail or south on the Santa Fe Trail with its deserts. Through the mid-nineteenth century, this meant walking the 2,000-mile five-month journey from Nebraska or Kansas. Southern California, today's Los Angeles and San Diego, was a desert and attracted fewer settlers.

Distances were longer in the West. St. Louis was settled in 1764 as a trading post; the first settlement in San Francisco (Yerba Buena) was in 1774. From St. Louis to San Francisco, it is 2,100 miles directly, but it was perhaps 2,500 miles when traveled by foot in the early nineteenth century. Future states would be larger as well. Montana, for example is 147,000 square miles, more than three times that of Virginia (41,000 square miles); Colorado is 104,000 square miles, more than twelve times that of Massachusetts (8,260 square miles).

As America moved across the continent, the land of the West provided natural resources, increased amounts of land, new animals and plants, and buffer boundaries. Whether the land could be peopled and they could be supported with goods was another question.

Without advances in transportation and communication, the West would not be able to be settled with large numbers of people and could easily have split off into new countries, topics that are explored in Chapters 5 and 6.

CHAPTER 3

Native Americans

by Daniel R. Wildcat

You've got to debunk the Indian, as you've got to debunk the Cowboy.
When you've debunked the Cowboy, there's not much left. But the
Indian bunk is not the Indian's invention. It is ours.
— **D. H. Lawrence**, Mornings in Mexico[1]

A Continuation: You Cannot Remember
What You Never Knew.[2]

A light shines in the American West that few people know and understand, other than the First Peoples of these lands now politically demarcated as United States of America. The light is the resilient sovereignty of the American Indians or, First Peoples, in other words, nations, of this land known as the American West. I say resilient because in spite of ongoing attempts to put that light out, it still shines.

The Standing Rock and the Dakota Access Pipeline (DAPL) protests, the Pawnee Nation of Oklahoma's legal challenge to fracking practices of big oil and gas interests, the tribal involvement in the Frack Off Greater Chaco movement in New Mexico, and the Northwest tribes' leadership role in opposition to international coal shipping port construction, to list but a few activities, demonstrate the persistence of this Light in the West about which most American's know almost nothing.

Why should Americans know anything about, much less understand, the reality of the First Peoples' sovereignty? They have never been taught *our* entangled settler-colonizer and First Peoples' histories. One cannot remember what one never knew.

Among important contributions the great Standing Rock Sioux intellect Vine Deloria Jr. made to the study of American Indian sovereignty was his consistent radical critique of Western conceptions

Vine Deloria Jr.

of history. He critiqued the overwhelmingly abstract linear temporal conception of history that infuses Western thinking, with deadly consequences.[3] Deloria also counterposed this abstract Western conception to an indigenous spatial conception of history that addresses both the most entrenched problems in American Indian historiography and many current conflicts found throughout the world.

The following, a modest non-alter-Native historical sketch, is presented to counter the still common deep prejudiced accounts of First Peoples' histories within the boundaries of the United States from 1800 to the present.

During the past five centuries, peoples who recently arrived in this land from Europe and those who have been here from their beginning have made histories embodied in a series of physical, social, and metaphysical collisions.[4] One problem an increasing number of historians recognize—then with few exceptions dismiss as unsolvable—is that the lens and narrative voice though which American Indian history is seen and recorded are those of the Western European immigrant. These Euro-American histories are rooted in the philosophy, values, and metaphysics of Western civilization.[5]

There is no romanticism in Deloria's views; rather, in their complex totality we find a realism. Deloria's fundamentally spatial conception of history is found throughout the recorded words of American Indian leaders and elders. As people try to wrap their minds around Deloria's spatial conception of history in all its richness, it is worth reflecting on Ten Bears's, Yamparika Comanche, words at one of the largest treaty-making events in US history at Medicine Lodge Creek in 1867. Ten Bears, after hearing of some of the government's plans for his people, stated:

> You said that you wanted to put us upon a reservation, to build us houses and make us medicine lodges. I do not want them. I was born upon the prairie, where the wind blew free and there was nothing to break the light of the sun. I was born where there were no enclosures and where everything drew a free breath. I want

to die there and not within walls. I know every stream and every wood between the Rio Grande and the Arkansas. I have hunted and lived over that country. I lived like my fathers before me, and, like them, I lived happily.

Great White Father told me that all the Comanche Land was ours, and that no one should hinder us from living upon it. So, why do you ask us to leave the rivers, and the sun, and the wind, and live in houses?[6]

Ten Bears, a Comanche Chief, shown ca. late 1860s.

Ten Bears eloquently speaks to what it means to be an indigenous—to be a Comanche— human being. Ten Bears's home was not a house, it was the southern Great Plains, its rivers, woods, the wind, and the sun which he knew well.[7]

A Historical Review of Three Federal Indian Policy Initiatives

The Boundary Line: Civilized Peoples and Savages

I am clear in my opinion, that policy and economy point very strongly to the expediency of being on good terms with the Indians, and the propriety of purchasing their lands in preference to attempting to drive them by force of arms out of their Country; which as we have already experienced is like driving the Wild beast of the Forest which will return as soon as the pursuit is at an end and fall perhaps on those that are left there; when the gradual extension of our Settlements will as certainly cause the Savage as the Wolf to retire; both being beasts of prey tho' they differ in shape.
—**George Washington to James Duane**, 1783[8]

In 1783, George Washington thought the United States of America large enough to contain both US citizens of European descent and savages, so long as a clear boundary line existed, as Washington stated, "between them and us."[9] No question existed in his mind about Indian title to the land. The primary issues addressed in the treaties that followed for the next thirty years focused on where the boundary lines should be drawn between the Indian tribes and the United States and how trade and intercourse should be enacted. But as we repeatedly see throughout the nineteenth century, the boundary line also represented a social and cultural demarcation between the civilized and the savage.

In 1791, Washington was even more committed to not only protecting citizens of the United States from Indian wars, but in relying on trade and intercourse to create a situation of Indian dependency on the government of the United States:

> It is sincerely desired that all need of coercion in future may cease and that an intimate intercourse may succeed, calculated to advance the happiness of the Indians and to attach them firmly to the United States.[10]

The Trade and Intercourse Acts of 1790, 1796, 1799, and 1802 sought to regulate political and economic interaction between non-Indians and Indians. Not until 1823 in John Marshall's landmark decision in *Johnson v. McIntosh*, when the European concept of "aboriginal possession" become fully explicated as an American doctrine of discovery, did the ironic fascination with boundary lines lessen. By the time Andrew Jackson became president, Washington's perception of a Unites States of America large enough for both Indians and citizens of the United States was lost in the shadows of a new policy of removal.

Removal Policy

Andrew Jackson set out his view on American Indian public policy in his First Annual Message to Congress in 1829:

> It has long been the policy of Government to introduce among them the arts of civilization, in the hope of gradually reclaiming

them from a wandering life... however.... Professing a desire to civilize and settle them, we have at the same time lost no opportunity to purchase their lands and thrust them further into the wilderness. By this means they have not only been kept in a wandering state, but been led to look upon us as unjust and indifferent to their fate.... Government has constantly defeated its own policy, and the Indians in general, receding farther and farther into the West, have retained their savage habits.[11]

Jackson goes on to declare that Indian "pretensions" to establish a government independent of the states of Alabama and Georgia would not be supported by his administration, since to support such a view in his mind would undermine the Constitutional provision that "no new State shall be formed or erected within the jurisdiction of any other state."

Furthermore, Jackson contended:

Our conduct toward these people is deeply interesting to our national character. Their present condition, contrasted with what they once were, makes a most powerful appeal to our sympathies. Our ancestors found them the uncontrolled possessors of these vast regions. By persuasion and force they have been made to retire from river to river and from mountain to mountain, until some of the tribes have become extinct and others have left but remnants to preserve for a while their once terrible names. Surrounded by the whites with their arts of civilization, which by destroying the resources of the savage doom him to weakness and decay, the fate of the Mohegan, the Narragansett, and the Delaware is fast overtaking the Choctaw, the Cherokee, and the Creek. That this fate surely awaits them if they remain within the limits of the States does not admit of a doubt. Humanity and national honor demand that every effort should be made to avert so great a calamity.[12]

How to avert "so great a calamity"? Jackson suggests removal to

an ample district west of the Mississippi, and without the limit of any State or Territory now formed, to be guaranteed to the

Indian tribes as long as they shall occupy it, each tribe having a
distinct control over the portion designated for its use.[13]

The cumulative effect of three Supreme Court decisions, *Johnson v.
McIntosh* (1823), *Cherokee Nation v. Georgia* (1831), and *Worcester v.
Georgia* (1832), was to provide a rationale for: (1) a denial of an abso-
lute and complete title in the land to Indians (note Jackson's phrase
"the uncontrolled possessors of these vast regions"); (2) denominating
Indians as members of "domestic dependent nations... in a state of
pupilage" with U.S.-Indian relations resembling "that of a ward to his
guardian"; and (3) reserving the right for political relations with Indian
nations to the federal government, thereby establishing what is now
referred to as a "nation-to-nation" relationship between the federal
government and Indian nations.

Although much is made of the Five Civilized Tribes, especially
the Cherokee's Trail of Tears, many tribes of the Great Lakes, the Ohio
Valley, and locations in the Appalachians and west to the Mississippi
experienced removal. Northeastern Kansas today is rich evidence of
this history of removal.

The well-known Trail of Tears narrative comports perfectly
with the historical moral complicity of the dominant Manifest Destiny narrative of Indian history. This narrative of inevitable defeat
leaves out the Cherokee, Creek, and Seminole Peoples' political and
military agency in addressing the threat of removal. Like the "End of
the Trail" statuette in tourist gift shops that cater to tourists buying
Indian souvenirs, this narrative obscures the fact that tribal resistance before removal affirmed the First People's sovereignty. What
most history textbooks fail to detail is the story of the First Peoples'
violent and nonviolent diplomatic resistance to an act that struck at
the heart of who they were.

Sovereignty, the act thereof inherent in choice, must be seen
in the nonviolent resistance to removal led by principal chief of the
Cherokee John Ross. Throughout the 1830s right up to the moment
of forced removal, Ross exercised diplomatic efforts to avert this
shameful US government act. In addition to repeated trips to Washington, Ross modeled keen political leadership among his people
within stable Cherokee institutions of governance. So stable, in fact,
that the Cherokee mounted consistent organized challenges to US
federal authority. Refusal to cooperate with federal officials took the

form of boycotting meetings with them and refusing to participate in a fraudulent treaty signing in 1835 that stipulated the Cherokee agreement to removal. In fact, the vast majority of Cherokees who followed Ross were noncooperative to the end—refusing to be moved unless by force of bayonet.

The Creeks waged what might be called today a guerilla war in 1835. The Seminole war of resistance to removal, known as the Second Seminole War, lasted seven years and cost the US government

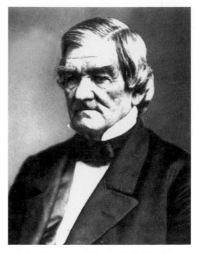

John Ross was Principal Chief of the Cherokee Nation from 1828 to 1866.

dearly at the time. Unlike the Creek and the Seminole, Ross chose to exercise Cherokee resistance using diplomatic and legal arguments. In the process, Ross demonstrated the Cherokee possessed sovereignty and a system of stable governance that was able to operate even amidst the political anxiety and fear many Cherokee felt.

With a brief exception, after the Civil War and through the 1870s, when a military subjugation program embodied in the so-called Plains Indian Wars, the dominant policy of the first three-quarters of the nineteenth century was geographic removal. However, the ultimate irony, as several scholars have pointed out, is that even this policy was less about geography than what Deloria has identified as the Western fixation on linear temporal notions of history—progress, civilization, industrialization, and advancement proved the necessity of erasing boundaries.

Early executive branch declarations on Indian policy and the lion's share of treaties understood Indian Country less as a place than as a concept invoked to mark the clear demarcation between the citizens of the United States of America and the recalcitrant heathen savages of the Americas. In short, spatial divisions were made on the basis of relative ideologies. The invocation of geography—of a place—was determined by an essentially ethnocentric ideology of racial and social superiority of the civilizers.

The first major federal Indian policy of the nineteenth century was basically geographical removal. The policy of removal explains why the Wyandottes ended up in Kansas, why my relatives the Yuchis ended up along with the Creeks, the Choctaws, the Chickasaws, the Cherokees, and the Seminoles in Oklahoma. During Jackson's presidency, the solution to the "Indian problem" was obvious—remove the Indians. The removal solution, while seeming perfectly feasible for Western European peoples who sought to solve their political and cultural problems by moving—moving to America—was experienced as traumatic to peoples shaped by cultures reflecting very directly the larger ecological and environmental community to which they held membership. Removal or relocation is really the beginning of much of the social and cultural dysfunctionality experienced today in Native communities.

The Classic Liberal Solution: Education

In the nineteenth century, some US citizens held that education would be the only way to deal with the host of problems accompanied by the extension of their settlements. Given the existence of the "boundary line" in the consciousness of citizens of the newly formed United States of America, it is not surprising that the first legislation directed at Indian education was called the Civilization Fund Act (1819). This act allowed the president discretionary funds

> for the purpose of providing against the further decline and final extinction of the Indian tribes, adjoining the frontier settlements of the United States, and for introducing among them the habits and arts of civilization... he is authorized, in every case where he shall judge improvement in the habits and conditions of such Indians practicable... to employ capable persons of good moral character, to instruct them in the mode of agriculture suited to their situation; and for teaching their children in reading, writing, and arithmetic, and performing other duties as may be enjoined.[14]

Even during the height of removal politics, Commissioner of Indian Affairs T. Hartley Crawford contended in his *Annual Report* of 1838 that education would be "the principle lever by which the Indians are to be lifted out of the mire of folly and vice in which they are sunk."[15] Hartley's report called for abolishment of tribally held lands, transferring instead to individual allotments, the creation of a large central school, and establishment of a political confederation for tribes in the West. However, it was not until the policy of removal was clearly untenable, some four decades after Crawford's 1838 report, that both off-reservation boarding schools and the imposition of individual private property ownership would emerge as the public policy solutions to the Indian problem.

The conclusion of the Civil War left eastern liberals looking for a new cause, and the general mistreatment and condition of the American Indians was increasingly in the public eye. It was increasingly clear that as settlers moved west into areas that 20 to 30 years before would have been unimaginable, that any hope of keeping Indians separate from the beneficent and malevolent elements of a society moving westward was impossible. With the opening of the Oregon and Santa Fe Trails and the granting of railroad homesteads in the 1860s, it became clear that a policy of removal or geographic separation was not going to be feasible Indian policy. The 1876 defeat of Custer's Seventh Calvary at the Battle of the Greasy Grass, the Little Big Horn, may have done more to undermine the extermination policy General Sheridan endorsed and the removal policy that had dominated the first half of the nineteenth century than any other single act. After the Greasy Grass battle, military subjugation seemed far too costly to be advanced as the sole solution to the Indian problem. Likewise, the policy of removal was untenable. Short of pushing all Indians into the Pacific Ocean, there was nowhere to remove Indians to.

The policy of Indian education in the late nineteenth century was essentially an inversion of the physical removal policy of the first half of the century. The motto placed above the entrance of Hampton Institute self-consciously declared the objective and evidenced the underlying philosophy of the boarding schools—"Destroy the Indian to Save the Man." It was your very nativeness as a Kiowa person, as a Comanche person, as a Creek person, as a Lakota, as a Pawnee, as a Cree, as a Crow, as a Cheyenne that was your obstacle to realizing your true fully developed humanity. Few policies have enjoyed such a wide consensus in interpretation in terms of their implementation, means, and goals.

In 1883, Richard Henry Pratt wrote, "In Indian civilization I am a Baptist, because I believe in immersing the Indians in our civilization

A small Ogalala tipi camp shown in front of the U.S. School for Indians at
Pine Ridge, South Dakota in 1891.

and when we get them under holding them there until they are thoroughly soaked."[16] Elsewhere Pratt stated, "Convert him in all ways but
color into a white man and in fact the Indian would be exterminated,
but humanely, and as beneficiary of the greatest gift at the command of
the white man—his own civilization."[17]

Pratt's firm conviction was that if young Indian boys and girls
were educated—in other words, civilized—completely culturally
assimilated to the dominant culture and society, the result would
be brown-skinned non-Indians. Pratt and a host of others reasoned
these young men and women would not really be Indians anymore.
They would be exactly like civilized members of the dominant society—capable of being fully integrated into American society and
empowered.

This "conversion in all ways but color" required the creation of
what sociologist Erving Goffman later identified as a "total institution"
in his study of modern prisons and mental institutions. Goffman's
"total institution" is exactly what Pratt had envisioned in his model of
cultural baptism by full immersion:

> I suppose the end to be gained... is the complete civilization of
> the Indian and his absorption into our national life.... If I am

correct in this supposition, then the sooner the Indian loses all his Indian ways, even his language, the better it will be for him and for the government and the greater will be the economy to both. Now, I do not believe that amongst his people an Indian can be made to feel the advantages of a civilized life.... To accomplish that, his removal and personal isolation is necessary. One year in the midst of a civilized community where, whichever way he may turn he can see the industrious farmer plowing his fields or reaping his grain, and the industrious mechanic building houses or engaged in other manufactures, with all the realities of wealth and happiness which these efforts bring to the farmer and mechanic is worth more as a means of implanting such aspirations... than a whole life time of camp surrounding with the best Agency schoolwork that can be done.[18]

The irony for much of federal Indian policy is that when policies appear geographical in nature, they typically center on cultural or ideological issues, for example, the boundary line of removal policies and the creation of "Indian Country." Conversely, when policies are targeted at the culture, civilization, or education questions, they inevitably use spatial strategies, for example, boarding schools and individual land allotments.

Harriet Beecher Stowe, meeting at Lake Mohawk in New York State, initiated conferences advocating Indian education in the 1880s, which continued through the first two decades of the twentieth century. Before-and-after photographs of children arriving at Carlisle, Haskell, Bacone, and other boarding schools in their beautiful traditional dress: buckskins, blankets, and so forth, their hair in braids, and after the first day dressed in starched military-style uniforms with hair cut, were offered as ex post facto evidence that the education process was under way and that this place was not like home. The photographs documented their first steps toward civilization, and they were prize photos to show people back East. Within days these same children were literally marching toward civilization. The military regiment at Haskell and other boarding schools included daily drill practice. Discipline—control of the wild Indian and the land itself—was central to boarding school philosophy and practice.

By the late nineteenth century, boarding schools became the internal, the psychological, or interior "contested terrain" of federal

Photos of Navajo Tom Toslino taken in 1882 before (left) and after (right) entering the Carlisle Boarding School.

Indian policy. But while the "hearts and minds" of Indian children would be redeemed in Pratt's institutionalized baptism, the ultimate problem remained: the land—land Indians were perfectly willing to live on, in spite of devastating changes, much as their ancestors had. In order for the West to truly be won, these recalcitrant and backward peoples had to be introduced to the proper civilized relationship between human beings and nature—individual private property. It is worth repeating Comanche leader Ten Bears's remarks at the Council of Medicine Lodge in 1868 to grasp how different the indigenous relationship to the land was from the Lockean view as espoused in his 1690 *Second Treatise on Government*. Ten Bears stated, "I know every stream and every wood between the Rio Grande and the Arkansas. I have hunted and lived over that country.... Why do you ask us to leave the rivers, and the sun, and the wind, and to live in houses?"

The oratory is dramatic, not just for its cadence or tone but because of its substance. Ten Bears lived on what Kiowa writer N. Scott Momaday called a "remembered earth." Only a little more than a century ago there were peoples, entire societies, which viewed their homes as immense landscapes and natural environments directly experienced, not as politically formed territories, jurisdictions, or townships. Ten Bears's famous speech at the Council of Medicine Lodge was speaking to the heart of what it meant to be Comanche—what it meant to have an Oikos—a home—that was, in fact, an ecosystem. This standpoint is hardly romantic, but rather a worldview deeply earth oriented; it is an example of spatial thinking.

The General Allotment (Dawes) Act

> *The General Allotment Act is a mighty pulverizing engine*
> *to break up the tribal mass. It acts directly upon*
> *the family and the individual.*
> —**President Theodore Roosevelt** in 1901[19]

A chronology of federal Indian policy in the nineteenth century becomes a sequence of attacks to the very existence of Indians insofar as their identities were explicitly and implicitly shaped by places, in other words, indigenous. Until 1887, only a few treaties stipulated individual allotments of land for tribal members, but Commissioner of Indian Affairs T. Hartley Crawford had identified individual allotments of land as the foundation for Indian self-government and appropriation of Western, that is, Anglo-Saxon-influenced laws and policies.

Almost forty years later, Indian Commissioner John Q. Smith wrote in his *Annual Report* of 1876:

> It is doubtful whether any high degree of civilization is possible without individual ownership of land.... I am not unaware that this proposition will meet with strenuous opposition from the Indians themselves. Like the whites, they have ambitious men, who will resist to the utmost of their power any change tending to reduce the [their] authority... but it is essential that these men and their claims should be pushed aside and that each individual should feel that his home is his own; that he owes no allegiance to any great man or to any faction; that he has direct personal interest in the soil on which he lives, and that that interest will be faithfully protected for him and for his children by the Government.[20]

Indian Commissioner Crawford's and Smith's goal to use the imposition of individual private property as the ultimate vehicle for cultural assimilation was realized with the passage of the General Allotment Act of 1887—easily the single most devastating piece of legislation in the entire history of federal Indian Law. Quite apart from an assimilationist impetus, it also provided for the "legal" dispossession of a full two-thirds of tribal land through a provision declaring all remaining land after the allotments were made as surplus and open to sale for a small fraction of its worth. In this respect, the effect of the General Allotment Act was to reduce Indian landholdings from 138 million acres to 48 million acres. It also created the jurisdiction issues that tribes wrestle with today as a result of the often checkerboard nature of landholding in what were once contiguous tribally held lands.

Tribes often fought mightily to maintain contiguous tribally held lands after individual allotments were made. The 1912 petition of the First Peoples of the Colville Reservation to maintain a plot of 300,000 acres as a contiguous tract of land is a good example. The Colville reservation was created on April 9 and July 2, 1872. Under the authority of the Indian Appropriation Act of 1890, an agreement was reached by which Indians ceded some 1,500,000 acres on the northern part of the reservation for $1.00 an acre. Congress balked at the payment and in a substituted act of July 1, 1892, allowed individual allotments to all Indians living on said land and made the rest surplus lands that were part of the public domain.

In 1905, a bill was introduced to open the southern part of the reservation to settlement after individual allotments were made. Although the bill never became law, the Interior Department instructed Inspector James McLaughlin to negotiate with the Colville Indians for the cession, grant, and relinquishment to the United States of the southern part of their reservation on essentially the same terms provided in the unsuccessful 1905 bill. As part of the agreement a very delinquent payment of $1,500,000 was arranged for the land ceded on the northern part of the reservation as stipulated in the earlier act of July 2, 1892.

Although this agreement was never ratified by Congress, it passed legislation on March 22, 1906, and June 21, 1906, which substantially adopted all the terms of the McLaughlin agreement. Individual allotments of 80 acres of agricultural land or 160 acres of grazing were proposed, with surplus lands again being offered for sale to non-Indians.

The petition of the Colville Indians stands as a testament to their awareness of what was at stake and the conscious effort of the Office of Indian Affairs to destroy any vestiges of tribal Indian identity tied to a sense of place standing outside the institution of private property. As the 1912 Colville Petition stated, the opening to white settlement would "leave the possessions of this tribe in isolated and unconnected land interests among the more numerous white settlers, and be a bar to retaining a community of interest and society among the present Indian residents."[21]

The petition points out the unsuitability of maintaining a living on the allotments proposed by the government, given the topography of the land. For the same reason (topography), the petition points out contiguous tracts would be difficult to establish. However, what is unmistakable in the petition is the recognition that if separated on individual tracts of land without a real social connectedness through the land, their earlier way of life and customs as well as "a community of interest and society among the present Indian residents" would be destroyed.

The petition states: "That the topography of this reservation is such that under any system of allotment it will be impossible for any number of us to obtain tracts contiguous to each other, thereby depriving us to a great extent, the enjoyment of the early life and customs of the Red Man."[22]

The Petition was so clear in its intent and rationale, then Second Assistant Commissioner Hauke summarized the signatories' goal in his equally clear rejection of the petition:

> The ultimate object in view for these Indians is breaking up the tribal interests in their land into individual allotments and aiding them as such individual owners of the soil to establish permanent homes. This object would be defeated by the retention of a large reserve wherein communal relations and old Indian customs could be continued.
>
> For the reasons set out herein, this Office believes that the Indians should be advised that their plan is impracticable and that it would not be in their best interests either individually or collectively. The petition and the accompanying note from the Secretary to the President are returned herewith.[23]

Even a decade into the twentieth century, the Office of Indian Affairs in the Department of Interior saw nothing positive in the continuation of their earlier lifeways. The office clearly recognized it would only cause them problems to entertain or indulge the Indians in any action that might acknowledge anything of their old environments and ways was of value.

All three federal policies: removal, boarding school education, and general allotment illustrate Deloria's general premise that political ideologies in American politics eclipse the importance of places or a sense of place in defining identities and political issues. Removal policies suggest the geographic separation functioned as much, if not more, as an abstract cultural demarcation rather than as an appreciation for geographic features of culture. When this policy inevitably failed, along with the short-lived genocidal military solution, assimilation through the institutionalized baptism of the Indian boarding schools seemed the only answer.

The first two solutions saw the Indian problem as geographic primarily in the sense that Indians were literally in the way. In the eyes of settlers Indians were not really connected to the places they inhabited, so much as merely in places that non-Indian settlers of the United States wanted to be. Assimilation policies, the boarding school educational policy, and the movement to impose private property relations were actually more spatially, in other words, environmentally and ecologically oriented than their advocates realized. The boarding schools almost accomplished what they set out to, but at a terrible price we still pay today.

If Christianity gave Western humans a theoretical/theological justification for seeing nature as corrupted and threatening, imagine the profound sense of guilt and shame foisted on children whose earliest experiences of life were tied to natural environments and landscapes—I do not mean in any Rousseauian "noble savage" sense—but in the simplest form of what today would be recognized as a cultural geographic or environment sense. What assimilationist policies, from educational policy to termination strategies, actually did was (not as non-Natives imagined—attack indigenous cultures as inferior, but) to literally attack the places and spaces from which indigenous cultures emerged. The logical result was a degree of self-hatred often unrecognized by its victims and the source of considerable dysfunctionality found in tribes today.

Time, Space,
and the Defense of Place

In the twentieth century, four federal government actions illustrate the continuing deep spatial historical problem the First Peoples of this land faced: the Meriam Report, or *The Problem of Indian Administration*; The Indian Reorganization Act, or the Wheeler-Howard Act; the US government policy of tribal termination; and the American Indian Religious Freedom Act embody, in varying degrees, a continuation of the same historical thinking, that is, ideology that sought to *displace* the First Peoples of the United States. In short, government policies promoted removal of the First Peoples from their cultures, lands, and unique existence as tribal nations. The *displacement* of the First Peoples was existential.

However, with the exception of the Meriam Report, the voices of the First Peoples increasingly found their strength to challenge the ideological narrative of US history so often found in textbook treatments of First Peoples of this land. The narrative of removal, displacement, and ultimately replacement when viewed in the light of current events is eclipsed by the resilient light of sovereignty found among the First Peoples of the landscapes and seascapes of not only the American West, but in the north, east, and south.

In the minds of the civilizers, the existential threats First Peoples faced were understood as a replacement logic. In the everyday lives of the First Peoples, federal government policy constituted an attempted erasure—a removal of their tribal identities and replacement, as the Meriam Report so succinctly put it, with one suited to the US society and the "advancement of productive efficiency, the acquisition of reasonable ability in the utilization of income and property."[24]

The scathing criticism of the Indian Service in the 1928 Meriam Report and conditions the First Peoples experienced under the federal administration of their affairs did nothing to assuage the overall tone of this still relevant report. Token acknowledgment is given in the Meriam Report to the fact that not all Indians wanted the life that was being imposed on them. The report also noted with almost a tone of regret that some value resided in the "Indian" cultures and encouraged government workers and missionaries to "take a sympathetic attitude toward Indian ways, Indian ethics, and Indian religion."[25] However, the overarching goal of the United

States Indian Service remained "the development and advancement of a retarded race."[26]

The morally duplicitous nature of the dominant historical narrative of inevitable movement to civilization permeates the report's first chapter, "General Summary of Findings and Recommendations." The ideologically driven history of progress, civilization, and, dare I say, enlightenment provides a rationalization for horrible wrongdoing. One can bemoan, even express regret over the injustices done to Indians in the past and, without missing a beat, find moral redemption in the full confidence that such is the manifest course of history.

This now legendary report in the annals of public policy treatments of the Indian problem shows that something felt so palpably half a century earlier was now explicitly embraced in the policies and administration of the Indian Service in 1928. The goal of all Indian policies and programs was the remaking of the maladjusted "Indian" so that she/he could productively assimilate into the civilized political and economic institutions of the United States. There could be no separate and unequal coexistence as George Washington and Andrew Jackson imagined little more than a century earlier. Both the physical and, more importantly, the social and cultural boundary line had to be removed.

In order to make this adjustment, the Meriam Report fundamentally reaffirmed the role education would play in this solving the Indian problem. Richard Henry Pratt's "killing" through education was now thoroughly understood as the work of the Indian Service. The necessity of continuing this crucial work by sanitized and civilized methods is the hallmark of the Meriam Report.

Much like Pratt had envisioned in his baptism allegory of Indian education,[27] solving the Indian problem required the destruction of the boundary line Washington and Jackson envisioned. For a United States now extending from sea to shining sea, there was no place to push the First Peoples of this land. The boundary line was obsolete and the removal now was a war on the personalities, or what Bob Thomas called the "Peoplehood of the First Peoples."[28]

The Meriam Report decried the failure to properly fund the civilized removal programs of education embodied in the killing of the Indian to save the man. It contended that, with proper funding and a complete focus on education, the work of erasing the unique character and personality, or rather *persons* of the hundreds of tribal nations in the United States of America, could be completed, after which time the celebration could begin and the work of the Indian Service would no longer be necessary, for the United States would no longer have Indians and consequently the Indian problem would be solved.

The Meriam Report embodies the paternalistic problem the civilizers must own. For if the civilized administrators failed to address the Indian problem who would? In the mind's eye of the progressive friends of the Indians, the Indian Service was doing the hard work of adjusting the maladjusted Indians to a modern advanced industrial society.

It would be immoral to leave the Indians to the systemic imperatives of the modern industrial society that was foreign to them. This task, rife with a complex moral complicity of regret, guilt, responsibility, righteousness, and, ultimately, an intrinsic pardoning logic—after all, no one stands in the way of history—that explains much about the still confused understanding most US citizens have of their government's history in the administration of the First Peoples of this land.

The ultimate proof of the prejudices of the Meriam Report is evident in its methodology. Nowhere is there any evidence that the First Peoples' view or opinion of the policies that shaped their lives were ever sought. How could they? This failure was intrinsic to the ideological view of history held by the civilizers—the administrators of the Indian and her/his problem.

Given the historical lenses of ideology through which the administrators saw the still lingering notion of the maladjusted savage, it would have been inconceivable to ask an "Indian" what they wanted—how could they know? The Indian was the problem.

In a very practical sense the Indian problem was and remains deeply situated in the psyche and historical worldview of Euro-Americans, as we so clearly witnessed at Standing Rock throughout the fall and winter of 2016–2017. Damn Indians! We just do not fit in the historical narrative of triumph, government depredations, tragedy, and the series of exceptional events that is the ideological narrative of manifest greatness the settlers want to tell.

The Indian Reorganization Act sought to change that, and its architect John Collier may to this day be one of the greatest friends of the Indians who, in spite of his good intentions, fell victim to the ideology of history as a forward march through time. Even when the "friends

John Collier, Commission for the Bureau of Indian Affairs, 1933-1945.

of the Indians," like John Collier, sought to help them, the deeply felt logic of Manifest Destiny continued to reveal itself, as in Collier's mammoth, far-ranging bill regarding government, education, economics, and courts.

As an advocate for the American Indian, Collier was indeed cut from a different cloth than the Indian commissioners who preceded him. He saw something valuable in what he called the Indian civilization—what we now call culture. Unfortunately, 150 years into federal Indian policy, he faced three problems. First, Indians were now successfully divided by governmental and nongovernmental institutions—most importantly, education—into traditionalist and progressives. Traditionalists wanted above all else the opportunity to continue active participation in their customs, habits, and lifeways. Progressives supported assimilation.

Second, for traditionalists, the continuation of cultures and ancient customs invariably meant the practice of a People possessing land in common, not dividing it up into individual private property. Collier's attempt to address the ever-declining land base of tribes in his mammoth legislation four decades after the General Allotment Act of 1887 illustrated the tension between "traditionalists" and "progressives." The General Allotment Act planted seeds of individual ownership of land as property and a source of income. After four decades of allotment policy and the complementary activities of the off-reservation boarding school education, a significant number of Indians objected to Collier's plan to restore land to the tribes.

Collier's plan was simple enough. He proposed that upon the death of a land owner the title to the land would revert to the tribe. What many Indians had learned through the Indian schools and as a result of the General Allotment Act was that property should be owned individually and go to the legal heirs upon the death of the owner. Any proposal to do otherwise would be seen as a gross injustice. Collier was surprised by the number of Indians at the so-called Indian Congresses, who very articulately criticized his notion of returning individually owned allotments to a form of communal landholding by the tribes.

In meeting after meeting with the tribes, the progressives who had decided to adopt the dominant society's practice of individual ownership got up and called this proposal, no matter how well-intentioned, anathema to what was now their custom and the habits that ensued from such ownership.[29] Collier found out in a very unexpected way that Indians had voices, and what they perceived as his paternalist meddling was unwelcome.

Traditionalists, of course, typically supported Colliers's approach to restoring ever-decreasing Indian landholdings.

Finally, throughout Collier's bill, the secretary of Indian Affairs was given extraordinary powers to make final determinations on a number of crucial issues on which the tribes would no doubt require assistance. Imagining a generation of administrators who would be enlightened like he was and dedicated to restoring more Indian participation in governance, education, economic development, and a court system, Collier was again surprised at how many Indians opposed what they saw as his paternalistic attitude.

While Colliers's efforts to honor, and when possible have unique tribal traditions shape the reforms he dedicated his life to promote, were well-intentioned, he seemed to misgauge just how independent the members of the First Nations could be. Ironically, for a friend of the Indians so intent on helping the Indian, he had fallen into the prejudicial "trap" of thinking they obviously lacked the vision and leadership to accomplish much of what he was proposing on their own. The Collier Bill did successfully promote self-government and the reform of education, but it failed to return the tribes to the "Native" vision he had of their economic systems and courts.

Collier learned from the Indians that they were now using the white man's education to shape their future, even if it meant not always doing it Collier's way. As the apocryphal quote attributed Mark Twain goes, he learned, "It ain't what you don't know that gets you in trouble it is what you know that just ain't so that causes all the problems."[30]

The "Termination" Policy

Immediately after World War II, those most concerned with the continuing Indian problem decided the full integration of the Indian into American society must entail the elimination of their tribes as nations within this larger nation. The policy that would end the status of the First Peoples as domestic dependent nations or "the nations within" was called termination.[31] The emerging policy of termination was greatly accelerated when Dillon Myer was named the commissioner of the Bureau of Indian Affairs. Philosophically Myer was the perfect choice for the termination task. He served during World War II as the director of the War Relocation Authority—the program that established the internment camps for Japanese Americans during the war.

Myer's experiences in the camps led him to see the impossibility of fostering civic and ethnic pride in people who were essentially prisoners segregated from the rest of society. In his mind, the Indian problem was a closely related issue. He saw reservations as little more than internment camps that segregated Indians from the rest of American society. Therefore his support for the destruction of geographic, treaty, economic, and political features of their segregation was unqualified.

The dire poverty and health issues facing many reservations was crippling in late 1940s and early 1950s. Never mind that many of these problems were a result of the chronic underfunding of Indian programs—the sentiment among lawmakers was that enough was enough. The prevailing attitude was much like that of President Ronald Reagan forty years later when he responded to a Russian student's question regarding the condition of the First Peoples of the United States. Reagan responded, "Maybe we made a mistake. Maybe we should not have humored them in that wanting to stay in that kind of primitive lifestyle. Maybe we should have said no, come join us; be citizens along with the rest of us."[32] Two decades after Collier's IRA reform, some lawmakers were beginning to see the Indian problem as unsolvable, unless the legal status of their tribal nations and their dual citizenship was solved with termination.

The historical amnesia present in this framing of the Indian problem was startling, for there was little recognition by lawmakers of the deep historical character of the problems clearly plaguing

American Indians that were, even as the Meriam Report had acknowledged, quite complex.

President Dwight D. Eisenhower named a new secretary of the interior in 1952. Unfortunately, his choice, Douglas McKay, had the same view of solving the Indian problem as did Myer. He only expressed the view less bluntly and in a more "civilized" manner. McKay presented termination as merely representing the government finally giving Indians full US citizenship. Of course, the irony is obvious for Indians who were made citizens in the 1924 Indian Citizenship Act. What McKay meant was to end the unique rights Indians held as citizens of their own unique "nations within." He selected Glenn Emmons to be his Indian commissioner, and Emmons, a moderate, felt little need to do anything to stop the growing movement of termination.

After several false starts, the 1954 Congress enacted termination bills, with the first successful bill terminating the Menominee Nation of Wisconsin. Later in the summer, legislation terminating the Alabama-Coushatta, the Paiutes, the Klamaths, and the western Oregon bands of Indians was put forward. The National Congress of American Indians stood firmly against this policy, as did John Collier and many of the liberal friends of the Indians. Several tribes, such as the Potawatomi and the Kickapoo, were scathing in their criticism of termination and were able to keep their Peoples safe. But lawmakers leading this initiative struck at, as they saw it, the weakest Peoples in order to avoid major pushback.

Unfortunately, what Congress had underestimated was how entrenched and complex the problems were that the tribes faced. They also could not fathom that a new generation of leadership in Indian Country was emerging. WWII veterans returned home determined they would not be second-class citizens on the land they fought to protect. Young leaders who knew the dominant system of politics and who valued their culture and the intrinsic tribal values represented in it were ready to make changes. Only twenty-five years after John Collier sought to engineer a federal policy to give Indians self-government with some semblance of appreciation for Indian culture, the First Peoples of this land demonstrated they were ready to act as sovereign Peoples or nations.

Within a few years the mobilization to fight for restoration began, and the American public started to understand that indeed the

First Peoples were different. They were more interested in achieving their vision of what a good and healthy tribal society looked like than buying into the American Dream that the "I like Ike" 1950s was selling. The enduring light of the West, flickering at best, was about to shine brightly again.

The fire of sovereignty saw old and young step forward to rekindle and build the fire anew. It would be nice to have a simple thesis to explain why this happened, but several factors figured prominently. Termination and urban relocation programs after WWII played a large part in the emerging Red Power Movement; so did the fact that during the 1950s and 1960s, a new generation of First Peoples were moving into colleges and universities, often as first-generation college students. Ironically, the very programs that sought to have First Peoples disappear into the fabric of American society had the opposite, unintended consequence of giving large intertribal communities in cities across American the opportunity to see the common issues their reservation communities faced across very different physical and cultural landscapes. The homogenizing one-size-fits all approach of the US government to *their* Indian problem gave the First Peoples of this land a clear target and a constant reminder of what they most valued: the right to be tribal peoples in the lands they honored as given to them by the Creator.

Urban Indians and their children began to realize they could be active participants in their Peoples' struggles for sovereignty rather than assimilated *good* Indians who honored their indigenousness as something like a romantic and noble past—simply a heritage to be acknowledged, but with little of value to be practically applied in the modern world. The American Indian Chicago Conference of 1961, attended by nearly 500 American Indians from across the United States, produced the first document, the Declaration of Indian Purpose, announcing that the so-called vanishing Americans were not going anywhere, and that, in fact, they had a lot on their minds.

In the next decade, so much was happening not only in large national meetings and conferences but also in urban Indian centers, community gatherings, and around kitchen tables in reservation and off-reservation households, that it would be foolish to point to any single catalytic event to explain what would become the Red Power Movement and the American Indian Movement. It was in this political environment that the forces for tribal restoration were emerging in unique ways across the country.

One of the best documented cases for the struggle for restoration of tribal nation status and the rekindling of the bright light of sovereignty is the Menominee. Under the leadership of two tribal members—Jim White and Ada Deer—the Determination of Rights and Unity for Menominee Shareholders (DRUMS)—came into being in 1970, only months after the Indians of All Tribes

Ada Deer in 2007

occupied Alcatraz on November 20, 1969. The power behind the story of the successful Menominee efforts to be restored to a tribal nation's status is found in the creation of the movement known as the DRUMS. As Nick Peroff's classic work on Menominee restoration effort documents, the struggle for recognition was a struggle for education and mobilization of a Menominee tribe deeply fractured and ill-informed of what had happened to them and a model of the complementary charismatic leadership of Jim White and the diplomatic skills of Ada Deer.

Quite significant and little recognized is the overall contributions Menominee women played in the successful restoration of their nation in 1974. In addition to Deer, Shirley Daly, and Sylvia Wilber played important roles in the DRUMS organization running the DRUMS newsletter and helping educate tribal members about what termination meant and why restoration was crucial for the continued existence of the Menominee People. The DRUMS newsletter also provided a media outlet for urban Indians and non-Indians nationwide about their movement's goals strategies and tactics. DRUMS launched a para-institutional approach to recognition, which constituted a co-optation of the methods and institutions of the dominant society, to take over the Menominee Enterprises, Inc., and the Menominee Common Stock Voting Trust—the corporate entities the Menominee First People was dissolved into.

Their ability to take indigenous Menominee culture and values into the DRUMS organization affirmed the long-standing international (tribal) diplomatic traditions of the Menominee First People. Through the early articulate public leadership of Jim White and the behind-the-scenes work of these three women and many others, we see a story of a resilient sovereignty—a modern example of Indigenous ingenuity at work.

In the documentary *Since 1634: In the Wake of Nicolett*, Ada Deer and Shirley Daly stress the significance of the Menominee relationship to their land and to the inextricable linkage between the land and their culture, values, and unique identity as Menominee People. The enduring and defining features of the First Peoples—the Indigenous Peoples—of the United States is that symbiotic relationship between the natural environments of their places—be they landscapes or seascapes—and the unique cultures and identities that emerge from this nature-culture nexus.

History
through Indigenous Eyes

When the history of the West is seen through indigenous eyes, it is not the West of the imagination, it is the particular place where a People came to be who they are—from the moment of creation. What becomes clear, even in a brief survey such as this, is that the idea of the West, like the East, takes on levels of collective meaning for immigrants when viewed through their unfolding story of discovery, civilization, and freedom over time that is foreign to Peoples who understand themselves as a part of unique places known experientially and honored in embodied customs, habits, and intellectual traditions—in short, in culture.

From the 1960s to the present, the most characteristic feature of the First Peoples' modern history is the extent to which their issues continue to be about places and spaces. The protests for Indian equality at Alcatraz, the battle for fishing rights in the Pacific Northwest, and the confrontation with federal agents at Wounded Knee all have taken place in the West and serve as iconic touch points in our entangled history, where the sovereign rights of First Peoples were on full display for all Americans to see. For the first time, through these events, many white Americans understood the hardships and injustice that First Peoples had been facing for centuries. The federal government, through laws such as the Indian Child Welfare Act, American Indian Religious Freedom Act (concerning sacred sites), the Indian Gaming Regulatory Act, and the Native American Grave Protection and Repatriation Act, all of which have had significant impacts in the West, have begun the difficult process of healing the painful silences and inequalities that have marked Native histories of the West. While there is a great deal of work to do, the new century offers signs of optimism.

As we move into the twenty-first century, there are indeed signs of improvement in relations between the settlers and the First Peoples of this land. Tribal leaders are fighting for their rights in the political process and in the courts. Many white Americans, especially younger ones, know the story of what was done to the First Peoples. They believe in the importance of land, defend the religious freedom of the First Peoples, and support the role of women. While bridges of understanding have been built, injustices continue to this day, as evidenced by the protests at Standing Rock. These protests against the Dakota pipeline, calling for protection of tribal water rights and the greater environment, resulted in the largest gathering of tribes in history, joined in the battle by many white Americans. For some, a Native reunification vision was coming to life, promising potentially an increased awareness and rekindling the alliances that were forged in the 1960s and 1970s. The opening of the Smithsonian National Museum of the American Indian in September 2004 highlighted the important history of American Indians and affirmed to many their pride in their ancestors and culture. Many religious artifacts and ancestral remains have been returned to their rightful owners, the tribal nations of America.

At the same time, federal and state governments as well as some business interests continue to make demands for access to water, oil and gas, mining, and energy resources on Native Lands. Some government and business leaders do not believe there are any rights for the nations of the First Peoples—only the right to optimize their own financial profits.

A light does shine in and on the history of the First Peoples, however, and there is a growing understanding and shared sense of purpose between the white and Native worlds. Hard work remains to be done to truly arrive at a place of equality, equity, and a common interest informed by Native worldviews emergent from a symbiotic relationship with the land. When, driven by fear, some want to build walls—the new "boundary line"—for homeland security, Native history teaches us that human security will be fleeting without fostering homeland maturity—a sense of place—where humankind recognizes the intrinsic value of the land, air, water, and diverse life that gives us a beautiful cultural diversity matching the geo-, eco-, and biological diversity of our mother, this blue-green planet called Earth.

Resilience resides in places, like the American West. Few can teach the lifeway lessons as well as those, little more than a century ago, who were thought of as the vanishing Americans. The First Peoples are still here, and they have stories to share—stories illuminated by a light a good number of people are beginning to see as they study our shared and entangled history.

CHAPTER 4

Changing Boundaries

by Robert C. Baron

There was never a good war or a bad peace.
—**Benjamin Franklin**[1]

In the field of world policy, I would dedicate this nation
to the policy of the good neighbor.
—**Franklin Delano Roosevelt's**
Inaugural Address, March 4, 1933[2]

This chapter is about our northern and southern neighbors; its purpose is to discuss US boundaries and the settlement of the North American continent. Together, Canada, the United States, and Mexico consist of 9.4 million square miles, more than twice the size of the fifty-one countries in Europe. Each of these three countries stretches from ocean to ocean, a situation that does not occur in any country in South America. How was North America settled by Europeans?

European Culture and Wars

To begin the story, consider the early history of French North America, English North America, and Spanish North America. France, Great Britain, and Spain have different histories, exploration objectives, religion, and culture, and these affected the early history of European settlements in North America.

Although France, Great Britain, and Spain are similar in population size today, they developed in different ways and peaked at different times. From the fifteenth to the nineteenth centuries they fought for dominance in Europe. The North American colonies were a small part of the European story.

Quebec was settled in 1608 and Montreal in 1642. Boston was founded in 1630. What would soon become Mexico City was conquered by Hernán Cortés in 1519, although the Aztecs had had a city there for centuries. Settlers from New Spain (Mexico) founded Santa Fe in 1609.

For the French, English, and Spanish colonists, there was an almost infinite wilderness to the south, west, and north of the first settlements. How would this land be explored and settled? Development and western migration were influenced by decisions made in Europe. The English were along the Atlantic Ocean, France was to the north and center of the continent, and Spain was to the south and west.

Columbus discovered the New World for Spain in 1492, and for more than two centuries it was the leading European country in the Americas. Brazil was a colony of Portugal and used its language, but the rest of South and Central America were Spanish. Cuba was settled in 1511, and Peru was conquered by Francisco Pizarro in 1532. The New World, especially South America and Mexico, were sources of substantial wealth in gold and silver for Spain. The major factors in Spanish colonization were the influence of the Spanish Grandee, the Catholic Church, and the Spanish Inquisition.

Spain was at war with France, England, or Holland through much of the sixteenth to eighteenth centuries, spending its wealth from the New World on the Anglo-Spanish Wars of 1585 to 1727, the Thirty Years War, the various Dutch wars, the War of Spanish Succession, the War of Quadruple Alliance, the Seven Years War, and various wars in the New World and elsewhere. Although Spain continued to be nominally in charge of much of Latin America until the nineteenth century, its influence in Europe declined after 1700.

France was the leading European power from the time of Louis XIV, who ruled France for seventy-two years, from 1643 until 1715. France was often at war with its neighbors—Holland, Spain, Italy, the German states, and the British—and this had an effect on its colonial empire. France was strongly Roman Catholic and sent Jesuit missionaries to the New World. In the seventeenth and eighteenth centuries, most decisions were made by the powers in Paris. Queen Anne's War (1702–1713) and the French and Indian War (1754–1763) resulted in France's defeat by Great Britain and the loss of its North American empire, with Canada going to England and Louisiana to Spain.

England entered the colonial race late. Beginning in the sixteenth century, Britain fought Spain with its navy for control of the seas. The British also supported buccaneers (pirates) to prey on the Spanish treasure ships returning from the New World. Britain's ultimate goals in North America were different from France's—to colonize the American landscape and to export some of the surplus population from England and Scotland.

From the seventeenth to the nineteenth century, the islands of the Caribbean were battlegrounds between the French, Spanish, Dutch, and the English. In North America, the Dutch had lost their colonies in Delaware and along the Hudson River to the British in the mid-sixteenth century when New Amsterdam became New York. But Holland, a great sea power, was very active in the Caribbean. Britain and France fought local battles to gain control of specific islands with their financially important sugar industry. With each European war and the resulting treaty, parts of North America and the Caribbean islands were traded at the bargaining table.

The peak of each country's power might be shown by listing the royal leader in each country at the time of its greatest power:

> Spain................ King Philip II.............. 1556–1598
> France.............. King Louis XIV 1643–1715
> England........... Queen Victoria........... 1837–1901

English colonial settlements and the migration across the continent by the people of the United States are covered in Chapters 5 and 6. Here, the settlement, movement west, and the boundaries with Canada and Mexico are reviewed.

Canada

Canada was visited by the Norsemen around 1,000 AD. In 1407, the Italian navigator Giovanni Caboto (John Cabot) discovered the Grand Banks and claimed this important fishing reserve for England. In 1534, Jacques Cartier explored the Gulf of St. Lawrence for France, and Humphrey Gilbert claimed Newfoundland for England in 1583. In 1608, Samuel de Champlain established a fur trading post in Quebec, and the following year he traveled to the Great Lakes. Sieur de LaSalle

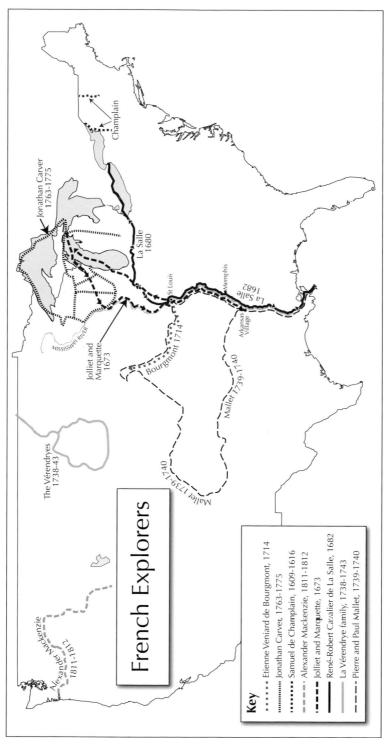

Fig. 4.1—Some French Explorers

visited the Ohio River area, and in 1673 the French explorers Louis Jolliet and Jacques Marquette navigated down the Mississippi River. Within a dozen years, there were French settlements in Mississippi and Louisiana. Figure 4.1 shows major French explorations in North America.

French North America (1534–1763)

For almost two centuries, France controlled a large portion of a North American empire, from the Gulf of St. Lawrence to the Gulf of Mexico. France governed New France despotically and from a distance. There were English-French rivalries, but French forces went deeper into the continent. Champlain decided to make the St. Lawrence Valley in what would become Canada the focus of New France and the gateway to the interior of North America. Champlain had established his fur trading post in Quebec, and Jesuit fathers soon arrived in Quebec as missionaries to the Indians. Beaver pelts and Catholic missionaries were the main reasons French forces explored much of North America.

In 1629, Quebec was captured by English forces but was returned to the French by the Treaty of St. Germaine. In King Philip's War, English colonial forces tried to take Quebec. The outbreak of the European War of Spanish Succession in 1701 brought another round of hostilities in North America as England once again attacked Quebec. The subsequent Treaty of Utrecht in 1713 gave Newfoundland and Acadia to the British and Cape Breton and St. John's Island to France. France was willing to sacrifice North American lands for losses in Europe. In following decades, 10,000 French-speaking Acadians would be expelled to Louisiana.

With the Death of Marquis de Montcalm in 1759, Quebec fell to General James Wolfe in the Battle of the Plains of Abraham during the French and Indian War, and the following year the French lost Montreal. The end of the conflict was marked by the Treaty of Paris in 1763, in which, as we saw earlier, France ceded New France and its people to Britain and Louisiana to Spain.

English Canada (1760–1867)

In 1670, the Hudson's Bay Company received a charter from Charles II in England and was granted all lands draining in Hudson's Bay (Rupert's

Land). Later, the Hudson's Bay Company became the authority over all Northwest Territories and regions west of the Rocky Mountains.

Canada became part of the British Empire with the Treaty of Paris. In 1774, the Quebec Act gave French Canadians a number of rights, including the French Civil Code, recognition of the Catholic Church with the ability to collect tithes, and the use of the French language. There were tensions between English- and French-speaking Canadians, especially between Upper (Ontario) and Lower (Quebec) Canada—the upper and lower parts of the St. Lawrence River.

Britain gave up claims to the Ohio Valley at the end of the Revolutionary War. In 1793, the Town of York (now Toronto) was established as the capital of Upper Quebec. Throughout the eighteenth and nineteenth centuries, there were explorers discovering the land in Canada. In 1789, Scotsman Alexander MacKenzie traveled to the Arctic Ocean; four years later, he reached the Pacific Ocean, a dozen years before Lewis and Clark.

During the nineteenth century, trade with Great Britain increased, and there was substantial migration from Great Britain to Canada of Scots, Irish, and English. One of the concerns in Canada was the fear of the United States and the possibility of absorption of parts of Canada—Alaska was bought from Russia and became part of the United States in 1867.

During most of the nineteenth century, the various parts of Canada were independent, as settlers slowly moved across the continent.

Canadian Nationhood

In 1867, the Dominion of Canada was established with Ontario, Quebec, Nova Scotia, and New Brunswick as founding provinces. Canada then became a federal state with powers divided between the capital in Ottawa and the provinces. The Hudson's Bay Company sold the Northwest Territories to the Dominion of Canada. In 1870, Manitoba entered the confederation, and in 1871, British Columbia did the same. They were followed by Prince Edward Island (1873), Alberta and Saskatchewan (1905), and finally Newfoundland/Labrador (1949). The ten Canadian provinces were now united by law if not physically.

The prairies, parkland, and forests of Alberta and Saskatchewan were carved out of the Northwest Territories and became part of the confederation. The question was, were the million acres of the western real estate to support old Canada? Discussed in Chapter 6 for the United States, the same question applied to Canada: was the West a colony of the East?

In 1880, the Canadian Pacific Railroad was founded and physically united the country with a route from Montreal to Vancouver. At that time, Canada was a country of 4 million people. In contrast, the United States at that time was a country of more than 50 million people. By 1904, three transcontinental railroads—the Canadian Northern, Grand Trunk, and Intercolonial Railway—became the Canadian National Railway System. Railroads connected Montreal to the empty plains of the West. As farms developed in the West, new forms of wheat increased yields, and western Canada was on its way to becoming a "breadbasket of the world." Substantial amounts of grain were shipped from Canadian prairies to England during World War I. When petroleum was discovered in Alberta, its population increased from 800,000 in 1941 to 2,200,000 by 1981.

In 1937, Trans-Canada Airlines was established. The construction of the Trans-Canada Highway system started in 1948, opened July 30, 1962, and was completed in 1970. This 4,860-mile-long highway went from Victoria, British Columbia, to St. John's, Newfoundland. Canada was now physically connected. The Canadian Broadcasting Company provided common news and entertainment to the nation of Canada beginning in 1922.

In 1920, Arthur Meighan was appointed prime minister of Canada, the first Canadian leader from the West. Since then, half of all Canadian leaders have been from the West, a situation similar to the United States.

Canadian–US Relations

As this chapter deals with boundaries, a review of the Canadian–US boundary is in order. During the Revolutionary War, there were American invasions of Quebec and Nova Scotia in an attempt to annex part of Canada to the American Republic. These invasions failed due in part to French Canadian neutrality. After the Revolutionary War, more than 30,000 English Loyalists from New England and New York migrated from the United States to Nova Scotia, and another 10,000 Loyalists settled along the St. Lawrence Valley and Great Lakes. In the War of 1812—a war for Canada's survival—US forces again invaded

Fig. 4.2—Canada Today

Canada, and French Canadian and British troops invaded Maine and upper New England. Americans burned down York (Toronto), and British troops burned down Washington in response. The war ended in a stalemate with no boundary changes, and anti-US sentiments increased after the War of 1812.

The Treaty of Paris, the Jay Treaty (1795), and the Webster-Ashburton Treaty (1842) had the 49th parallel established as the continental boundary from Lake Superior to the Rocky Mountains. In the US election of 1846, the political slogan "54-40 or Fight" was used, an attempt to seize all of Oregon and much of western Canada. President James K. Polk, in office at the time, was looking to expand both north and south. The forested areas west of the Rockies (Oregon) had been left to British and American joint management, and the dispute between the two countries was ultimately settled by diplomacy. Britain benefited by American troubles with Mexico. On June 15, 1846, the Oregon Boundary Treaty made the 49th parallel the boundary from the Rockies to the Pacific Coast.

For more than two centuries, the United States and Canada have been neighbors at peace. This is the world's longest undefended, open border—3,987 miles of open boundary between Canada and the lower forty-eight states and an additional 1,538 miles of open border between Canada and Alaska.

In 1923, the United States replaced Britain as Canada's leading trading partner. Today, Canada is the United States' most important trading partner, second only to China in imports. (For example, in 2016, US exports to Canada were $266,826K and imports were $278,056K.) The two countries' trade is in many areas, from agricultural products to minerals to timber and hydroelectric power. This has been a mutually beneficial relationship between the two neighbors for 200 years.

Roads travel north and south in British Columbia and Washington; Alberta, Idaho, and Montana; Saskatchewan and Manitoba; and North Dakota and Minnesota for trade and travel through a friendly boundary.

The US relationship with its southern neighbor has not been quite as peaceful, however.

Mexico

Early History

Spanish explorers visited most of the New World during the sixteenth, seventeenth, and eighteenth centuries. In 1519, Hernán Cortés anchored his ships off the Veracruz coast, and in 1521 the Spanish defeated the Aztec leaders and founded Mexico City (which had been Tenochtitlan to the Aztecs). By 1550, Mexico City had a printing press, and in 1551 the Real y Pontificia Universidad became the first university in the New World. Mexico City's population reached 70,000, making it the largest city in the New World.

In 1528, Spaniards explored Florida, and Álvar Núñez Cabeza de Vaca returned overland through Texas into Mexico. Hernando de Soto explored Florida to beyond the Mississippi River; from 1540 to 1542 Francisco Vázquez de Coronado explored Arizona and New Mexico; in 1542, Juan Rodríguez Cabrillo explored the California coast.

If we dimly recall America's colonial origins, it is not for lack of
written records. Bundles of documents relating to North America and dating back to Ponce de Leon's discovery of Florida in
1513, repose in public and private archives in Spain, Mexico
and the United States. The first book devoted entirely to North
America, Cabeza de Vaca's account of his stranger than fiction
journey from Florida to the Pacific slope, appeared in Spain in
1542. From Spain's first contact with North American shores,
historians began to fashion the first-hand accounts of explorers
into comprehensive narratives.

—**David Weber**[3]

Spanish Explorers

Figure 4.3 is a map of the early Spanish explorers in North America.
including Ponce de León, Álvarez de Pineda, de Vaca, De Soto, Coronado, Alarcón, Cabrillo, de Anza, Serra, and Bartholeum Ferrier.

In April 1598, Juan de Oñate took possession of New Mexico and
in 1610 founded a colony in Santa Fe. The Church had a large impact
on Mexican society and settlements; shortly after Oñate founded his
colony, the Franciscans began to build missions in New Mexico.

Mexico was a colony of New Spain and as such was governed
by Spain until 1821. Leadership of New Spain was from Spain, with
Spain's government specifying all aspects of its colonies, including the
locations of new churches, the types of crops that could be grown, and
the New World's institutions. There was a wealth of silver, and Spanish
galleons brought back New World riches including silver bullion. The
silver from Mexico financed the various Spanish wars in Europe.

During the eighteenth century, with Spanish reconnaissance
in California, the Spanish began to build missions from Monterey to
San Jose. The settlers focused on converting the Indians, planting, and
ranching.

Meanwhile, Spanish influence in the country that would become
the United States was being challenged on the East Coast by the American colonies and in the middle of the country by French commercial
interest. Spain got all of Louisiana in 1763, viewing it as a buffer
between the English colonists on the Atlantic and its Mexican lands to
the west and south.

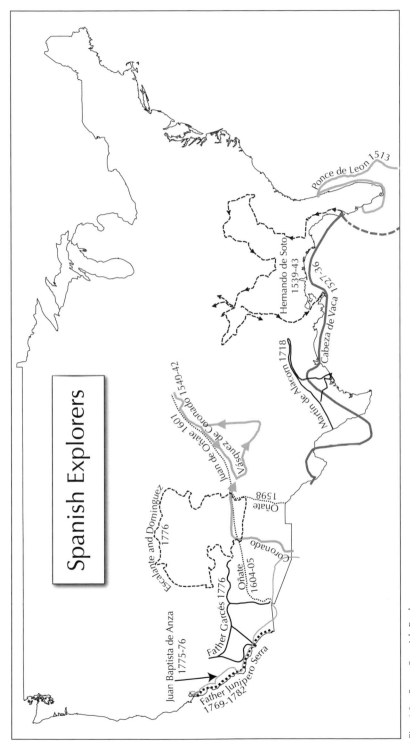

Fig. 4.3—Some Spanish Explorers

Greater Mexico

Mexico in the nineteenth century was in the last stages of the Spanish Empire's collapse. The Adams-Onís Treaty with Spain in 1819 fixed the boundary of Mexico at the Sabine River, then to the Red and Arkansas Rivers and westward to the Pacific Ocean along the 42nd parallel. In 1821, there was a new constitution in Spain, and Spain signed a treaty to give Mexico its independence. In 1823, the Central American countries (Belize, Costa Rica, El Salvador, Guatemala, Honduras, and Nicaragua) seceded from Mexico. In 1824, Mexico became a federal republic under its first constitution.

Meanwhile, Mexico had been spreading north. There were permanent settlements in southern California, Arizona, the Rio Grande Basin of New Mexico, and the San Antonio Valley of Texas. San Antonio was founded in 1718, San Diego in 1769, and Los Angeles in 1781. Greater Mexico included the land that would become Texas, Arizona, New Mexico, and California. There was significant trade along the Santa Fe Trail from the eastern United States to Mexico.

Texas was first settled by 300 American families in 1821, led by Stephen F. Austin. Most came from Louisiana, Mississippi, and other southern states, and they brought their slaves with them. One in five people in Austin's colony was a slave. Spanish law said that the children of slaves would become free, and Mexican law forbade slavery entirely. In 1835, Texas began a rebellion against Mexico known as the Texas Revolution and in 1836 would declare itself independent.

In the United States, the idea of Manifest Destiny was developing as a basis for territorial expansion. Most North American land west of Texas was occupied by foreign powers—Mexico, England, and Russia. The United States felt it had an obligation to take over the land of the West, Canada, Mexico, Cuba, and even much of Latin America and bring its culture and ideas to an expanding area.

Mexican-American War (1846–1848)

After the success of the Texas Revolution in 1836, Texas applied for statehood. Meanwhile, Mexico made it apparent than the permanent loss of Texas would lead to war with the United States, and northerners opposed the annexation of Texas and the addition of another slave state. President Martin Van Buren also opposed statehood. William Henry Harrison was elected president in 1840, but died within two months and was succeeded by his vice president, John Tyler. In April 1844, President Tyler approved a treaty for the annexation of Texas, but the Senate refused to ratify it.

When James K. Polk became president in 1845, the country had changed its position and wanted to annex Texas as well as the Oregon Territory. Polk was prepared for two wars—with Great Britain and Mexico, a war north and a war south. The Oregon question was resolved by treaty with Great Britain, but Polk wanted California in order to make the United States a Pacific trading nation, even if it led to war with Mexico. America annexed Texas in March 3, 1845, and, after negotiations failed about the boundaries of Texas, went to war with Mexico. A declaration of war was signed by President Polk in May 1846.

There was significant opposition to the war. Henry Clay, a three-time Whig candidate for president, declared: "This is no war of defense but of unnecessary and of aversive aggression. It is Mexico that is defending her firesides, her castles, and her alters, not we."[4] A new member of Congress from Illinois, Abraham Lincoln, also opposed the war. The morality of Manifest Destiny was challenged by several Americans, including Henry David Thoreau. While there were negotiations between the two countries, American expansion broke the truce.

Neither country was ready for war, but President Polk sent General Zachary Taylor to march into Texas and General Stephen Kearny into California and New Mexico. The war was fought by both the small regular US Army and a large number of volunteers.

General John C. Fremont invaded California, and General Taylor reached the Rio Grande. There were a number of battles as American troops entered Mexico. General Taylor's troops fought General Antonio López de Santa Anna's troops at the important city of Monterrey. General Kearny's troops took Santa Fe. There were battles at La Angostura, Carmago, Veracruz, San Pedro, El Brazito, and Cerro Gordo. American troops under the command of General Winfield Scott landed in Veracruz in March 1847 and went south. Mexico City fell on September 14, 1847, and the war was effectively over. Future Civil War leaders such as Robert E. Lee, Ulysses S. Grant, George B. McLennan, George Meade, William T. Sherman, and Jefferson Davis were young officers in this war.

The question then was, should the United States absorb all of Mexico? There was opposition on both religious and linguistic grounds, so the border was drawn farther north.

Fig. 4.4—Mexican land lost in the Mexican-American War of 1846-1848

The Treaty of Guadalupe Hidalgo was signed and the treaty ratified by the Senate on March 10, 1848, ending the war. The United States
received the California Territory, which included the present states of
California, Nevada, Utah, Arizona, New Mexico, and parts of Wyoming and Colorado. With this treaty and the loss of Texas, Mexico lost
half its territory to the United States. In 1853, Mexico sold southern
Arizona and New Mexico to the United States with the Gadsden Purchase, giving the United States the land to build the Southern Pacific
Railroad to Los Angeles. Figure 4.4 shows the land Mexico lost in the
1840s and 1850s.

In 1862, French, Spanish, and British forces blockaded Veracruz,
demanding payment of loans. And from 1863 to 1867, French installed
a monarchy in Mexico, with Maximilian becoming emperor.

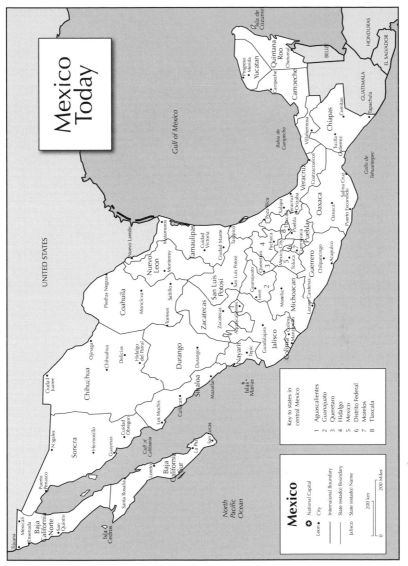

Fig. 4.5—Mexico Today

Mexican–US Relations

In 1910, another Mexican Revolution began. In 1914, President Woodrow Wilson sent American troops to blockade Veracruz. In 1935, Mexico expropriated foreign oil companies, and in 1942 the United States and Mexico agreed on the Bracero Program for Mexican contract labor in the United States. Then, in 1993, the North American Free Trade Agreement (NAFTA) was signed by Mexico, the United States, and Canada, with financial benefits to all three countries. Since then, there has been significant growth in resulting trade.[5]

Trade with Mexico	1986	2015
US Exports	12.39 billion	236 billion
US Imports	17.3 billion	295 billion
Total Trade	30 billion	531 billion

Hispanics in America

Before the Mexican-American War, there were many families who had been living in that country for generations. Few returned to Mexico after the war. And throughout the nineteenth, twentieth, and twenty-first centuries, immigrants from Mexico continued to arrive in the United States. Let's look at some numbers.

States percentage Latino population, including both recent immigrants and families up to ten generation in America[6]

New Mexico	48%	California	39%
Texas	39%	Arizona	32%
Nevada	28%	Colorado	23%

CHAPTER 5

Migration from the East

by Robert C. Baron

Rivers are moving roads
which carry us wherever we wish to go.
—**Blaise Pascal**[1]

Throughout American history, there have been a number of westward visitors—explorers, trappers, traders, miners, and missionaries. Behind them were farmers and ranchers who would settle in the new areas. As America grew, there were two major trends: a movement of people toward the West and the use of rivers to get them there and get their products out.

Rivers and Settlements

Almost every city in the world that is not on an ocean or a lake is on a river—London on the Thames, Cairo on the Nile, Shanghai on the Yangtze, Buenos Aires on the Rio de la Plata, Moscow on the Volga, Montreal and Quebec on the St. Lawrence, Léopoldville on the Congo, Baghdad on the Tigris and Euphrates, Budapest and Vienna on the Danube, Delhi on the Ganges, Berlin on the Elbe, Rome on the Tiber, Phnom Penh on the Mekong, Cologne and Basel on the Rhine, Lyon on the Rhone.

This method of settlement continued in the New World. New York and Albany are on the Hudson; Philadelphia on the Delaware; Hartford on the Connecticut; Minneapolis, St. Louis, and New Orleans on the Mississippi; Cincinnati and Pittsburgh on the Ohio, Little Rock on the Arkansas; Chattanooga on the Tennessee; Albuquerque on the Rio Grande; Kansas City and Omaha on the Missouri River.

Rivers provide water for drinking, for bathing, and for agriculture. They may be sources of fish and of recreation. They have historically been the method of transportation and trade. Rivers have been used by industry for power, and as a method of disposing both personal and industrial waste. A region's history and contemporary society is shaped by its rivers. To understand America, we should know the stories of its rivers.

In 1937, the editor Constance Lindsay Skinner conceived of a series of books called The Rivers of America. The first book published by Farrar and Rinehart was *Kennebec: Cradle of Americans* by Robert P. Tristram Coffin. Over the next thirty-seven years, the series expanded to sixty-five titles by major American writers covering every part of North America and its rivers. They wrote of the story, people, and natural history of their river; they were novelists, historians, and poets rather than scientists, and their love of a special river comes through in their writing. There are books on the Missouri, Lower Mississippi, Upper Mississippi, Arkansas, Illinois, Columbia, Ohio, Tennessee, Colorado, Rio Grande, and the other rivers that drain the continent and are important to America's history. These books also tell the story of America's movement west.

During the eighteenth century, colonial settlements were within a few miles of the Atlantic coast. Trade and communication were by sea. With the Revolution, and especially with the Louisiana Purchase in 1803, the United States moved westward. How were these new settlements to be reached and how was trade to be accomplished?

Walking, Wagons, Water

For centuries, there were three methods of traveling. The first was to walk. The second was by wagon or horseback. The third was by water— at sea by sailing, on the rivers by either oar or relying on the current to take the boat downstream.

Distance is measured not only in miles but also in the time it takes to go a certain distance. It might take a day to walk three miles through a thick New England forest. On a clear path, one can walk two to four miles in an hour or twenty to twenty-five miles in a day. Greater distances can be done on horseback. In David McCullough's biography *John Adams*, the author recounts how in January 1776 it took two weeks for Adams to ride the 275 miles from Philadelphia to Boston along the Post Road from the first Continental Congress.

Democracy in America
Alexis De Tocqueville, 1835

There may be no other book that has analyzed America better than *Democracy in America*, written by Alexis De Tocqueville. Which of these quotations still apply today?

• • •

"If there is a single country in the world where one can hope to appreciate the dogma of the sovereignty of the people at its just value, to study it in its applications to the affairs of society, and to judge its dangers, that country is surely America…"

"The Mississippi Valley is all in all the most magnificent dwelling that God has ever prepared for the habitation of man, and nonetheless one can say that it still forms only a vast wilderness…"

"At the moment I am speaking, thirteen million civilized Europeans are quietly spreading into the fertile wilderness whose resources and extent that themselves still do not know exactly. Three or four thousand soldiers push the wandering race of natives before them; behind the armed men advance woodcutters who pierce through the forests, ward off ferocious beasts, explore the course of rivers and prepare the triumphant march of wilderness across the wilderness…"

"The Americans who move away from the coast of the Atlantic Ocean to plunge into the West are adventurers impatient with every kind of yoke, greedy for wealth often thrown out by the states that saw them born. They arrive in the wilderness without knowing one another…"

"Of all the political effects that equality of conditions produces, it is this love of independence that first strikes one's regard and most frightens timid spirits…"

"Local freedoms, which make many citizens put value on the affection of their neighbors and those close to them, therefore constantly bring men closer to one another, despite the instincts that separate them, and force them to aid each other."[2]

Although the nation had unlimited land to the west, it needed a way to get there. The Allegheny Mountains slowed westward migration, and westerners required a high degree of self-sufficiency to survive the trip. Many of those who moved west logically settled near the Ohio and Mississippi Rivers and their tributaries so that agricultural products could be floated to market. It was easy, for example, for river traffic to go downstream from the Ohio or Missouri River basins down the Mississippi to New Orleans on canoes, rafts, flatboat, and keelboats. However, getting goods upstream was difficult. Often the crew took several months to walk home and then built another boat for the next trip south. Sometimes they hauled or polled the boat upstream, a trip that could take many months.

If people were to continue their movement west, there had to be ways of getting supplies to them as well as their farm products out. Fortunately, the years between 1770 and 1860 saw major changes in transportation. In addition to increased ocean trade, there were several major developments in travel during this period: the development of roads and pikes, the building of canals—especially the Erie Canal— and steam engines and the advent of the railroad system.

Improved transportation increased trade, lowered distribution costs, and helped create a national market. Westerners became producers and consumers of goods, with grain and lumber sent from the West and leather, textiles, wagons, tools, and other products sent from the East.

Roadways

The initial transportation innovation came with the development of turnpikes and toll bridges. In 1790, the first private turnpike was built in Pennsylvania. In 1811, the federal government authorized the construction of the Cumberland Road from Cumberland, Maryland, to the Mississippi River in Vandalia, Illinois. The need for roads was heightened during the War of 1812 as problems with transporting troops and supplies to the Canadian border became apparent. This growth in turnpikes resulted in a network that by 1820 had connected most of the major eastern cities. Stagecoaches went on the roads with passengers, and every ten miles or so, there were changes in horses pulling the wagons.

The toll gate is raised on a turnpike in this 1864 photo by
Frances Benjamin Johnston.

Turnpikes were often privately financed, with the tolls charged paying the investors and financing improvements. In New York alone there were 900 miles of toll roads by 1807. However, these roads did not solve the problem of transporting large amounts of goods and raw materials. Freight could only be moved by horse- or ox-drawn wagons, and roads were limited and often in bad condition—usually compacted dirt that was not kept in good condition. During summer the roads were muddy, and they were snow-covered during the winter. Only in spring and fall were they passable, and even then mud could delay movement.

Short on capital, the young United States was still one of the more developed countries with a population that was relatively well educated, had a strong interest in technology, pushed to explore new lands, and was eager to exploit natural resources and develop a flourishing commerce. Between 1800 and 1850, the population of the United States grew from 5.3 million to 23.2 million, and the proportion living west of the Alleghenies increased from 27 percent to 45 percent.

Canals

While most eastern rivers flowed a short distance to the sea, the major East Coast rivers did not connect together. To address this, construction began on several canals in the 1790s, including the Santee Canal in South Carolina to connect the Santee River to the Cooper River and then into Charleston Harbor, the Middlesex Canal in Massachusetts to connect the Merrimac River to the Concord River, and the Schuylkill Canal near Philadelphia.

At the time, much of America's capital investment went to infrastructure development. Support for both roads and canals were the responsibility of the states. Of the $188 million provided by the national government for canal construction, about 30 percent was raised through loans from British banks. One cannot overemphasize the importance of these British investments to the growth of the American economy. Prior to the expansion of canal construction beginning in the 1790s, midwestern farmers faced transportation costs that virtually prohibited their contact with eastern markets. By the 1840s, the development of direct transportation routes made possible the expansion of commercial farming in the states of the Old Northwest, raising per capita income and leading to the growth of a national market for commodities.

In the 1780s, it was proposed that a canal be dug across New York from Albany westward connecting the Hudson River to the Great Lakes and the West. Gouverneur Morris in 1800 advocated a waterway to link the Hudson River and Lake Erie, and a route was laid out in 1809. New York mayor and later governor DeWitt Clinton and steamboat inventor John Stevens promoted the idea, and in 1817 the New York legislature authorized construction of the Erie Canal with DeWitt Clinton as chairman.[3] Parts of it were opened in 1820, and by 1825 the Erie Canal was completed, allowing boats to travel from New York City to Buffalo and then onward to the Great Lakes. The Erie Canal, originally 363 miles long and with 83 locks, was four feet deep and forty-two feet wide at the top. The canal took in $700,000 of tolls in 1826. It reduced the cost of shipping one ton of goods from Albany to Buffalo from $100 to $15 and cut travel time between Albany and Buffalo from twenty days to ten, with passengers able to travel a mile and a half per hour for a cent and a half per mile. A flood of immigrants began their journey west by the Hudson River, Erie Canal, and on to the Great Lakes and the West. New York City became the commercial metropolis of the country and Buffalo, Cleveland, Chicago, and Detroit became major cities.

By 1840, many canals had been built, including from Portsmouth on the Ohio River to Cleveland, and from Cincinnati to Lake Erie. And while the era of building large canals had slowed, they continued to be constructed, including the Chesapeake and Ohio Canal; the Wabash Canal in Indiana, which allowed shipments south to the Ohio River and then on to New Orleans or north to the Great Lakes and via the Erie Canal to New York City; a canal system partway from Philadelphia to Pittsburgh; a canal from Washington, D.C., to Cumberland, Maryland; from Portsmouth on the Ohio River to Cleveland; and a canal from Lake Michigan at Chicago to the Illinois River. Canals were supported at both the state and federal levels, both of which, in some cases, granted right-of-way to the canal builders, a forerunner of the financing of railroad expansion by giving land to the developers.

In 1830, there were 1,277 miles of canals in the United States, by 1840, there were 3,326, and by 1850, 3,698 miles. Ultimately, some canal companies failed because revenue never met costs, and canals do have problems as a method of transportation. Floods and droughts affect them, and they can freeze in winter and become impassible when water is low. In addition, they can only be built on level ground.

The Steam Engine and Steamboat

The steam engine was invented in England by Thomas Newcomen and James Watt, and its first application was in factories and mines. Eventually, steam engines were used in transportation with the invention and production of the steamboat by Oliver Evans, John Fitch, John Stevens, and Robert Fulton.

Evans developed an automated flour mill and received the third patent given by the new government in 1790. He designed a high-pressure steam engine in 1804 and developed a steam-driven boat that went down the Schuylkill River in Pennsylvania. It was amphibious, and Evans drove it onto land and into the city center of Philadelphia. On August 26, 1791, Nathan Reede of Warren, Massachusetts, received a land carriage patent signed by Thomas Jefferson and George Washington for "a simple method of moving land carriages by means of steam." Samuel Morey of Fairleee, Vermont; William Henry of Lancaster, Pennsylvania; James Rumsey of Virginia; and John Fitch of Connecticut all built and operated steam-driven vessels before 1790. Rumsey probably deserves credit for the steamboat since in 1786 he had designed a mechanically driven boat. Fitch was granted a patent

Steamboat on the Red River, Dakota Territory, 1800s.

for the steamboat, but it was John Stevens and Robert Fulton who commercialized it.

Born in Pennsylvania, Robert Fulton was a painter who went to London to study with Benjamin West. He was also interested in engineering, designing and patenting a method of raising boats in a canal. He continued work as a painter and an inventor in both London and Paris. Fulton's work was financed by Robert Livingston, and 1803 he built an experimental boat that operated on the Seine. In 1806, he returned to the United States and completed the design of the *Clermont*, a steam-driven ship. In 1807, Fulton demonstrated the steamboat with a trip upriver on the Hudson from New York to Albany. Two years later he had a successor on Lake Champlain. He received a twenty-year monopoly on New York waters and a similar exclusive contract on the waters of the Lower Mississippi. In 1814, Fulton and Livingston began to offer regular steamboat service between New Orleans and Natchez, Mississippi. Fulton steamboats on the Hudson and ferries connected Manhattan with New Jersey and Long Island. After 1830, the entire East Coast came alive with steamboats, some complete with luxurious dining and sleeping quarters. In 1848, steamships began running between the East Coast and California by traveling around the tip of South America.

Development continued in the United States, as the Hudson and the Mississippi Rivers were ideally suited for steamboat travel. Livingston, a signer of the Declaration of Independence and negotiator for the Louisiana Purchase, started the Mississippi Steamboat Company in 1809, and built the boat *New Orleans* in 1812. By 1820, there were sixty steamboats on western rivers, with many traveling the Lower Mississippi.

Steamboats were largely responsible for the growth of

Manifest Destiny

Americans thought that they had a responsibility and duty to spread their institutions, government and mode of law across the American continent.

"....our manifest destiny is to oversee and to possess the whole of the continent which Providence has given us for the development of the great experiment of liberty and federated self-government entrusted to us."[4]

—John Louis O'Sullivan
New York Morning News
December 27, 1845

Mississippi River commerce and travel on the Great Lakes. Steam engines solved the problem of getting goods and people upstream, growing from seventeen boats handling 3,290 tons of freight in 1817 to 727 boats handling 170,000 tons in 1855. There were both sidewheel and paddlewheel steamboats. They could, however, be dangerous, and frequent explosions of the boiler resulted in thousands of deaths.

In the twenty years after 1814, annual steamboat arrivals in New Orleans increased from 20 to 1,200. By 1838, 684 steamboats were on the Ohio River, with the Pittsburgh district 304, Cincinnati district 221, and the Louisville district 103. In 1846, there were 1,190 steamboats on western waters, and the Mississippi Valley began to develop. The first steamship on the Missouri River was in 1819, the Tennessee in 1821, the Upper Mississippi in 1823, and the Illinois in 1828. Steamships competed with railroads until the 1870s.

The Growth of Midwestern Farm States and Beyond

With the river system and the steamboat, some states increased in population and were able to enter the Union. Illinois entered the union in 1818, Missouri in 1821, Arkansas in 1836, Iowa in 1846,

Farmers working the land in 1899.

Wisconsin in 1848, Minnesota in 1858, and Kansas in 1861. Four of these states (Illinois, Iowa, Missouri, and Wisconsin) reached a population of more than 1 million by 1870, and the remaining three states each topped a million by 1890. These were agricultural states that had good soil and adequate rainfall; their settlements and growth were possible because of the river and canal system and the development of the steamship.

As shown in Table 5.1, in 1900 and in 1940 before World War II, these seven states had significant population densities. They were comparable to Virginia, which had forty-six people per square mile in 1900 and sixty-seven by 1940. The upper midwestern farm states prospered.

Immigration has a push-pull component. Europeans were attracted to America by the jobs in industry and the new farmland available in the Midwest. Famine, laws controlling the poor, and the desire for religious and economic freedom caused many to leave Europe. In 1848, there was an unsuccessful revolution in Germany, and many Germans left to come to the United States and South America. In 1846, there was famine in Ireland, and many Irish came to the New World. Some of these immigrants settled on the East Coast; some came to the West. Economic problems in Scotland, Scandinavia, and other parts of Europe also encouraged immigration to the New World. In every census from 1800 to 1880, the population of the United Sates grew between 26.6 percent and 36.4 percent. A good part of that growth was due to immigration.

TABLE 5.1

Population of seven western states entering Union before the Civil War and population density

State	Became State	State Size Sq. Miles	Population K[5]			
			1900	People per sq. mile	1940	People per sq. mile
Arkansas	1836	52.1K	1312	25	1949	37
Illinois	1818	55.59K	4822	87	7897	142
Iowa	1846	55.87K	2231	40	2538	45
Kansas	1861	81.8K	1470	18	1802	22
Minnesota	1858	79.6K	1751	22	2792	35
Missouri	1821	68.9K	3106	45	3785	55
Wisconsin	1848	54.3K	2068	38	3138	58

In the nineteenth century, new threshing machines, corn huskers, and other farm machinery were developed. Simplicity of design meant that a farmer could repair equipment without having to send it back to the factory. Farmers could now produce more food and feed more city dwellers, and these advances solved the labor-shortage problem in farming.

By the end of the nineteenth century, giant combines pulled by large teams of horses worked the wheat fields of the Midwest. McCormick and John Deere increased western food production and enabled more people to leave the farm and go to the city, or, in the 1860s, to the Civil War. In the seventeenth and eighteenth centuries, 90 percent of the American population was involved in agriculture. Even into the 1860s, 80 percent of people lived on farms, which made up half the nation's wealth. That percentage decreased as farming became more efficient.

In 1838, the total shipment of wheat from Chicago was only seventy-eight bushels. Ten years later, it was more than 2 million bushels. But while wheat was easy to sow and grow, reaping was another matter. A farmer had to go through a field swinging a scythe in backbreaking labor, and he would only grow as much wheat as he and his family could harvest by hand. With the advent of the reaper, horsepower was substituted for manpower. In 1831, Cyrus McCormick, a young

Virginia mechanic, introduced the horse-drawn reaper that could cut through six acres of oats in one day. Jerome Case began to manufacture threshing machines that efficiently separated wheat from chaff. In 1841, McCormick sold only 2 machines, but in 1852 that number rose to 1,000, and in 1857, 23,000 reapers were sold.

People wanted to go west to coastal Oregon and California with their excellent farmland, moderate climate, and adequate moisture, and they headed out on the Oregon, Mormon, and California Trails. From the 1840s to the 1860s, approximately half a million Americans traveled west on the Oregon Trail alone; along the way, more than 30,000 would die from cholera, typhoid, smallpox, dysentery, or drowning and other accidents.

33-horse team combined harvester

A team of horses was needed to haul this giant log that measured 30 feet around in the Cascade Mountains of Washington, 1905.

To reach the Oregon Territory on foot from the East took a journey of 2,000 miles and four months. Weather on parts of the road was extreme, with very hot and dry summers in the plains and windy and snowy winters in the mountains. Leaving from St. Joseph or Independence, Missouri, or Omaha, Nebraska, the travelers had to worry about weather, steep grades, flooded streams and rivers, and the need for water, food, and firewood daily. Mules and oxen died from exhaustion or inadequate food and water. Possessions were discarded along the trail to lighten the load. On a good day, it might be possible to make twenty-five miles. On a bad day, the travelers might only make five miles.

As mentioned, some sailed by ship around the tip of South America, but most travelers took the Oregon Trail from the Missouri River to the Columbia River and the Willamette Valley or Astoria. There were many guidebooks published for the Oregon Trail. People traveled together for safety or support. Wagon trains of thirty to fifty wagons, with some wagon trains longer than one third of a mile, were formed in Omaha or Missouri. Leavenworth, Kansas, sometimes saw

500 wagons per day headed to California and Colorado.

Because they were on the ocean, three other states entered the Union before the Civil War: Texas on the Gulf Coast in 1845, California in 1850, and Oregon in 1859 on the Pacific. The latter two states were isolated and closer to Asia than to the East and England. A trip from California by ship had to go around the tip of South America, a voyage of more than 6,500 miles to reach Boston and 8,000 miles to reach England. The population density of these three states in 1900 and 1940 are shown in Table 5.2.

To settle the interior of the country, however, a new method of transportation would be needed: railroads.

TABLE 5.2
Three ocean states admitted before the Civil War

State	Became State	State Size Sq. Miles	Population K[6]			
			1900	People per sq. mile	1940	People per sq. mile
California	1850	155.97K	1485	9.5	6907	44
Oregon	1859	96K	414	4.3	1090	10
Texas	1845	261.9K	3048	12	6415	24

The Railroad

Unlike canals, railroads could run year-round, navigate up and down hills, and were cheaper to build. They had the added advantage of being faster and safer than steamboats, and unlike turnpike travel, railroads could supply their own power. In 1826, John Stevens demonstrated the feasibility of steam locomotion on a circular track in Hoboken, New Jersey, and the era of railroads in America began. Over the next few decades, steam-driven railroads began to eclipse canals and turnpikes as the main mode of transportation the world over. The railroad industry became the first large, national business with improvements in technology, finance, marketing, and management. In 1828, work began on a railroad between Baltimore and Ohio, and it took thirty-five years for the railroad to reach Wheeling, West Virginia. In 1830,

TABLE 5.3.
Railroad active mileage by region[7]

Region	1830	1840	1850	1860	1870	1880	1890
New England	30	513	2,570	3,860	4,495	5,982	6,631
East	—	1,484	3,206	11,927	18,292	28,155	40,826
South	10	737	2,082	7,908	10,610	14,458	27,933
Midwest	—	—	46	4,951	11,031	22,213	35,580
South Central		21	107	250	331	1,621	5,154
West	—	—	—	239	4,578	15,466	47,451
Total	40	2,755	8,565	29,135	49,337	87,895	163,475

there were 40 railroad miles in operation in the United States; there were 2,800 miles in 1840; 8,600 miles in 1850; and more than 30,000 miles by 1860.

Initially, most railroads were in the Northeast, with the Boston and Lowell Railroad, the Boston and Worcester, and a variety of lines in New York and Pennsylvania. In 1852, the management of the Pennsylvania Railroad announced that they had officially opened to trade and travel a single-track railroad between Philadelphia and Pittsburgh,

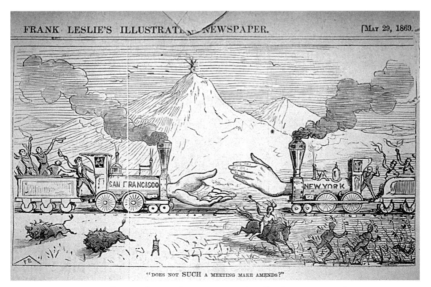

Cartoon by Frank Beard commemorating the 1869 connection
of the transcontinental railroad.

connecting the headwaters of the Ohio River with the Atlantic seaboard. Pittsburgh became the "Gateway to the West."

By 1860, 18 percent of the railroad mileage was in the Midwest and West, and by 1890 it was more than half. Railroads reached Chicago in 1852, the Mississippi River in 1854, and the first bridge across the Mississippi River opened in 1856 at Davenport, Iowa. In 1874, a railroad bridge with three arches was built at St. Louis.

In the 1850s, Secretary of War Jefferson Davis sent out survey teams to plan a transcontinental railroad to reach the new state of California where gold had been discovered. Because of regional differences between the North and the South about the desired route, the railroad was not built until after the Civil War.

The North had a substantial lead in miles of railroads and miles of telegraph wires by 1860—one of the major factors that enabled the North to win the Civil War. In 1862, President Abraham Lincoln signed the Homestead Act that sold settlers 160 acres for $200, encouraging thousands to head west and build farms. But drought killed many hopes. Lincoln also signed the Morrill Act that used the sale of public lands for the benefit of agriculture and education, which is discussed in Chapters 8 and 10.

The building of the transcontinental railroad in the 1870s allowed settlers to access the lands of the West. In the Midwest, most farms were a short distance from a railroad or a spur, enabling grain, hogs, and cattle to be shipped back East.

From 1800 to 1910, the average growth in population for the United States was 30 percent per decade. Much of this growth was in the West. Population density is part of the story that is told in Chapters 6 and 9.

CHAPTER 6

The Country Moves West

by Robert C. Baron

The long term consequences of this migration of Americans
towards the West are still hidden from us by the future
but the immediate results are easy to recognize:
as a portion of the former inhabitants
move away each year from the states
where they are born.
—**Alexis de Tocqueville**[1]

Once I thought to write a history of the immigrants
in America. Then I discovered that the
immigrants were American history.
—**Oscar Handlin**, *The Americans,*
Little Brown, 1963[2]

National Railroads

Steamboats increased speed and the distance that could be traveled in a given time, but it was the railroad that gave promise of dealing with the vast distances of the Far West. Railroads were, however, expensive to build and maintain. A mile of track could cost as much to build as an entire steamboat. Iron rails, wooden bridges, and heavy locomotives increased costs further. In short, railroads needed lots of capital, and for much of the nineteenth century it was supplied by the government and Wall Street.

On January 44, 1852, railroads reached Chicago. The first railroad bridge across the Mississippi was completed on April 21, 1856. By 1857, trains were running to St. Louis via Cincinnati. By 1859, a railroad reached the Missouri River.

Passengers pose in front of their train in the Black Hills of the Dakotas.

In 1853, three years after California became a state and six years before Oregon entered the Union, Secretary of War Jefferson Davis sent Army Pacific Railroad Survey teams to plan a route for a national railroad to reach the Pacific Coast. There was a possible northern route along the Missouri River along the 48th parallel, led by Isaac Stevens; a central route by the Arkansas River to Salt Lake City along the 37th to 39th parallel, led by John Gunnison; another route along the 35th parallel through New Mexico and Arizona and across the Mojave Desert, led by Amiel Whipple; and a far southern route, traveling from Texas to San Diego and up the coast, led by

John Pope. There were political differences between the North and South about the route.

In 1862, Congress approved a bill for a transcontinental railroad, and, after the Civil War, the United States built a national railroad system. The first route was to be from Omaha to Sacramento—the central route the South had opposed.

The Central Pacific laid tracks east from Sacramento, and the Union Pacific west from Omaha. Both organizations were given government loans and millions of acres to support the company. On May 10, 1869, they met in Promontory, Utah. There was now a 1,775-mile rail line between San Francisco and Omaha, and so California was connected to the rest of the country. A trip from New York to San Francisco, which had previously taken six months, now took only seven days.

This was not, however, an intercontinental system. A passenger had to change trains in Chicago as well as Ogden, Utah. On the Union Pacific, another change was required, with a ferryboat crossing from Council Bluffs to Omaha until a bridge was built over the Missouri River.

By the 1880s, three more railroad lines had crossed to the Pacific, and parts of the prairies bloomed. Southern Pacific completed a transcontinental railroad line on January 12, 1883, that went from New Orleans to Texas across Arizona and New Mexico, the territory of the Gadsden Purchase from Mexico, and on to Los Angeles.

Northern Pacific construction started in 1864 to connect the Great Lakes with Puget Sound on the Pacific Ocean, linking the Pacific Northwest with the rest of the country. By 1883, the Northern Pacific went from Lake Superior across Minnesota through the Badlands of the Dakota Territory and the Rockies at Bozeman, Montana, to Portland, Oregon.

The Pacific Railroad Act of 1862 gave ten square miles of federal land for every mile of track laid. It also loaned $16,000 per mile of track laid on the level and $48,000 per mile of track in the mountains. Most of the land was granted to five companies: Union Pacific, Central Pacific, Southern Pacific, Northern Pacific, and Santa Fe. The government also loaned the railroads thirty-year federal bonds. These were easier to sell than land in the Rocky Mountain states.

Railroads opened the Rocky Mountain West to farming, ranching, lumbering, and mining. Railroad trackage, which was 30,000 miles in 1860, reached 93,000 miles in 1880 and 193,000 miles in 1900. Much of that growth was in the West.

In order to expand track mileage and allow trains to run faster, the railroads needed a stronger metal than wrought iron to absorb the shock of passing wheels. Iron rails were too soft, wore down on one side, and had to be turned frequently. They also broke or cracked and had to be continually inspected to prevent accidents. Gradually, the use of steel rails became widespread and replaced the iron rails in service. Steel was also used for the manufacture of locomotives and railroad cars, providing stronger and lighter trains, improving the carrying capacity of trains by a factor of ten, reducing car weights, increasing locomotive power, and decreasing transportation costs. The expansion of the railroad system was only possible because of advances in the manufacture of steel.

The railroads were the parent and major market of the steel industry. From 1880 to 1900, the majority of steel produced in the United States was used by the railroads. Steel was equally dependent on the railroads. The expansion of railroads made possible the hauling of the large amounts of material required for modern steel making; railroads and steel making were highly interdependent, each needing the other to succeed.

Railroads brought people to the West for settlement. The federal government developed a system by which new railroad companies in the West were granted land that they could sell or pledge to bondholders. A total of 208 million acres were granted to the railroads, with 51 million additional acres granted by the states and various municipalities.

The Rocky Mountain West

Immigration increased significantly during the nineteenth century. Between 1821 and 1830, 143,000 immigrants entered the United Sates. Between 1871 and 1880, there were 2,812,000 immigrants, and in the period between 1881 and 1890, there were 5,426,000. As we saw in Chapter 5, some came because of famine in their home country and some because of political events and financial conditions in Europe, but the major motivation was economic—to obtain jobs and land.

With the development of the transcontinental railroad in the 1870s and 1880s, other states entered the Union before the turn of the century—Nebraska in 1867; Colorado in 1876; North Dakota, South Dakota, Washington, and Montana in 1889; Utah in 1896; and Idaho and Wyoming in 1890. After the Civil War, many thousands migrated west to the Great Plains and the Rocky Mountain and Pacific Coast states, and because of the Homestead Act, these states were able to develop significant agricultural industry.[3] The Midwest states grew a variety of crops. California, Oregon, and Washington grew fruits and vegetables. Some of the Rocky Mountain states grew wheat, while others used dryland farming or irrigation water for sugar beets and alfalfa. In general, though, Rocky Mountain residents were more dependent on ranching and mining for their economy.

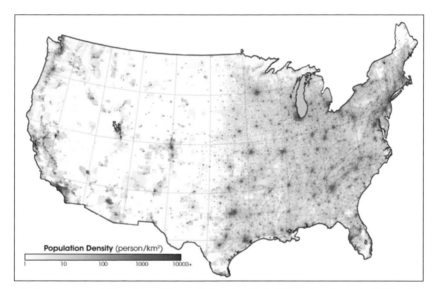

A visual representation of the US population density in 2006 when it reached 300 million. Based on data archived by the Socioeconomic Data and Applications Center

The western states were sparsely populated. Population densities were low (a few people per square mile, substantially below that of the midwestern states), not only as they entered the Union but also at the turn of the twentieth century and as late as 1940 and the advent of World War II. Their population and population densities in 1900 and 1940 are shown in Table 6.1.

Railroads needed not only financial support to be built but also customers and freight to continue in business and pay off debt.

TABLE 6.1

Thirteen far western states and population density[10]

State	Became State	% Public	Size Sq Mi	1900 Pop	Pop per Sq Mi	1940 Pop	Pop per Sq Mi
Arizona	1912	44.3%	114K	123	1	499	4.3
Colorado	1876	38.9%	103.7K	540	5	1123	11
Idaho	1890	65.2%	82.75K	162	2	525	6
Montana	1889	31.9%	144.55K	243	2	559	4
Nebraska	1867	2.3%	76.88K	1066	14	1315	17
Nevada	1864	89.6%	109.8K	42	0.4	110	1
New Mexico	1912	36.2%	121.36K	195	1.6	532	4
North Dakota	1889	7.3%	68.99K	319	4.6	642	9
Oklahoma	1907	3.6%	68.68K	790	11.5	2336	34
South Dakota	1889	8.7%	75.9K	402	5	643	8.5
Utah	1896	67.9%	82.17K	277	3.4	550	6.7
Washington	1889	32.8%	66.58K	518	8	1736	36
Wyoming	1890	49.7%	97.1K	93	1	251	4

In order to get enough customers, they brought immigrants west and gave or sold them land. Table 6.2 shows the date of admission of these states and the number of foreign-born residents in the census taken closest to their admission. In some cases, before statehood the state might have had more than half their inhabitants foreign born.

These settlers came mainly from northern and western Europe and were often educated and skilled. Germans came in large numbers as political refugees after the failed revolution of 1848 and the Franco-Prussian War. Germans farmers came to Minnesota, the Dakotas, Illinois, Missouri, Iowa, and Wisconsin. They grew wheat, which was shipped to Minneapolis. Norwegian and Danish immigration started in 1825 to Wisconsin and Minnesota. Between 1846 and 1930, about 20 percent of the population left Sweden. In 1886, the Northern Pacific Railroad opened colonization offices in Germany and Scandinavia, offering low-cost transportation to America and land-purchase deals.

Sometimes an entire European town might come together to the American West. In other cases, people were met at a boat in New York

TABLE 6.2.

Nine Rocky Mountain states and the number of foreign born residents[11]

State	Admission	Census Year	% Foreign Born
Nebraska	1867	1870	25.8%
Colorado	1876	1880	20.5%
N. Dakota	1889	1890	44.0%
S. Dakota	1889	1890	38.3%
Washington	1889	1890	25.8%
Montana	1889	1890	32.6%
Wyoming	1890	1890	24.6%
Idaho	1890	1890	20.7%
Utah	1896	1890	28.0%

City, put on a train, and then dumped in a strange prairie. Gradually, the population of the Rocky Mountain states increased.

Most farms were close to a railroad. When one railroad served a city or region, they could charge whatever they wanted. In addition, unless you were close to a railroad or spur, you couldn't get your crops out. In 1887, the first Interstate Commerce Commission (ICC) rules were passed to regulate commerce with the first regulations for railroad charges.

Railroads had borrowed heavily to add to their size, but insufficient business meant they could not pay interest on their debt. The Panic of 1873 was led by railroads that were building and borrowing too much, and this led to the bankruptcy of many railroads, including the Northern Pacific, Union Pacific, and Santa Fe. Because railroads were the major consumer of steel, timber, coal, and furniture as well as being a major employer, a national depression ensued. Railroad financing was the major activity of Wall Street, and when railroads defaulted on their loans, New York investors took over the companies, reorganized them, fired people, cut service, and raised rates. Many towns and farmers suffered.

Early in the twentieth century, the last three states entered the union—Oklahoma in 1907 and Arizona and New Mexico in 1912. The map of the continent was complete, and forty-eight states were in the Union.

Placer mining for gold in December 1888, at Rockerville, Dakota

Mining, Cattle, Sheep, and Timbering

Besides farming, gold and silver mining were major players in the growth of the West. Between 1849 and 1899, news of gold and silver discoveries and the possibility of instant fortune led tens of thousands of Americans westward. There was temporary growth as new gold, silver, and quartz deposits were found—new towns were developed and then abandoned. When Nevada entered the union in 1864, it was partially due to the influx of miners. California, the mountains of Colorado, Virginia City in Nevada, Idaho, Montana, the Black Hills of the Dakota Territory, Arizona, and finally Alaska in 1899 were scenes of mass migration of miners from the United States and around the world. Most returned home after a few years, but some settled in these territories.

The digging for precious minerals along with oil and gas drilling and coal mining profoundly affected the history of the Rocky Mountain West. In Montana, copper mines even led to company domination of the state for a century.

The mining wealth went back East, which supplied the capital for large-scale, hard-rock mining. The value of gold from the earth in California was more than $82 million by 1851. By law, the miner's right to exploit transcends all other individual and local government rights.

The cattlemen also came into the empty West, using large amounts of public land for their cattle that were then shipped back East. Cattlemen drove cattle north from Texas to railroads in Kansas. Overcrowding and overgrazing of cattle and a deteriorating open range ultimately led to the 1934 Taylor Grazing Act.

Until the Forestry Act of 1905, the forests of much of the West were clear-cut, leaving only stumps—there was no replanting. Timber interests simply moved to another location.

The West as a Colony of the East

Bernard DeVoto in essays for *Harper's Magazine* and Dick Lamm in *The Angry West* point out that for much of its history, the Far West was run for the benefit of easterners. In his essay "The West Against Itself" published in January 1947, DeVoto writes about the wealth of the West that ended up in the East. First it was the trapping of the beaver, then the development of the gold and silver mineral wealth, oil and gas, coal and copper, the cattlemen who were peons of their eastern bankers, lumbering, and then, finally, power were all shipped east.[4] In his book, Dick Lamm reviews the boom-and-bust nature of western history and points out that most of the decisions and most of the money ended up in the East.

DeVoto believed in the 1930s that the West had always been a province of the East, and it had always been plundered. While that may have been true at the time, it is not today.

Changes during the Past
Three-Quarters of a Century

As shown in Table 6.3, western states grew after World War II. California and Texas added the most citizens and are the largest western states today. Nevada and Arizona each started with a low population and grew significantly, in part due to the development of air conditioning and in part a desire for some to retire in a warmer climate. Colorado and Utah grew by a factor of four, and many other far western states grew by a factor of two to three after 1940. Much of this growth was in cities—Los Angeles, San Diego, Houston, Phoenix, Denver, and Salt Lake City.

TABLE 6.3

State Growth Since World War II[12]

State	Became State	Population K		Times Growth
		1940	2010	
Mid-West				
Arkansas	1836	1949	2916	1.5
Illinois	1818	7897	12830	1.6
Iowa	1846	2538	3046	1.2
Kansas	1861	1801	2853	1.6
Minnesota	1858	2792	5304	1.9
Missouri	1821	3785	5989	1.6
Wisconsin	1848	3138	5686	1.8
Pacific West				
California	1850	6907	37254	5.4
Oregon	1859	1090	3831	3.5
Washington	1889	1736	6725	3.9
Rocky Mountain West				
Colorado	1876	1123	5029	4.5
Idaho	1890	525	1568	3.0
Montana	1889	559	989	1.8
Nebraska	1867	1315	1826	1.4
Nevada	1864	110	2701	24.5
N. Dakota	1889	642	673	1.0
S. Dakota	1889	643	814	1.3
Utah	1896	550	2764	5.0
Wyoming	1890	251	564	2.2
Southwest				
Arizona	1912	499	6392	12.8
New Mexico	1912	532	2059	3.9
Oklahoma	1907	2336	3751	1.6
Texas	1845	6415	25146	3.9
Total West		49133	140701	2.9
Total US		132165	308745	2.3

Of course, it's not just the number of people in an area that tell the story, it's also the population density—that is, the number of people per square mile.

First, consider the crowded East. Based on the 2010 Census, high-population-density states included New Jersey with 1,260 people per square mile, Rhode Island with 1,016, Massachusetts with 850, Connecticut with 742, Maryland with 610, and New York with 485.

In contrast, however, the western landscape remains relatively open, despite the growth in western cities. A good way to put this in perspective is to look at a study by Conservation International,[5] which has many rules for designating an area as wilderness. One is that it has a population density of fewer than five people per square kilometer, equivalent to 12.6 people per square mile. (Another study uses six people per square mile to qualify as wilderness.) By this measure, the states of South Dakota (10), North Dakota (10), Montana (7), Wyoming (5), and Alaska (1) qualify. New Mexico (14), Idaho (15), and Nevada (18) come close. And in many other western states, there are large areas with few people. Parts of Arizona, Colorado, Utah, and even California have low population densities. California, the most populous state, has 9 national parks and 140 wilderness areas.

And while parts of the developing West were on or near railroads, much of the land was connected only by trails or rough roads. Growth in population required something better.

Transportation

In 1900, there were 21 million horses in the United Sates and 4,000 automobiles. Important roads were unsurfaced and often impassible, and there were few signs or maps to guide a motorist. The country was still a vast land with scattered communities in need of

1905 Baltimore Surrey by Griffith and Turner Co.

better transportation. A steamship could run on the smooth surface of lakes and rivers, and the railroads on smooth tracks. The automobile also had to run on a smooth surface—or at least smoother than open land. Without good roads, the auto would have made little impact on America.

Before cars, America had bad roads. For example, it took four months for a wagon to get halfway across the country during the California Gold Rush of 1848. Roads were wagon or horse tracks, and some went across private land where one had to open and close gates as one traveled. The development of roads was necessary for the development of the auto industry.

At the beginning of the twentieth century, streets existed in the cities and towns, but there were only dirt roads and trails in the country leading from the city to the surrounding farms, with nothing beyond. These country dirt roads were impassible both in the winter and during the spring months, when snow and rain turned them into pools of mud. Attempting to drive on these bad roads resulted in broken transmissions, flat tires, and boiled-over engines.

The first concrete road outside a city was built in 1908, when Woodward Avenue in Detroit was extended a mile past the city limits. But for most of the country, roads consisted of wagon ruts across the prairie. Automobiles were only for the city until better roads could be built.

The following figures from the *Engineering News* in 1912 show how bad the road situation was.

TABLE 6.4		
February 1, 1912, Mileage of Public Roads in the United States[6]		
	1904	**1912**
Total Mileage	2,151,379	2,199,645
Mileage of improved roads		
Stone	36,818	59,237
Gravel	109,925	102,870
Other materials	6,807	28,372
Total	153,530	190,479
% all roads improved	7.14%	8.66%

In 1912, Carl Fisher of Indianapolis proposed a coast-to-coast highway, with route markers and directional signs. The fledging automobile manufacturers and their customers immediately backed the idea. Since there were no national highway funds and few local sources of finance, Fisher proposed an organization, later known as the Lincoln Highway Association, to fund the national road. The choice of a route was announced in Colorado Springs on August 1913 and work began shortly thereafter. The Lincoln Highway started in New York City and then went across New Jersey, Pennsylvania, Ohio, Indiana, Illinois, Iowa, Nebraska, northern Colorado and southern Wyoming, Utah, and then on to San Francisco. Over the next few years, the 3,300-mile Lincoln Highway was completed and then improved. The army sent heavy vehicles over the road in 1919 to show its potential for military use, and the federal government took over responsibility for finishing and maintaining it in 1923.

The Federal Aid Highway Act of 1921 authorized the Bureau of Public Roads to provide funding and help state highway departments construct paved two-lane interstate highways around the country. Roads in general did not keep up with developments of the automobile, however. While city streets and surrounding suburbs had adequate roadways, travel across longer distances was another story. From the 1920s through the 1950s, a coast-to-coast automobile trip involved numerous two- and three-lane highways, frequent stops, and top speeds of forty miles per hour, often through the centers of cities and towns. Most goods were still shipped by railroad, and most long-distance travel was by train.

General John J. Pershing had originally proposed the concept of an interstate highway system in 1918 on military and national defense grounds. The German Autobahn, built by Hitler in the 1930s as a military highway, set the standards for roads and was the first major national highway in the world.

Until the end of World War II, there were only minor improvements in American roads, although there were some good individual roads built—for example, the Pennsylvania Turnpike, the parkways north of New York City, and US Routes 1, 40, 50, and 66. The national routes often went through small towns, benefiting local businesses but slowing the traveler down considerably. The Pennsylvania Turnpike sped the driver across Pennsylvania but then dumped a car into narrow highways on both its western and eastern sides.

In 1956, President Dwight D. Eisenhower signed into law the Federal Highway Act, which sponsored an Interstate Highway System and authorized the construction of a 42,000-mile national system. Justified in part on national security grounds and in part as a public works project, this highway system unified the country, changed the face of America, and was one of the most important events of the twentieth century. The building of roads led to growth in many areas, including construction and leisure activities. The federal government agreed to pay 90 percent of the cost from gas taxes, with state and towns paying the remaining 10 percent. The system committed federal-state highway spending of $33.5 billion, financed by a penny-a-gallon tax on gasoline over the next dozen years. These taxes were increased over time, and the Federal Highway Trust Fund had annual receipts of $3 to $5 billion in the 1960s and is now running about $35 billion per year. This amount is raised by taxes on gasoline, gasohol, diesel, special taxes on trucks and trailers, and the sale of tires.

Until the 1960s, most of the West was physically isolated. With better roads, parts of the Far West were connected to the country by car, truck or bus, no longer dependent on the railroads and their arbitrary pricing.

Communication

The United States had a technology revolution in the nineteenth and early twentieth centuries. The cities of the West (e.g., San Francisco, Dallas, Denver, Salt Lake City, and Minneapolis) participated in this change, but much of the western countryside did not. In terms of communications, some of the Far West was still isolated until recently. (For a complete description of the history of the automobile, telegraph, telephone, radio, and television and the computer networks, reference my book *Pioneers and Plodders: The American Entrepreneurial System.*[7])

Electric power was developed by Thomas Edison, and the Edison Electric Light Company was incorporated in 1878. Nikola Tesla and George Westinghouse developed long-range power distribution systems in the late nineteenth century. Most western cities had electric power by the turn of the century, but power was not provided to many in Kansas, Colorado, Nebraska, and other western farms until the 1930s or 1940s.

Under President Franklin Delano Roosevelt and the New Deal, power and water control came to the West. (For those interested, the story of the rise and fall of the big dams is told in the Rivers of America series.[8])

The Rural Electrification Administration was established in 1936, providing loans to hundreds of rural organizations to set up their own power systems. Within five years, the number of farms with electricity and electric light and power increased from 750,000 to 2,500,000; by 1950, 90 percent of farmers in the United States were electrified.

Samuel Morse developed the telegraph, and on May 24, 1844, he publicly demonstrated its feasibility. By 1861, the telegraph spanned the continent and thousands of miles of wire had been strung. Railroads and many businesspeople were using the telegraph. While some small towns had a telegraph office and a local newspaper, other towns and farms did not and remained isolated. The weather bureau used the telegraph to communicate weather information in 1898, but many farmers and ranchers still had to look at the sky to predict their own weather.

The Rural Electrification Administration (REA) erects telephone lines in a rural area.

Alexander Graham Bell invented the telephone and demonstrated it in Boston in 1876. By 1880, there were 237,000 phones in operation by and more than 6 million by 1907. By 1930, there were 13.5 million telephones installed in American homes, fifty-four years after the first telephone. Again, however, many farms and remote areas did not get phone service until the 1940s, and even then it might have been a twelve-party line.

In 1905, more than half of the American population lived either in towns smaller than 5,000 inhabitants or on farms. Information came from newspapers, mail, and word of mouth.

Radio was demonstrated in 1906, and the first commercial radio station, KDKA in Pittsburgh, went on the air on November 20, 1920. There were 2.5 million radios by 1924 and 570 licensed stations. But much of the West either could not receive signals or got a program from just one station. By 1934, radios were reaching 60 percent of American homes, but that meant 40 percent had no radio service. Many of those were in the American West.

Television came on the scene in the 1950s. At first it was restricted to large cities on the East Coast, but by 1970, there were 680 stations serving 95 percent of the country's population. Once again, those not served were in the sparsely populated West. Cable television was started in the 1950s as a way of reaching customers in areas that had trouble receiving broadcast signals. In 1953, Bill Daniels built his first cable system in Casper, Wyoming, and soon there were 800 cable systems, most around the West.

It was only with the advent of communication satellites in the 1980s and 1990s and the development of the internet that people in low-populated areas could access information and entertainment and become less isolated.

Isolation and Integration

In the census of 1900, more than half of the American population lived in cities and suburbs, and that trend of increasing urban population continues today. And although it varies among states, four out of five Americans live in an urban environment.

For example, in Arkansas, 34 percent of the population lives in rural areas; in Idaho, it's 29.4 percent; in Iowa, 36 percent; Kansas, 25.8 percent; Minnesota, 26.7 percent; Missouri, 29.6 percent; Nebraska,

26.9 percent; North Dakota, 40.1 percent; Oklahoma, 33.8 percent; South Dakota, 43.3 percent; Wisconsin, 29.8 percent; and in Wyoming, 35.2 percent.[9]

That is only part of the story, however. People may move, but the land doesn't. In Colorado, for example, there has been large increase in population on the Front Range—the area bordering the east side of the Rockies between Colorado Springs and Fort Collins. Yet of the 63 Colorado counties, 34 are called rural or predominately rural by the Census Bureau; in California, 11 of the 58 counties are rural or predominately rural; in Kansas, it's 85 of the 105 counties; in Nevada, 15 of the 17 counties are rural or predominately rural; in Oregon, 28 of the 36 counties are rural or predominately rural; and in Texas, 121 of the 254 counties are rural.[10] Not everyone chooses to live in a city.

Who are these rural people? Some are ranchers and farmers and the businesses that support them. Some are people who want to raise their children away from the crowds and problems of the large-city schools. Some are small businesspeople who may sell their products to a worldwide market. Some are people who have retired and sold their home for a profit, preferring the neighbors and slower pace of country living.

People have always moved to cities for education and jobs as well as the cultural advantages. Yet there are benefits of living in a city while still being able to easily access rural areas for camping, hiking, biking, climbing, skiing, hunting, fishing, and the benefits of nature nearby. There is a difference between the western cities and suburbs and the rural West. Denver, Omaha, Dallas, Boise, and other cities shared in the technological progress of the nineteenth and twentieth centuries. Rural areas might not have. Most people in the nineteenth century lived on farms with a small town within riding distance on a horse or buggy. They did not get electric power until the 1940s, good interstate roads until the 1950s, access to radio and television until the 1950s to 1970s, and satellite connection to communication and computer networks until the 1980s or later. The rural West is no longer isolated.

It has been said that the story of the West is the story of water, and whoever controls water controls the region. While this is true, it is not the entire story. It ignores the importance of electric power, since neither cities nor farms can prosper without it. It ignores the importance of communication. An American, no matter where she or he lives, can watch a baseball game or a college basketball team, can read the latest book or see the newest movie, and can even attend a concert by their favorite entertainer or watch an opera broadcast from New York, thanks to modern communications systems.

There was a difference between the pre– and post–Civil War West. There was an even greater change between the pre– and post–World War II West. The following quote by Charles Colton was true when it was written in the nineteenth century. It is no longer true.

> If you would be known, and not know, vegetate in a village; if you would know, and not be known, live in a city.[11]

Today, rural isolation is no longer always the case. That is why some people who retire are selling their expensive city homes and moving to the country for a better quality of life; they can still visit the city for shopping, cultural events, and medical services. Examples include southern Missouri and Arkansas (nearest major medical center is Springfield), the mountains of Colorado (nearest medical center is Denver), or much of rural Utah (nearest center is Salt Lake City). Most of the time, however, one is healthy and wants to enjoy the twenty or so years one may have ahead.

The rural West provides food, water, energy, and a story of our past. It helps us understand who we are. We are a restless people, and the open lands of the West are part of our heritage. In 1845, Alexis de Tocqueville wrote about Americans:

> Sometimes the progress of man is so rapid that the desert reappears behind him. The woods stoop to give him a passage, and spring up again when he has passed. It is not uncommon in crossing the new States of the West to meet with deserted dwellings in the midst of the wilds; the traveller frequently discovers the vestiges of a log house in the midst of the most solitary retreat, which bear witness to the power, and no less to the inconstancy of man.[12]

CHAPTER 7

Women of the West

by Elizabeth Darby

*There is often a difference between what a culture tells us
we ought to do and what we in fact do.*
—Elizabeth Jameson

Independent spirit.
Fierce courage.
Melancholia.
Pioneer. Adventurer.
Entrepreneur. Madam.
Reluctant companion facing a challenging wilderness.
Landowner. Cattle owner. Farmer.
Politician. Lawyer. Teacher. Justice. Marshal. Mayor.
Bank robber. Cattle rustler. Stagecoach driver.
Heartbroken mother. Tireless workhorse. Angel of Mercy.
Equally tireless champion of women's and children's rights.
Cook. Laundress. Slave. Self-possessed freed woman.
Matriarch of family or extended family (kinship).
Doctor. Healer. Midwife. Wise woman.

This is but a small list of adjectives and modifiers that describe the experience of women who came to live in the American West, as it grew into a vast domain soon including the Spanish and Texas Territories north of Mexico and extending to the previously Russian and British claims of the Oregon Territory.

No one experience was the norm for a woman in a land that was this vast and inherently multicultural from the very beginning of human arrival to the North American continent.

Indigenous women lived at "home" with a sense of well-being and intimate comfort in a landscape and habitat the Europeans would later call the "wilderness" or "terra sauvage" of North America. They prospered and thrived, raised families, were matriarchs of their people, healers, wise women, and businesswomen and artisans before the arrival of later waves of other women of differing ethnic backgrounds.

Hispanic women moved north from Nueva España in Mexico and were often landed, powerful women who came to rule over their ranchos of thousands of acres, settling into a home of the southwestern deserts.

Women of African descent traveled thousands of miles on foot, coming both west and north, not only as slaves or servants but also as freed women seeking new lives in a territory where, they hoped, racial prejudice played second fiddle to cooperative survival. Some made the trek alone, buying their freedom for themselves and their extended family with their earned wages, while others coming north from Mexico arrived already without the shackles of slavery, women of African Mexican descent who had self-possession and respect and were part of the West from early as the 1600s.

Anglo immigrant women sought opportunities for farms and new livelihoods, some as daughters of the Revolution who marched west to the frenzied drumbeat of Manifest Destiny from their socially significant East Coast lineage, while newly emigrated European and Anglo women came west fresh off ships laden with those, often impoverished in their homeland, eagerly seeking new opportunity.

Chinese women first arrived as sex slaves often smuggled to the mining camps of Golden Mountain, but were able, much later, to come to the West to begin businesses away from the straits of cultural oppression in their homelands. Destitute and oppressed, these women nevertheless finally gained the status that comes with education and the savvy that comes with business acumen, as many became the West's first Asian teachers, lawyers, and white-collar workers.

No one experience for the women of the West was necessarily unique despite their multiethnic backgrounds, however. The common experience was one of "wrasslin" cultural norms that defined what "women's work" could be and was in its grim reality of the day in the mid-eighteenth and nineteenth centuries. Individually and together as a sex, women struggled through the hard work of their daily lives. For all but the indigenous women, they did so in a land far away from what was thought to be "civilization," meeting the demands of a territory without infrastructure or "niceties" inherent in the most basic of urban or village communities of the US Eastern seaboard or of their homes of origin in Europe or Mexico. While in the more populated eastern states a woman had female companionship—a few miles' walk to church or plentiful dry goods, easy access to flowing water—women of the West had none of these. Only the indigenous women knew how to thrive in a land where there were miles and miles between water sources and without European city–styled infrastructure.

Regardless of background, there was an overlap in what women from any background did as daily work, and it included some measure of the basic yet most powerful work of all: that of creating a "home." A woman's work for all cultural backgrounds included ensuring the survival of her family, her extended family, and even her newfound family of community through her long hours of labor. It may not have been included, or much less heralded, as historically or economically important by mostly male writers. But the simple fact is the West would not have been populated or "settled" from all but the indigenous point of view without such backbreaking work of "home" being made in a wild and unforgiving climate. Thus the role of women in the West is of paramount power and importance, if too often marginalized, taken for granted or worst of all, simply disregarded.

In the West, these norms of what constituted women's work were often radically different from the rules and expectations of the immigrant women's lands of origin. There were also fluid cultural rules in the open territorial canvas that was the West that allowed women who had emigrated a gambit to reach for a free and independent life experience unmatched at the time anywhere else in the world, and that rose beyond their specific circumstances.

Any attempt to capture this fluidity is a study in itself, and thus one chapter on it risks error through generalization, but to better understand the multiculturalism and rules of power for women of the West, some broad brush is necessary. Historians began putting women back into the story of the American West only in the last thirty years, as anything other than the long-suffering Madonna of the Plains. Their work, highlighting the economic and cultural importance of the many women of multiple ethnic origins, is a rich and largely untold story with much to explore still.

Journals and diaries of the women who came to the West are full of wonder, of cross-cultural incredulity at the land and its extremes, and of a yearning for—and more importantly, a taking of—power where they could that was unusual if not unique for the time in any other part of the world. What a strange new world, replete with opportunities for living a life of their own franchise and economic power, women who came west found. Here are a few of the differences these women might have observed in the multiculturalism that surrounded them, if they could have seen beyond the circumscription of their cultures of origin:

- Native American women held respect and equal, vital footing in their extended families and tribes (although their workload wasn't usually understood that way by Anglo culture). They enjoyed a strength through matriarchy and matrilineal inheritance that puzzled the later arrivals to the West.
- Spanish-culture women were able to legally own property, married or not, in contrast to many American or European immigrant women who came West as virtual nobodies, with no rights to property or custody of their own children should their husbands divorce or abandon them.
- African-descent women came to the West and were able to petition for rights and freedoms, as well as equality under the law, not before experienced for former slaves. Those of Mexican African descent arrived free and with economic independence. Both waves of women of African heritage soon found themselves in a land where they were able to build communities and become the rock of the cities of the West.
- Chinese women, uncounted and too often unnamed during the 1800s even in their homeland, struggled against both a patriarchal and prejudicial system that had control of their bodies and their lives. Their strength would be recognized later, as with the power of education and of becoming teachers and lawyers, they would soon create an emerging middle and professional class of women of the American West.

This is not to say there was not racial or societal prejudice and discrimination between the groups of women who came and built the West. Sadly, far from it. With each wave of women arriving to make their mark on the vast natural lands and perceived wilderness of the West, new sets of definitions of "respectable" or "acceptable" came to be overlaid on the women already here and building the West. The new social strictures were ugly, racist, and too often as divisive as the societies the women left behind, often still fueled by a sense of entitlement and privilege predicated on skin color and definitions of otherness of the time.

With, or perhaps despite, the multiculturalism found in a land where such groups coexisted, however, it would be safe to say that women of all backgrounds experienced in the West a sense of personal franchise and freedom as the common experience. It was one that was unknown elsewhere in the United States. For some immigrating settlers, the uprooting and loss of their status and culture of the "more civilized" areas of their points of origin caused unending melancholia, while the very same experience of life in "uncivilized territory" was every day an eager adventure for others. The tapestry of women's experience in the American West is complex, varied, and one of many emotions, as often colored by what they felt they lost in security or status as by what they found they suddenly could do at a time when "nice women didn't do that..."—including owning land, hunting, cow punching, owning their own businesses of all sorts, dealing cards, bank robbing, to even simply foregoing a corset and wearing men's clothes for parts of each week.

All of these generalizations proffered here to reach for an understanding of the experience of the Women of the West are best set against the facts of the fluid cultural exchange that took place during the populating of Jefferson's Louisiana Purchase, and later the purchases of the kingdom of Nueva Expaña and the annexation of Texas and the Oregon Territories, which became the American West.

The West wasn't empty territory, of course, at the time of the Louisiana Purchase in 1803. Although uncounted in the census of the mid-1800s, thousands of Native Americans had made the verdant habitat that was the West a fertile and abundant home for millennia.

The Spanish arrived during and after their conquest of the West as kingdom and colony in the 1500s, and the southwestern deserts, coastal California, and Mexican Texas territories absorbed another wave of women who came from Europe via the long trek from Mexico. Their daughters settled Santa Fe and other outposts of the arid West, but they also lived amid the beauty along the California coast, where power and vast ranchos combined into the making of a Spanish political elite. Spaniards and their descendants had occupied the land decades before the arrival of English settlers to the original thirteen colonies. It would be another two hundred years before Anglos began pushing in on the Spanish settlements of the West.

When Anglo immigrants began to travel to the territories in the fabled wagon trains, it became a kind of culturally biased set point created by historians of old for when the "West began," but the West was already home to women. They left their mark on the land by having already created home and a way of living in the "wilderness." There was already a rhythm to the life of a woman in the West, whether indigenous or of Hispanic descent. There was a culture, a system of power and of service, but not servitude, and an organized civilization of government, family, economy, and religion, that remains too often untold in the history books.

Women of African ancestry, too, came west early on, before the mass migrations of the late 1800s, coming north with the Hispanic expansion from Mexico into the Southwest, and as others had, they too came in search of opportunity as well as freedom. In 1833, the Third Annual Convention for the Improvement of the Free People of Color encouraged immigration to Mexican Texas over returning to Africa for African-American women. Mexico had declared independence from Spain in 1821 and in doing so abolished slavery and guaranteed full citizenship rights to all, regardless of color. Women who were fugitive slaves or who were brought west as slaves could buy or claim their freedom once reaching Alta California. African American women joined the ranks of other women in becoming entrepreneurs as laundresses or cooks, baking bread or owning boarding houses, as domestics, or in doing the hard work of homesteading while husbands worked at neighboring homesteads.

After the Civil War, the "Bonneted Madonna of the Prairie," the long bannered stereotype of women in the West, began the trek in companies of wagon trains sometimes twelve across, or by walking with a handcart across what they called the "wilds." This, of course, is the westward journey depicted of women settling a "wilderness," but one that ignores all these prior waves of women who came before. The journals and stories the Anglo women left describe their hard work in making a home in an empty, beautiful paradise. It's a very different story from the Hollywood version of long-suffering, docile women.

These Anglo and European women also sometimes came alone, sometimes with sisters, sometimes as widows with several children walking with them, or as part of extended families, or with husbands and having babies as they covered the 2,000-mile trek overland. And indeed they buried children along the route as well, as dysentery and common illnesses of cholera, typhoid, small pox, and measles ravaged the westward trails as they made the journey from the Missouri through the Mountain West to the Pacific Coast. On the Overland Trail between 1862 and 1868, 20,000 people traveled *each year*, and the trail itself quickly morphed from a favorite path through prairie used by Lakota or other Plains people to a path consisting of a smelly string of trash and human and animal waste. Some women reported there seemed to be a grave every few yards left by those who traveled before them.

In the early mining-camp days of the mid-1800s, women were in the minority, as is demonstrated by the 1860 Census at the Comstock Lode in Nevada, which counted 2,379 men and a mere 147 women. "As a result of the western gold rushes and later extractive economies that attracted men, the gender ratio in the territory west of the Rocky Mountains remained imbalanced well into the 20th century. According to the U.S. Census Bureau, in 1850 there were 593 white women for every 1000 men in the Rocky Mountain and Pacific Coast states and territories."[1]

But the census did not count a number of non-white groups of women. Of the 800,000 women living west of the Mississippi in 1900, "12,000 were black, 4500 Chinese, 370 Japanese, some 6000 Indian."[2] So many more women remained uncounted, as they were living in Indian Territory. Not surprisingly, the 1880 Census shows that in those western states where mining and gold had been the driver for immigration, women remained at half of the male population, while in the farming states of the High Plains, Northwest, Utah, and California, numbers of men and women were closer to equal.

"From the fields to the franchises, women have worked to sustain their households in the midst of a wider terrain. And at the same time, gendered ideas about the ways humans make and claim homes have shaped social worlds, public life, and political decisions, throughout the history and across the spaces of the American West," notes historian Virginia Scharff. "Despite the influence of gendered ideas on social life and even federal policy, the West offered women unprecedented opportunities to do what so many men did: to reinvent themselves."[3]

What the westering women found was a clean slate of potential and possibility that would lead the country in women's rights and women's ability. The image of the strong woman brandishing a gun and running her ranch is as much a truth as the madam, the woman who was at once an entrepreneur and, in today's terms, a pimp who knew what was wanted in a land where men outnumbered women. There were also many opportunities for creating economic opportunity, using the skills of her hands. "Bread baked by a woman's hand" was a skill not found easily in the mining camps and so was highly sought after, while other women entered business with cooking and as the "needed" laundress. For the woman making a home, the work was no less but the wages were.

"Weary days of labor and pain," a western woman confided to her diary in the late 1800s. "Have made 175 loaves and 450 pies. Taken care of the children and done all the housework but the washing."[4]

Where there were few doctors in a vast land, women learned healing and herbal remedies from the women who had used them for years in their indigenous family groups. Incredibly resourceful, women were perhaps the original survivalists, finding solutions so that their children might survive if not also thrive. For the later arrivals, a first year's survival in the wilderness might rely on teachings from the original indigenous women of the West. Such healing skills were apparent across social and cultural groups, as women of all ethnic backgrounds opened their homes and hearts to become the hospitals, emergency shelters, and canteens for the poor, hungry, and homeless.

> "The historian Elsa Barkley Brown reminds us that, 'We have still to recognize that being a woman is, in fact, not extractable from the context in which one is a woman—that is race, class, time and place.' For westering women, their context was one of a blank slate, opportunity to redefine the woman's traditional role from one of drudge to one of helpmate as well as one of powerful independence."[5]

In 1869, Wyoming became the first territory to give women the unrestricted right to vote, with the territory of Idaho following in 1870, then Washington and Montana, in each case before statehood. Colorado in 1893 was the first state in which women's right to vote was created by the electorate. By 1914, women could vote in the territory of Alaska and in eleven states, all except one of which were west of the Mississippi. The Nineteenth Amendment finally granted women the right to vote throughout the remaining United States in 1920.

Widows and single women were also able to lay claim to land in their own name under the Homestead Act of 1862 as well as under other government land offers to "settle" the West. A few women also patented mining claims and panned for gold, while others tried their hands as stagecoach drivers; some even cross-dressed to join the cavalry or ran their own gambling salons—women who could deal cards were highly sought after, with men traveling hundreds of miles to sit at their tables.

As a result, there is a formidable list of "firsts" in American society to come from the women of the West. Here's a short version:

Bridget (Biddy) Mason was born a slave in 1818 and taken by her owner to California, a slave-free state. She then resisted a move to Texas and petitioned the California court for her freedom. After it was granted, Biddy worked in Los Angeles as a nurse and midwife and became a real estate entrepreneur and philanthropist.

First woman justice of the peace: **Esther Hobart Morris**, Wyoming, 1870

First woman elected US mayor: **Susanna "Dora" Salter**, Argonia, Kansas, 1887 (daughter of pioneers from Ohio); also mother of nine children, one of whom was born during her tenure

First licensed African American medical doctor: **Dr. Justina Ford**, Colorado, 1902

First woman elected to US Congress: **Jeannette Rankin**, Montana, 1916

First woman elected US governor: **Nellie Tayloe Ross**, Wyoming, 1924

First female elected senator to serve full term: **Hattie Ophelia Wyatt Caraway**, Arkansas, 1932

As we have continued into the twentieth and twenty-first centuries, the list of firsts goes on, from first female Supreme Court justice (Sandra Day O'Connor, Arizona, 1981); to the first woman in space, astronaut Sally Ride (California, 1983); to the first female commercial airline pilot, Emily Howell Warner (Colorado, 1973); to the first female US secretaries of the Departments of Health and Human Services and of the Interior, Shirley Hufstedler and Gale Norton, respectively.

The endurance required of the women who came to make a home in the extremes of the western habitat has become legend. The women who populated the western territories had not only their women's work to do—essentially *all* the work of making a home function, of course as her counterparts in more "civilized society" traditionally had to do, but these homes were made in a wilderness. Fetching clean water and wood, doing the laundry, cleaning, growing food, handling livestock, all aspects of food and cooking, and making clothes and dressing their family was on the daily to-do list. In addition, there was the unique work of pregnancy, birth, nursing, and childcare, as well as medical care of family and neighbors. Let's not forget it was an age when childbirth was feared as deadly in any location, yet one in five women were pregnant while on the overland trails.

Women in the West also took on more of the men's sphere of work, whether on the trail or in encampments or in the growing communities. Whatever was needed to be done to survive and thrive would become "women's work," altering the definition from her counterparts in the more "settled" eastern and southern regions. This included starting businesses, whether as laundress or baker or at a saloon or dry goods store; buying and selling land and cattle; or becoming some of the most powerful property owners in their territory, whether in Santa Fe or Los Angeles. Often women became the "angel of the community," for as women of the many cultures prospered, they provided shelter, food, and sometimes a stake or loan of money to help newly arrived poor get on their feet. They became the founding benefactors of hospitals, schools, and social service missions throughout the West.

Where one would love to imagine a sisterhood of strong women of many cultures joining supportively in a live-and-let-live tapestry, the reality was closer to waves of ever-changing social rules begetting winners and losers. Although the madam and her house of women serving men was also a savvy and often highly respected entrepreneur in the mining camps, with a new wave of immigrating settlers a few years later, she would become a social pariah, her staff ostracized by newer waves of "civilized" women coming West and bringing with them stricter societal norms. The freedom of the West where women could overcome the boundaries of their ability without social hurdles would soon become a land in which women again would be subject to racial divisiveness by the women who followed. With increased population and new arrivals, heaps of predefined cultural, social, and racial norms of acceptability would be shellacked onto the land, where previously women were free to see what was possible for themselves, or to live as women had for millennia before them in indigenous cultures. It's not a new story, but it is the underbelly of the shining American myth of the West. For every woman who found her adventure, a life she would otherwise only dream of had she stayed in a more civilized or settled city or country, there was a woman dragged from all she knew to start over, not by her choice—and yet another, such as the indigenous women, whose very existence was suddenly anathema to the newer wave of social straits.

> Still I must sweep, and churn and brew,
>   And make my dresses nice to view;
> And nurse the baby, read the news,
>   Darn socks, keep buttons on the shoes,
> Play the piano, beat the steak,
>   Then last, not least, this undertake.
> Not Euclid's problem intricate,
>   Have half so puzzled my poor pate.
> If men to such a task were set,
>   They'd lock their doors and swear and fret,
> And send for all their counselors.
>   And say an age were time too short
>   To learn this trade, perfect this art.
> But we must learn a hundred trades
>   Without apprenticeship or aids,
> And practice all with equal skill,
>   'Tis their good pleasure, our good will.[6]

Hard work unimaginable to most people today was the unifying experience for women in the vast open spaces of the American West. An excerpt of a woman's journal records such hard work on "wash day," as women often divided the week into days totally given over to one household task, whether baking fifteen loaves of bread twice a week or sewing and mending day, while still undertaking all the other demands of her women's work. Here is one women's list of work on wash day, during a time when turning on a tap for water to flow into a sink—barely three generations ago in the West—would have been a miracle. The hand-cranked washing machine was not introduced into the majority of the West until 1915. (All spellings as in original.)

1. bild fire in back yard to het kettle of rain water.
2. set tubs so smoke won't blow in eyes if wind is peart.
3. shave 1 hole cake like sope in bilin water
4. sort things. make 3 piles. 1 pile white, 1 pile cullord, 1 pile work briches and rags.
5. stuf flour in cold water to smooth then thin down with bilin water
6. rub dirty spots on board. scrub hard. then bile. rub cullord but don't bile just rench and starch.
7. take white things out of kettle with broom stick handel then rench, blew and starch.
8. pore rench water in flower bed
9. scrub porch with hot sopy water
10. turn tubs upside down
11. go put on a cleen dress, smooth hair with side combs, brew cup of tee, set and rest and rock a spell and count blessings.

In the end, a glimpse into the lives of women in the West offers not only a multitude of freedom and rights unheard of throughout other nations and cultures of the same time but also into the commonality of a creed of endurance that is, perhaps, the theme throughout all women's history. There are firsts alongside the stories of subjugation and loss that should leave us shaking our heads in appreciation of the sacrifices made, but also in shared sorrow at the pain caused by cultural collision in a landscape of such open possibilities for women.

"We argue that claiming a home is a potent way of changing the world," note Virginia Scharff and Carolyn Brucken. "Instead of worrying that the association of women with home will trivialize women's history in the west, we want to expand our definition of home beyond domesticity to encompass the process of inhabiting places. In the name of home, women have done everything from gathering food and building houses to speculating in real estate and running governments."[7]

There is, in the subject of women of the West, much to be celebrated and to laud in wonderment, considering how the hardy and enduring women of all cultures reached for lives that were otherwise impossible in more restricted economic strata of the time. Perhaps it is to this spirit that we look when defining the spirit of the West in myth and in reality, amid all the modifiers that cling to it still: a light-filled canvas on which individuals, including women of all ethnic backgrounds, could paint the lives of their dreams in a landscape of immense and incredible beauty and possibility, and where dreams as large as the vast sky could be lived.

Western women of each background and cultural heritage lived facing different stresses and challenges, hopes and opportunities. Some of these were based on their culture, while others were specific to their "time of arrival" to the wide open spaces of the West. Here are a few details amid the multicultural array of women in the West.

Western Native American Women

Living for millennia on the North American continent before the arrival of women of other cultural roots, the West for the Native American woman was already "home" in every way. Life, celebrations, homemaking, and the sacred were interwoven into the vast habitat of the North American landscape the indigenous people knew simply as home and as often revered as mother of life. Never a wilderness per se for the indigenous women, instead the environment and culture were the woven warp and weft of their lives on earth. That is not to say daily life wasn't a challenge; through a multitude of generations women and men had learned how to survive seasons, climate, and the harsh varieties and extremes of weather in such a varied land. And as with all women making their home in the extremes of nature in the West, days were filled with hard work for Native American women: the work of making a home and a living that is the work of life. Native American women were not just "reproducing units" as women were so often counted in history; they were also warriors, leaders, builders, and craftswomen, a nuance overlooked by the women and men of different cultures who came later.

There are too many varia-
tions in culture to really describe
the lives of indigenous women
in the vast and varied lands west
of the Mississippi to the Pacific
Coast. Lewis and Clark came
in contact with *only* about fifty
Native American tribes in their
exploration, just a fragment of the
many different cultures calling
the West home at the time. Many
more peoples, especially along
the Pacific Coast, had already
been wiped out when the Spanish
arrived with European diseases by
the time Lewis and Clark made
their journey in 1803.

Navajo woman, 1904.

Before the arrival of Spanish explorers, for example, the
Tongva lived in what is now the Los Angeles area, where they grew and
foraged buckwheat, prickly pear, and hunted abundant wild game. But,
by 1844, nearly two-thirds of their population had been killed by small
pox. The story would be the same across the West with the arrival of
first the military and then waves of settlers from the 1600s through to
the late 1800s, when the surviving Native Americans were forced onto
reservations, usually the land no one else wanted—veritable waste-
lands where their way of life and culture were further destroyed.

For these original women of the West, what was true was a sense
of sacred and home that was integrated into the land itself. In many
tribes, the women were responsible for the actual building of the home
from traditional raw materials, a feat that would astonish later cultures,
despite its vital and important role. The land provided all that was needed
for living, and the vegetation was a pharmacopoeia the women learned
to use to help their families and kin survive. These early herbalists also
helped later arriving women of all cultures greatly, teaching them which
plants would supply winter nourishment and which herbs would aid in
fever, childbirth, and nursing, as well as many of the other illnesses of
both child- and adulthood that proved so dangerous to newly arriving
settlers far from the western medicine of European practice.

"When traditional indigenous people speak of their relatives, they are referring to every living thing, not just human kinship," writes the late Wilma Mankiller. "The very identity of traditional tribal people is derived from the natural world, the land, and the community. They understand their own insignificance in the totality of things."[8] Before her passing in 2010, Mankiller had been a former principal chief of the Cherokee Nation of Oklahoma.

The indigenous first women of the West were also masters at crafts, creating their family's clothing, needed tools, and other essentials for survival, all with their hands and abilities from the materials nature provided. Many tribes were also matriarchies, where leadership was conferred on women, and they took part in the governing of their people. So many of these roles were misunderstood by the later settlers to the West, perhaps largely due to the low status of the women within those later cultures, especially the European and English immigrants.

"Most people know very little about indigenous women, except for a few almost mythical icons such as Sacajawea, an intelligent, resourceful Shoshone interpreter who accompanied the Lewis and Clark expedition in the early nineteenth century," writes Mankiller. She continues,

> This appalling lack of accurate information about indigenous women fuels negative stereotypes.... [In film, as in the larger society], the power, strength, and complexity of indigenous women are rarely acknowledged or recognized. While the role of indigenous women in the family and community, now and in the past, differs from nation to nation each of the women at this gathering [for her book] stated unequivocally that there was a point in time when there was a greater equity between men and women, and that balance between men and women must be restored if we are ever to have whole, healthy communities again.[9]

Mankiller notes that Navajo women once controlled the economy by owning and managing the livestock, while Ojibwa women trapped small animals, dressed furs, and built canoes. There were even women who chose roles in their nations that transcended gender, in which the women sat on tribal councils and even took wives. Sometimes it was out of necessity, or by choice from a vision or dream and willed by the Creator. A woman might take on a hunter and warrior role to feed and protect her children and siblings, while also taking "wives" to do the rest of the necessary women's work so vital to survival, notes Professor Ramona Ford.[10]

"As a matriarch, I think I could write an entire book on the challenges and responsibilities of womanhood," wrote Rosalie Little Thunder who is Sicangu Lakota. "We are the creators of 'home,' caretakers of the spiritual and physical needs of the *tiwahe*, or household, and our *tiospaye*, or extended family. We are teachers, healers, storytellers, peacemakers, problem solvers, and visionaries. The roles and responsibilities in indigenous cultures are different and dynamic."[11] The Sicangu Lakota's original territory extended through the northern plains states from Minnesota through the Dakotas and Nebraska to Wyoming, but they were eventually placed on the Rosebud Reservation in South Dakota.

Quickly subjugated by new waves of settlers, causing the destruction of their people and their culture and the taking of their lands, the Native American women of the West were still resourceful, taking on "seasonal income" through what work they could find while still holding family together on the reservations, notes historian Jane Simonson.[12]

Native American women are finding their strong voice to put themselves back into the story of the American West. They are an essential part of this story to be seen anew, and there is much that is yet to be understood, given the diverse and rich culture of so many different peoples and cultures that called the West home. More research that questions the old stereotypes handed to history by Anglo "victors" who encountered the Native American people is increasingly being undertaken but so much more can be done. In these new views of Native American women, it has become evident that so much was misunderstood or simply seen through a European- or male-dominated worldview. Military explorers and dominating settlers preferred to do "business" with the men of the tribe rather than the women—who often held franchise to do trading—and the women suffered from both the cultural and the male-dominated point of view. Among the Lakota, for example, "women gained status through participation in the Buffalo ceremony and Virgin Fire ritual. Many groups also reserved a high position for the holy women who could sponsor the Sun Dance," notes Ramona Ford.[13] Plains women made ceremonial objects and elaborate arts and crafts through which they gained status. Women of the Dakota and Lakota, Arapaho and Cheyenne formed craft guilds (with prizes for designs that were passed to heirs with a sort of patent on use).

"Euro-Americans overwhelmed native systems by disease and conquest. European ideas of proper gender roles became more difficult to resist. Native American women often lost their economic base, their formal political rights as clan matrons... their sexual freedom, their reproductive rights, and their right to be cross-gender or different in their roles when they chose," writes Ford.[14]

For the original women of the West, there was no "settlement" or separation between their lives and the land that provided for them. "Western Shoshone women are taught that a woman is like the Earth: she gives and nurtures life," write Mary and Carrie Dann, ranchers who live and work in their home territory of northern Montana. "The Earth and women have the same properties: The Earth provides for us, just as we provide for our children. The way we were taught, if the Earth is treated with disrespect by a woman, she is disrespecting herself. We are one and the same."[15]

The generosity of these indigenous women teaching and helping the women who later came west was instrumental to learning how to survive in the challenging landscape. This is a powerful narrative of women in the West, and one whose time has come to be included, taught, understood, and the wisdom of it learned, as it was the foundation of strength and resilience that became the national narrative of resilience and strength we tell ourselves that was born in the American West.

Hispanic Women of the West

Living in a former colony of Spain in the late 1500s and early 1600s, the American kingdom of Nueva España, women had legal rights to property ownership that other western women did not yet enjoy. "Under English common law, women, when they married, became *feme covert* (effectively dead in the eyes of the legal system) and thus unable to own property separately from their husbands. Conversely, Spanish Mexican women retained control of their land after marriage and held one-half interest in the community property they shared with their spouses," writes Vicki L. Ruiz, distinguished professor of history and Chicano/Latino studies at the University of California, Irvine.[16]

1850 portrait of a
"Californio Woman"

Coming from the Kingdom of New Spain (which included most of South and Central America as well as Florida, Mexico, the American Southwest, and up the Pacific Coast), Spanish colonists moved into the territory of what became Mexico and later the American Southwest between the early 1500s and 1821.

Colonists settled at the northern edge of the vast Spanish territory, far from the society and rules of cities in Spanish Mexico, in an area considered a backwater when compared to the urban vibrancy of Mexico City. Life for the early explorers presented them with remote existence and a decidedly vast but sparsely populated landscape in the American Southwest. Ironically, parts of what were known as the Spanish Borderlands more resembled the sedge and rocky Spanish landscapes they were accustomed to, whether in what would become Texas or along the California coast, while the borderlands (New Mexico, Arizona, part of Colorado and Utah) challenged them with an arid desert environment in which the indigenous people had already created a thriving home.

By the late 1700s, Spanish settlements of the El Camino Real missions in Alta California (as opposed to Baja California, still part of Mexico) followed the Spanish system of conquest—first military arrived, immediately followed by missions to spread Catholicism and the creation of civilian settlements, and always with women as part of family units coming along with the priests to inhabit the newly conquered territory and establish home. For example, two years after the first expedition of Juan de Oñate to establish the city of Santa Fe in 1598 at the northern edge of New Spain, women and families followed under military guard. In 1600, a party of civilians accompanied the Juan de Resa expedition to Santa Fe to increase the Spanish population in the region. Among them was Isabel de Olvera of Querétaro, daughter of an African-descent father and Indian mother, who before coming sought an affidavit from the mayor of Querétaro declaring her freedom and status, in case she might be "annoyed," she wrote, as a woman of mixed ancestry. Her arrival in the West predates by nineteen years the creation of Jamestown on the American East Coast. De Olvera was a lady-servant for one of the Spanish elite women who came to Santa Fe.

The women who found their way to Santa Fe and to the ranchos of California would have been the daughters and granddaughters of the women who made a home in the kingdom of Nueva España that was Mexico in the 1500s. Accustomed to the rigors of nature in the New World, and sometimes the result of Spanish marrying indigenous people, they would have felt at home in the wide open spaces and perhaps would even have found the milder climate of California or the high deserts of Santa Fe almost a luxury if the raids by Zuni, Comanche, Apache, and Navajo locals hadn't been so frequent.

"Despite an abhorrence of racial and religious impurity [among the Spanish] and a preference for Spanish marriage partners, centuries of ethnic admixture in Spanish society promoted an acceptance of intermarriage in the New World that was unparalleled by any other European colonial culture," notes anthropologist Bonnie G. McEwan. "While heavy physical labor was usually allocated to indigenous and, later African men, women were more often incorporated into Spanish colonial life where they played an active role as wives, domestics, craft specialists, and most importantly, cultural brokers."[17]

A Spanish elite was soon established in the Spanish territories, one based on wealth, land ownership, and home education of women. "By all accounts women provided a measure of balance and stability to the colonial enterprises with which they were involved (Lockhard 1968; 163; McAlister 1984; 97)," writes McEwan.[18]

In California as early as 1775, women were among the colonists brought from Sonora, New Spain, along the Gila River overland trail accompanying friars and soldiers led by Colonel Juan Bautista de Anza to settle missions near San Francisco and Santa Clara. The role of women in balancing otherwise military outposts continued, even through the arrival of immigrants from Europe and the eastern United States to the borderlands of the American Southwest, after the territory was ceded to the United States. With the new arrivals, a fresh wave of culture clash took place in which the Spanish-culture women who had called the land home for more than a hundred years found themselves suddenly a lower class than the new Anglo arrivals. The Spanish manner of dress was often mistaken for "hussy" compared to the high-collared prim and prudish norms for the newly arrived Victorian-influenced Anglos.

Intermarriage was common, and Anglo men who married Hispanic women they met in these remote outposts then accessed the women's land and holdings as well. Intermarriage was encouraged by Mexico in Texas, in that American men who did so would receive a land allotment of their own in the borderlands as well as Mexican citizenship. When Mexico lost its northwestern territories to the United States, however, those of Spanish culture experienced prejudice in Texas and California as Anglos took territory and relegated Hispanics to second-class citizens.

A few of the land-owning women of the old Spanish families remain legends to this day. Among them was Maria Rita Valdez de Villa. Her family was among the original eleven families recruited from Sinaloa and Sonora to help to establish the new pueblo (city) of El Pueblo de Nuestra Señora la Reina de los Ángeles del Rio Porciuncula. As one of the granddaughters of the original families of Los Angeles, Maria Rita Valdez de Villa would in 1838 come to be deeded Rancho Rodeo de las Aguas, a 4,500-acre land grant where three sources of water came together; today the area is known as Beverly Hills. Another large land owner, Doña Vicenta Sepulveda, ran her Rancho Valle de San Jose, a 17,634-acre area in the northeast of present-day San Diego County. It was sold to her in 1858, and she owned and managed it until 1869.

Another enterprising woman in the early west of New Mexico, known as Madame La Tules, became legend in her own right. Doña Maria Gertrudis Barceló is thought to have been born at the turn of the century (1800) and was of a high-ranking family living on a rancho south of Santa Fe. She was renowned for her beauty, wit, her fashionable if shocking (to starched Anglo women who described her in the mid-1800s) dress, and her brilliant ability at Monte, a card game wildly popular at the time. Her two sons died in infancy, and it is guessed that this may have been what took her from her role as Doña (a woman of high family) and mother to become a businesswoman, opening one of the most famed gambling casinos of the early West. She was politically influential, and foresaw that the US arrival in New Spain would mean decline for the people already there. "Many modern historians give great credit to Doña Tules for the cultural bridge her Sala provided accustoming Euro-Americans to the Nuevo-Mexicano lifestyle."[19]

She became quite wealthy from her business success, and she left, at her death in 1852, a building an entire block long in the center of Santa Fe filled with European carpets and crystal chandeliers that had been brought across the Santa Fe Trail by wagons from St. Louis. She left it, as well as a residence and her wealth, to her sister, while also receiving a funeral of a *rica* (a rich woman) in the main cathedral of the city.[20]

African Descent Women of the West

Lost in the myth of the American cowboy West, women of African ancestry were nevertheless among the first women to immigrate to the vast territory, joining or accompanying the earliest Spanish settlers to the area. Although we are finally more commonly aware of the histories of Buffalo soldiers and the legendary Black cowboy tales, like many of their female counterparts, women of African-Mexican or African-American ancestry were simply overlooked and their contributions remained untold. "Black women were an integral part of the western and American tradition," writes Era Bell Thompson. "It both impairs their sense of identity and unbalances the historical record to continue to overlook the role of Black women in the development of the American West."[21]

As with others seeking opportunity and freedom for men and women alike, the open spaces of the West offered a new beginning for many women of African ancestry. Coming north first as daughters of Africans originally brought by the Spanish to central Mexico from the mid-1500s to 1821, thousands more came as refugees from slavery in the United States to Mexican Texas when Mexico declared its freedom from Spain in 1821, thereby establishing a slave-free territory where all

Mary Fields, shown here in 1895, was the first African-American woman employed as a mail carrier in the United States.

would find equal treatment under the law. The same was true for other Spanish territories of the Southwest and included California. Thus women of African descent, many former slaves who walked across the deserts of the west, were among the founders of San Francisco, Albuquerque, Laredo, San Antonio, Santa Fe, El Paso, and Tucson.

Among the settlers who, with military protection, made the 500-mile, two-month journey from Sinaloa in 1781 to a site that would become known as Nuestra Señora la Reina de Los Angeles de Porciuncula, just south of the mission at San Gabriel, were nineteen-year-old Maria Guadalupe, twenty-seven-year-old Gertrudis Perez, and forty-nine-year-old Maria Petra Rubio, all noted to be of African ancestry. Such freedom of movement and opportunity in the Spanish territories continued for another fifty years, until the Republic of Texas gained its freedom from Mexico in 1836. Then Texas became one of the largest slave-owning empires in the union, while in California, current and former slaves were able to petition for their freedom, as the state had included equality for all in its founding charter.

After the Civil War, freed African American women found work in the West as cooks or domestics, some traveling still as servants of white families. Famous now for their courage, for example, Polly Holmes and husband Robin "were granted freedom in 1849, and obtained freedom of their three children, through a lawsuit decided by the Territorial Supreme Court. Three years later a California court freed Bridget 'Biddy' Mason and her extended family of thirteen women and children in a celebrated trial," Quintard Taylor writes.[22] A slave to a Mormon family, Mason accompanied them on foot and with pushcart from Missouri to Utah, and then on to California when they moved. There, she asked for protective custody from the Los Angeles sheriff and petitioned the state for freedom. California Supreme Court judge Benjamin Hayes ruled "all of the said persons of color are entitled to their freedom and are free forever."[23] As with many women who had before experienced hardship and destitution, Mason set up a house open to serving the homeless, destitute, and other women who made it to California to attain their freedom.

Following the Civil War, the frontier loomed large in imagination as a land of freedom and where the hope for "being equal" might be more than a dream. Kansas, for example, had seen the start of John Brown's abolitionist revolution and seemed a shining new land for newly freed African American women and men to set up home, farm, and community. The reality of life on the prairie, however, was as challenging for these women as for others when they first set eyes on the flat, arid, and treeless land where living in dugouts was the norm for early settlers. The winters were bitterly cold, the summers too hot, the wind fierce, and the land difficult to farm. That didn't stop them from acquiring 160 acres when they could or giving farming a try on the High Plains, as well as creating communities of color in Kansas, Colorado, and Nebraska. The African American population in the West increased from 627 in 1860 to 12,000 in 1865.

Yet life free of racism remained elusive for all but those in sparsely populated areas where families of all backgrounds *had* to come together to survive the winters and summers and harvest failures. In the face of hardship, inequality faded, while it lasted in feeling and fact through segregation laws in the growing cities. Many African American families eventually gave up farming and moved to help build the cities of Denver, Lincoln, Leavenworth, Lawrence, Pasadena, Berkeley, and San Francisco. The women also created Ladies Aid societies, becoming the cement of social assistance in the growing cities—collecting food, clothing, and helping newly arrived freed people find their footing.

"The clubs offered black women the opportunity for self-expression and informal education while linking them to an emerging national network of black women's organization," notes Taylor. "These women took charge of their collective lives and fates and avoided victimization by the world around them. As the Kansas Federation of Women's clubs stated in its motto, they were 'rowing, not drifting.'"[24]

The cause of serving community became the women's work of so many African-American women in the West. Taylor notes that they were "disproportionately active in creating and maintaining churches, literary societies, women's clubs and civil rights organizations."[25] In 1902, for example, Dr. Justina Ford became one of the first African-American female doctors west of the Mississippi, where she served women and children of all backgrounds. She had been denied her license in Chicago due to her gender and her ancestry; in Denver, she was denied membership in the Colorado Medical Society or ability to practice in a hospital. So she opened up her home as a clinic and served women and children, many of whom were poor or non-English speaking and had been turned away from the local hospitals.

Lutie Lytle, daughter of a Topeka policeman, became the second female lawyer of African-American ancestry in the nation in the mid-1890s, while other women started newspapers or became stock investors in mining firms.

As with women of other ethnic backgrounds, the story of African American women of the West is still being collected and told. "Historians have begun to incorporate the voices of women and people of color precisely because they complete the mosaic of experience formed through encounters of diverse peoples and cultures in this region over the past five centuries," notes Taylor.[26]

Anglo Women of the West

The stereotype of the women of the West, dubbed the "Bonneted Madonnas of the Prairie" and immortalized by a fanciful painting by W. H. D. Koerner, emerges from the Anglo women who came west in the mid- to late-1800s. Koerner painted the work in his New York studio, having never gone west, yet the painting became the iconic image of the westering women for nearly a century. There were, however, two differing experiences for the Anglo women who came west, depending greatly on their starting point.

For the woman who was a daughter of immigrants to America who arrived in North America in Revolutionary times, she might be the third, fourth, or fifth generation of the new model of American individualist. Her familial lines would have been Pilgrims or religious refugees, landed gentry, or earlier opportunity-seeking working class, but who had already fought a Revolutionary War, built a new democracy, and were now seeking to fulfill the dream of Manifest Destiny "from sea to shining sea." They sought to settle the whole of the American continent, which was considered devoid of people and full of resources belonging to them, rather than a land already occupied with people of other cultures. These women left behind society, friends, and extended family along the East Coast and the Ohio Valley to come with their husbands 2,000 miles on the overland trails to create new homes and communities.

Many came unwillingly, experiencing loss and what was known at the time as sometimes fatal melancholia as they settled

Two women and their children (circa 1887-1889) pose in front of a building in the Arizona Territory.

in the "wilderness," as they saw it, while bringing overland their silver, carpets, chiffoniers, wedding beds, or even pianos and china to "civilize" the land and make it a home much like they left behind. Many of the carried items had to be left beside the trail to unburden oxen or be traded for supplies as they came west.

It is from these women we read most of the journals and letters regarding their sense of mission, their worries, their exhaustion, and their heartaches, sent home to their families in Ohio and in the original thirteen American colonies. If they were from the South, these women often brought slaves with them, bringing along as well the acculturation of social status that defined how women of any non-Anglo ancestry would be seen and treated in the West. Other women came from the tradition of abolition and reform and, after the Civil War, with a sense of building a new nation, perhaps one without official subjugation of other people, yet still with an already established judgment of how the races *should* engage and a strict definition of what was appropriate in the manner of an individual's life. Misunderstanding or perhaps not wanting to see the nuance of indigenous culture, it would be these women working to Christianize the "primitives" who would lend to the destruction of the native cultures, with all "good intent" of the times to "raise them from their low class." Equally, the judgment of other ethnic cultures created a social caste creating separation rather than a sisterhood of women with those who came west before them, even as all were doing similar backbreaking work as they created home in the western lands.

"The very nature of the overland travel precluded the likelihood of the sanitized Madonna—well-worn clothes, few items for personal hygiene, limits of diet, demands of pregnancy and childbirth, daily chores, rigors of the trek and uncertainty of the road ahead—all combined to produce a far more weathered collection of women than Koerner suggested," note historians Anne M. Butler and Ona Siporin. "If their photographs are scanned for less of the romance and more of the humanity, pioneer women radiate a far different kind of beauty. Theirs is a beauty forged from the reality of life's constant and oven searing experiences."[27]

More unexpected were those women who came west willingly, setting off for new adventure and opportunity, and as often came solo. Whether leaving alone for the mining camps or with husbands, as widows, or with sisters, they would quickly take on the roles of businesswomen and entrepreneurs, providing cook tents or boarding-houses or laundry services to augment their income and would equally take on whatever "men's work" was needed to keep the homestead functioning. Widows with children were able to claim land under the Homestead Act and thus could find a way to start anew that was not possible in the crowded cities of the East Coast.

Until 1849, women made up only 15 to 20 percent of these immigrants, and women's diaries left behind portray not only the adventure but also the hardship and the loneliness that accompanied them on trail, as many write that they missed female companionship.[28]

Then there were the newly immigrated Anglo and European women who had arrived only lately by ship to the United States and with full intent to "Go West." Wave after wave of new immigrants to America, many of them single women or recently widowed in the mid- to late-1800s brought yet another cultural dimension to the West. Fleeing famine or a shortage of work or to find land they could own rather than rent, these European and Anglo immigrants came west seeking economic opportunity and land ownership. Once they passed through the ports of the East Coast and Ohio, they often found jobs and housing there in short supply, so they willingly undertook the westward journey. Between the 1830s and 1860s, some 250,000 to 500,000 people traveled from St. Louis to California, encouraged by letters from friends and families portraying the opportunity of a sparsely populated land agreeable for farming, especially in the Midwest and the Great Plains regions, or for gold. Nearly 10 percent died en route, as dysentery, typhoid, malaria, diphtheria, and childbed fever took a steep toll. "Their travels changed their lives in ways they had never anticipated before they become pilgrims to the West," conclude Butler and Siporin.[29]

Faced with mercurial weather, where in winter winds commonly whipped over sixty miles per hour and temperatures fell well below zero in drifting snow, to summers with temperatures over 100 degrees and frequent drought or fire, the land presented a wholly new environment for both sets of Anglo women, whether migrating from the East or newly arrived in the country from Ireland, the British Isles, and Europe. A testament to their fortitude was the daily habit of sweeping the dirt floor of the dugout or "soddy" until a "normal" house could be built, using the broom to create a "clean swept floor" as the definition of civilized living. This was done despite cows falling through the roof, insects bursting through the walls in springtime, or a rattlesnake coming in over the transom, and killed with a buggy whip as my own Welsh great-grandmother did to protect her five young children.

A sense of isolation was keen for the Anglo westering women, having come from closely inhabited cities or small communities, regardless of origin in Europe, Britain, or the East Coast of the United States. Thus church gatherings were important in any season, as were visiting days, the tradition after the Sunday meal of "setting with your nearest neighbors." Quilting bees, weddings, Fourth of July celebrations, or the creation of a grange were vital to creating a sense of community for these westering women. Sickness, childbirth, or death also brought women together in a community of shared concern and grief. The commandment of the plains, when thinly settled, was generally one of hospitality to strangers.

As among earlier-arriving women of other cultures, Anglo women of the West also broke stereotypes set fast for women in the culture of the time and in the civilization of the East Coast. Some became famous madams of the West, while others later became mayors and senators. "By virtue of class or ethnicity, most western women did not fit the prescriptions of True Womanhood," notes historian Elizabeth Jameson. "Moreover ideology does not describe behavior."[30] As one early female westerner wrote: "There is often a difference between what a culture tells us what we ought to do and what we in fact do."[31]

Whether a wage earner in the mining camps or vital center of the economic unit that was the homestead, Anglo women also had to find a personal balance between the Victorian ideals of womanhood they brought with them and the gritty reality of life in the early West. For many it was a battle within of whether to do the daily hard work with or without laces of corsets and fashionable multiple petticoats, or the practicality of men's work boots traded for dainty high-button heeled shoes.

Some, such as Nellie Cashman, did it all. Born in Ireland in 1845, she, along with her sister and mother, emigrated when Nellie was five, refugees from the potato famine in the mid-1800s. During her first job in Washington, D.C., during the Civil War as an elevator operator, it is said that General Ulysses S. Grant himself encouraged her to "go West." She made her way to San Francisco in the 1860s, and from there to the mining camps in Nevada where she panned for gold herself, while also opening and running a boardinghouse for the miners, offering a roof over their heads even if they didn't yet have funds to pay her, and tending to them when they were ill. Nellie did this in other early mining camps as well throughout the West, from Arizona to British Columbia and beyond to the Yukon, and was described to be "pretty as a Victorian cameo and, when necessary, tougher than two-penny nails."[32] At one point, she mounted an expedition to rescue miners stranded in the mountains of British Columbia, refusing to leave the snowed-in area until all seventy-five men were rescued. She raised funds for the Salvation Army and for the building of hospitals as she continued to move around the West, whether in Tombstone, Arizona, or Montana, raising her dead sister's five children while still opening restaurants and funding hospitals. Her legend as an "Angel of Mercy" grew until her death in 1925. She led quite a life, whether dressed as a man or in heavy Victorian skirts and other trappings of the "decent woman" of the time.

"The women... did just as much to make this western country as any of the men did," said one Canadian pioneer woman. "They were just taken for granted... women sat in the background while the men got praised."[33]

Chinese Women of the West

In smaller numbers, women from China came to the United States in the mid-1800s via a 7,000-mile, two- to three-month voyage, before the advent of steamships cut the journey to one month (compared to the 2,000-mile overland journey, which took three to six months). Many of the earliest immigrant Chinese women were put on the boat and made to work off their passage once they arrived in the United States, or were sold by destitute parents into servitude or kidnapped outright to find themselves placed in pens or "cribs" as forced prostitutes for the male-dominated mining camps of the West Coast. Their lives were hell at the lowest rung of social status, even compared with other women who journeyed to the camps and set up shop in the sex trade for the same reason. Those of other cultures might find work in a "respectable" brothel where a high-class madam and savvy entrepreneur held rein, while Chinese women lost even their names into a kind of cultural anonymity of "Chinese Mary."

Chinese women, unvalued at home due to cultural norms, found themselves equally so in the New World, essentially leading grim lives as sex slaves with Chinese or Anglo men plying them as wares to any willing customer from their caged cribs just off the street curb. Gary

Okihiro writes that the economic labor of the sex trade resulting in the exploitation of Asian women in America "was also an extension of social relations in Asia, where patriarchy controls women's bodies and lives." Okihiro goes on to say, "In nineteenth-century Guangdong Province... women's prostitution was an alternative to infanticide, abandonment, and the selling of daughters."[34]

Still, many of the working women sent money home to fathers and family, while others were exploited by pimps or owners who kept all their earnings and hired them out as seamstresses, cooks, or washerwomen as well. "Prostitutes ran away, married their patrons, committed suicide, or died of disease and abuse," notes Okihiro.[35] The more fortunate might have found a way to create work for

Polly Bemis in her wedding dress in 1894 Idaho.

themselves in their own laundry shops, as so many of the other women of the early West did, but in the end there were very few due to overwhelming racism and xenophobia that defined the Chinese woman as at once exotic and other.

It is thought that the first Chinese woman to immigrate to the United States was Marie Seise, about which very little is known, save her registration in the Trinity Episcopal Church (San Francisco) records. Historians have pieced together that she ran away from her family in Guangzhou to escape being sold into slavery. She married a Portuguese sailor and after his death became a servant to a family that took her to Hawaii. Later, she was servant to a family who took her to California in 1848, where she went to work in the mining camps at the fabled Golden Mountain.

Other Chinese women made their own way by dint of courage and strength, immigrating as children of barely nine or ten years old and then outliving husbands once in the American West. Annette White-Parks writes of one woman, Ah Yuen, who after outliving three husbands, became in Wyoming "the toast of her countrymen," where she was a cook in the days of the Pony Express, while another woman, Mary Tape, sailed from China at age eleven, and after working as an interpreter and "contractor" of labor in California, taught herself telegraphy and succeeded in winning in court the right for her daughter to attend school.[36] It would not be until the arrival of Donaldina Cameron, an Anglo woman of Presbyterian faith who was active in setting up missions in San Francisco, that many of the women enslaved would find a champion and a way out. Too often, however, that way out was one of substituting prostitution for marriage, and the refugees in Cameron's care were forced to continue to dress in native Chinese outfits, further enhancing their being seen as other.

Due to laws enacted to prevent the continual immigration of Chinese men to the mining camps and railroad labor camps, it would not be until the very late 1800s when Chinese women would immigrate to join husbands to create what Anglos might deem "respectable" family units in the day. The Chinese Exclusion Act of 1882 stopped all Chinese women, except the wives or wives-to-be of Chinese American merchants, from being allowed to legally migrate. The New American experience for these enterprising women would have been totally different from their land of origin. Here, as wife and mother, the Chinese woman would have been able to help her husband in business, while also able to enjoy more freedom from the domination of her mother-in-law to whom she would have been inferior in the family unit at home in China. By the early twentieth century, laws were newly written to deport alleged prostitutes, which included most Chinese women.[37]

The association between opium dens, prostitution, otherness, and houses of "ill repute" made it difficult for Chinese women in the West to be seen as individuals and "firmly relegated Chinese women to the margins of American society," writes Sucheta Mazumdar. "The arrival in 1902 of sixteen-year-old Xue Jinqin as a student at the University of California, Berkeley, and her lecture to an audience numbering around a thousand in San Francisco's Chinatown on women's education and on 'women's obligations to break the old Chinese practices' passed unnoted by the East Coast media."[38]

In the twentieth century, Chinese women finally found new avenues through education and through community organizations such as the Chinese YWCA, which helped with social services. With access to more education, by the 1920s a few Chinese women could find work using language skills, such as becoming operators for the Chinatown telephone exchange, "where they were required to speak fluent English, several Chinese dialects and sub-dialects, memorize 2,200 phone numbers, in an exchange that handled an average of 13,000 calls a day,"[39] while other second-generation daughters challenged the status quo to become schoolteachers, nurses, and even dentists and bank managers. Faith So Leung, for example, is believed to have become the first Chinese American female dentist in the country. It would be the beginning of Chinese American women able to take on the work that would create the rise of an American-born Chinese female middle class.

Women of the West lived their lives as part of a multiethnic tapestry that was woven into the beautiful yet challenging land itself. The isolation and remoteness of the landscape provided the warp and weft for the independent spirit and freedom that became a hallmark of the West, offering women an opportunity to define their lives in a way unique to anywhere else in the world of that time. If there were limitations placed on these strong, enduring women who lived in the West, and there certainly were, they were cultural in nature, where the possibility for women of the time was as large as the land itself. Some of the limits were borne of the male and societal view of women in the years between 1500 and 2000, and the women who lived in or emigrated to the American West challenged these at every turn in ways not undertaken anywhere else in the world. Some limits were self-imposed, as women brought with them the corseted thinking they tried to leave behind or were dragged from in the name of "settling a wilderness." Saddest of all, limits were imposed by women on their multiethnic neighbors and predecessors, even as they learned from them the needed tools to survive such a harsh and challenging climate.

Yet, the unifying strength of all the women who lived in the American West was fierce fortitude and independence of spirit augmented by a backdrop of immense possibility. The story of the American West is the myth our nation tells itself to remind us of our own persistence, fortitude, and grand self-image. It's long past time that the story of the women of the West—*all* women of the West—is put firmly into the center of the American West story as both the strength and the heart of this colorful multiethnic history.

CHAPTER 8

Politics in the West

by Donald A. Yale

Go west, young man,
and grow up with the country.
—**Horace Greeley**[1]

Politics should be the part-time profession
of every citizen.
—**Dwight David Eisenhower**[2]

Overview

As we saw in the introduction, westward migration happened for many reasons—financial opportunities, land, and/or a new start. To understand the politics of the West, how they evolved, and what forces molded them, it is helpful to understand some underlying existing cultural biases these western migrants brought with them.

In Europe, it was difficult for the common person to own land; most land was owned by the monarchy, church, or nobility. Farmland was cultivated by commoners, who paid the landowners for their use. Usually, what was left for the farmer was meager, and any chance of improvement for their own or their children's lives, slim. In the New World, land was plentiful and accessible, especially in the West, and farming methods did not recognize the need to rejuvenate the land. Tobacco was especially demanding, extracting the land's many nutrients. Thus, as the land became unproductive, farmers moved west to new land. Land seemed infinite.

Land speculation was a way of life in the New World. Our colonial ancestors pursued it with vigor. Even while George Washington was president, he was involved in speculation in the Ohio Valley.

Thomas Jefferson speculated in land as well. (His interest in the West is described in Chapter 1). With the Louisiana Purchase, the concept of land owned by the federal government was accepted. Jefferson, not a believer in a strong central government, agreed with the concept of states transferring lands nominally under their control to the federal government. For example, Virginia claimed all land to the Mississippi River, even though it was under Spanish and French control; with the Louisiana Purchase, these became federal lands. And the lands were not empty. They were filled with Native Americans as well as French, British, and Spanish. In the Far West, lands on the Pacific Ocean included Russians and later Asians to help build the railroad.

Jefferson believed that the future of America and American democracy depended on a strong agricultural class. He was always experimenting with new crops and farming methods, including water conservation. He was skeptical of the industrialists and, as a result, the Federalists. He was for local control, strong communities, and a limited federal presence. It was he who concluded the Louisiana Purchase, and it was the federal government, under his control, that conducted exploration of these new lands, the most famous, of course, being the Corps of Discovery—the Lewis and Clark Expedition. It was the federal government that owned these lands.

A second concept brought from the Old World was what we call the "Protestant work ethic," which evolved along with Protestantism after the Reformation. As Max Weber argued, Protestantism fostered the "spirit of capitalism." But the more important aspect of the Reformation was that a person does not need an intermediary for access to God. Further, it elevated the individuality and responsibility of humans. When John Knox, founder of the Presbyterian Church in Scotland, espoused that "all men are equal," he was expressing his belief that it was an individual's responsibility to stand up against tyranny. Since a person's religion was personal, conflicting beliefs were to be embraced, not just tolerated. The reformers were also challenging the existing "experts"—the priests. With a newly emboldened sense of self, the experts were to be questioned and sometimes held in contempt. Our founders were primarily deists, and their beliefs led to such radical thought as separation of church and state.

Jefferson was a student of religion and felt strongly that his religious beliefs were personal and not to be in the public eye. He was not alone in his attitudes. Further, the strong message was for people to be left alone to pursue their own life without interference from others, especially government. This is best documented in the US Constitution, the arguments for and against ratification, and the first political parties—the Federalists and the anti-Federalists or Democratic-Republicans. These beliefs were passed on to the future generations that traveled westward.

The West was a wild land. Population density was and continues to be low. By the 1920 Census, more people were living in cities than in rural areas. Today, roughly 85 percent of the population lives in urban centers. The 15 percent living in rural areas constitutes 72 percent of the land. In the West, 89 percent lives in urban areas. However, because of state political districting, rural areas either control or have significant influence in state legislatures. Smaller numbers of representatives can have greater control of state legislation. In fact, rural area influence in state politics has increased, even though the populations have decreased. (For more information, see Chapters 6 and 9.) The US Constitution dealt with political power between the large states and the small states by having a House of Representatives with number of members based on population and a Senate with two members from every state. All states, with the exception of Nebraska, are bicameral to balance the interests between large centers of population and rural areas.

The American West

During the country's early days, people had to rely on themselves and their neighbors to survive. Rugged individualism emerged from the self-reliant trapper, explorer, emigrant, miner, rancher, and farmer. The ideas from the Reformation, as described earlier, reinforced individualism. Geography and demographics informed political beliefs as well. Low population levels also compelled settlers to rely primarily on themselves and help from their neighbors. They grew their own food, built many of their own tools, and used their ingenuity to survive. They relied not only on family and neighbors but also on their towns and churches, their states, and then their country. Settlers believed strongly in local control for school, religion, and enforcement of laws.

As part of its rugged individualism, the West has been more fractionalized than the East and less inclined to be labeled. People were judged as neighbors, not as co-religionists or by their ethnic and national backgrounds. Democracy and social stability were best achieved with peaceful diversity rather than trying to enforce homogeneity. The common good could only be achieved by non-violent means. Truth and trust were necessary for commerce, government, and survival. These new westerners valued honor and competence over class or relationships, resulting in more personality-driven politics. It also made for more difficulty in defining or directing party loyalty. To survive, cooperation and compromise with neighbors was essential. Civility and acceptance of diverse peoples were both necessary for communities to function. There was a component of innocence in this belief system. Acceptance didn't include all, but was still more open than in the East. "A traditional marker for the frontier's arrival was the organization of the first primitive county governments."[3]

It was not the county, state, or federal apparatus that got voters to the voting booth; democracy lived in local politics. Participation in democratically elected government was expected and embraced. Unfortunately, eastern political and business interests often controlled state politics. The federal government was too far away and controlled by people the westerners felt did not have their best interests at heart. Westerners feared the federal government's control over them and constantly resisted it. However, there were some rights that western migrants demanded. As defined in the Constitution and articulated in the *Federalist Papers*, the government was to promote and ensure common defense, general welfare, and blessings of liberty for all people. In this regard, since, as established in the Louisiana Purchase, all the land was initially owned by the federal government, ownership was conveyed by the federal government.

At the height of the Civil War, President Abraham Lincoln signed the Homestead Act of 1862, another major factor in populating the West. It provided that "any adult citizen, or intended citizen, who had never borne arms against the U.S. Government could claim 160 acres of surveyed government land."

The Morrill Act of 1862 was another federal government handout. The government gave each state 30,000 acres of land for each of their senators and representatives based on the 1860 Census. The land was to be sold to provide endowment for higher education to promote agriculture and mechanical education. Thus were spawned the land grant colleges many called "A&M."

The third landmark legislation Lincoln promoted was creating the Department of Agriculture. Currently, the department oversees services to rural America, including agricultural research, conservation, price supports, marketing, loans for purchase and operation of farms, food safety, nutrition, rural electrification, and telephone services. Air travel to rural areas in the West is controlled and promoted by the FAA, another federal agency. The South was against government measures that might help western development, and those measures were defeated in years before the Civil War. They did not want the rapid population of the West to diminish their majority of slave state representation in Congress.

The other major requirement for western migration was to clear the land of "others." As mentioned, the land was not empty. Spain still held significant land in the Southwest, including the Pacific states. Russians, French, British (Canadians), and others still occupied territory. And, of course, Native Americans were there in great numbers. The federal government, through its army, was needed to push these people out for the migrants. The Native Americans had no chance against the forces hostile to them, and the Spanish were pushed out with the Mexican-American War from 1846 to 1848 and the Gadsden Purchase of 1853. President James Polk did more for westward expansion than any president since Thomas Jefferson. The army "removed" these other people, and they continued to provide protection for the new wave of westerners.

Native Americans faced an extraordinarily difficult future with the tide of settlement. They had established significant trade routes from the Mississippi to the Pacific. The Plains Indians particularly, having come from the East either by choice or forced by American expansion, had adapted to their new environment. Francisco Vázquez de Coronado had brought and left the horse to the continent in the sixteenth century, which allowed Native Americans to use larger tracts of land than they had prior. They needed ten to twelve horses per person, and the abundant grass of the prairie provided ample food, but they also needed wintering grounds when the grass was dormant and not nutritious.

Horses also enabled Native Americans to become more efficient buffalo hunters, killing the animal for meat and other uses, including trading hides to the East. As their land was encroached upon, their water controlled by others, their wintering spots not accessible, and with buffalo hunting and trade declining, the government encouraged Native Americans to go to reservations and learn farming. During that time, the government promised them food, clothing and shelter as well as land, farming equipment and seed. However, the government did not keep its part of the bargain and provided very little. The Indians began to starve. They also contracted European diseases, which killed them in large numbers.

The federal government's other major benefit to the settlement of the West was subsidizing the building of the Transcontinental Railroad and expansion of telegraph service. Railroad building was a risky business and was difficult to finance through traditional means. The Civil War underlined the necessity and importance of railroad systems "to secure the safe and speedy transportation of the mails, troops, munitions of war, and public stores" (Section 3 of the 1862 act). The Pacific Railroad Acts of 1862 and 1864 were to create incentives for the building and running of the Transcontinental Railroad and for the stringing of telegraph wire along the same right of way. The acts provided right of way, utilization of natural resources, and ownership of mineral and mining rights and land grants up to "the amount of five alternate sections per mile on each side of said railroad ... and within the limits of twenty miles on each side of said road" (Section 3 of the 1862 act as amended from ten miles to twenty miles in Section 4 of the 1864 act) creating a checkerboard of railroad and federal land ownership. "And the United States shall extinguish, as rapidly as may be consistent with public policy and the welfare of the said Indians, the Indian titles to all lands falling under the operation of this section and required for the said right-of-way and grant of land herein made" (Section 18 of the 1864 act). The acts also directed the creation and sale of bonds for additional financing.

Railroads were controlled by eastern industrialists, a fact that also informed evolving political beliefs. They were exploitative of the farmers and ranchers, who had capital outlays for housing, draft animals, wagons, plows, wells, fencing, and seed grain. Farmers were perpetually in debt. As outlined in *The American Political Tradition*[4] by Hofstadter, the farmers' and ranchers' products declined in value as the dollar appreciated. As a debt-driven business and with a shortage of hard currency, farmers wanted an increase in the money supply, generating a desire for free silver. The ensuing Panic of 1893 and the decades of exploitation led to William Jennings Bryan's famous "Cross of Gold" speech,[5] calling for free silver and rejection of the gold standard. In his speech, Bryan quoted an old motto attributed to Thomas Jefferson, "Equal rights to all, special privileges to none." He asked "for nothing from the government but 'even-handed justice.'" The progressive and

William Jennings Bryan ran unsuccessfully for president three times in 1896,
1900 and 1908. He later became
Woodrow Wilson's Secretary of State,
serving from 1912-1914.

populist movements of the later nineteenth and early twentieth centuries are examples of that.

As James Chace stated in his book *1912: Wilson, Roosevelt, Taft
and Debs*, "Disenchanted with mainstream political parties, it seemed
that the only avenue open was the populist or People's Party with its
roots in southern and western agrarian sentiment directed primarily at
the great corporations."[6] The progressives, including William Jennings
Bryan of Nebraska and Robert M. La Follette of Wisconsin, were trying to undo the injustices of Reconstruction and the robber barons and
re-create a nation of limited and decentralized power, genuine competition, democratic opportunity, and enterprise. These concepts are still
in play today.

Law enforcement in the West was always a problem. The settlers ignored existing treaties and agreements and preexisting land and
water ownership, and they occupied federal lands. This mentality continues today, with people like the Bundys not paying federal permit
fees and occupying federal facilities based on the belief that it is their
right as citizens to do so. Historically, people have simply gotten away
with it. The land and resources were owned by the federal government.
And while all agreed to that, westerners believed it was their right to
exploit these resources and the government's obligation to either sell or
give them the land and its resources. "Whatever laws Congress passed,

land distribution could not keep up with the settlement. Orderly surveys were to precede sales; once a district had been divided and platted, a competitive auction could be held…. Using the U.S. Army to remove citizens by force was never an attractive political option, and presidential proclamations were exercises in futility."[7] "The settlers of the West," Malcolm Rohrbough has remarked, "took the view that the land was there to be taken, and that the rules and regulations of the government did not change their natural rights as citizens… all men were far from equal…. The advantage always accrued to the wealthy man of influence, regardless of what the law said."[8] The settlers didn't wish to cooperate with federal authorities, as land and water use were local issues, even though the federal government provided funds and expertise to exploit them.

"In the early development of the far West, five principal resources lay ready for exploitation: furs, farmland, timber, minerals, and federal money. Territorial experience got Westerners in the habit of asking for federal subsidies, and the habit persisted long after other elements of the Old West had vanished."[9] The federal government was not helpful when calamities such as drought, fires, insect infestations, and the Great Depression occurred. That is, until the New Deal.

The geography of the West also necessitated overland travel, ultimately spawning the railroad. Before that, however, north–south navigation was limited to the Mississippi and Missouri Rivers. The invention of the steam engine and resulting steamboat travel opened land on either side of these rivers, but westward travel did not have the luxury of navigable waterways. Travel by oxcart, wagon, stagecoach, or foot were the only methods for traveling west until the railroad.

As people traveled west to the Pacific coast, they found that water was scarce. Water law was first established in the arid lands of the West, and its value, some suggest, exceeded gold. In fact, water is the one resource in the West that continues to define development. The resources used during the first migrations were grass and water and sheltered wintering grounds. Native Americans and new settlers clashed in using and controlling these natural resources, which, ultimately, Native Americans lost. Eventually, managed water required healthy watersheds, including storage behind dams. Otto Mears of Colorado became a wealthy man by controlling the headwaters of streams and rivers. As time went on, water was less controlled by states and more by the federal government. Dams were built, and water was transferred to areas lacking sufficient supply.

Western History

As quoted from *The Legacy of Conquest* by Patty Limerick,

> "The Reclamation Act of 1902 put the national government in the center of the control and development of water, the West's key resource… expert management of the national forests, using federal powers to guide resource users…. The Taylor Grazing Act of 1934 finally centralized the control of grazing on the public domain."[10] The act marked the effective end of the era in which the goal of the federal government was to transfer public lands to private ownership and development. Within two years, the Taylor Act removed 142 million acres of western lands from potential sale and reserved them for grazing under federal control. President Franklin Delano Roosevelt reinforced the act by officially removing the majority of the public domain from private land claims at the end of 1934. The Taylor Act established the principle that virtually the entire remaining public domain should be set aside for federal management rather than sale.

The federal government controlled national parks, Indian reservations, grazing permits, reclamation projects, dams, timber, and oil subsidies and other economic supplements. "As the historian, Robert Athearn has commented: 'The West was inclined to bite the hand that fed it…. What it amounted to was the unwillingness or inability of the states to reconcile what they conceived to be their rugged individualism, born of the frontier, with the planned society that was implied by the New Deal.'"[11] Whole books can be—and have been—devoted to water and other natural resources in the West.

How slavery became ingrained in the Americas is also a subject for a different book. Slavery, however, was a significant factor in molding the politics of the early West. The Missouri Compromise of 1820 was needed to keep a balance between slave and non-slave states. Missouri was admitted as a slave state and Maine (formerly part of Massachusetts) as free, and, except for Missouri, slavery was to be excluded from the Louisiana Purchase lands north of latitude 36°30'. However, the House of Representatives was overrepresented by slave states, as representation was based on population, and slaves were counted as three-fifths of a person for purpose of the population census.

Of the first seven presidents, five came from southern states. Jefferson was certainly visionary with the Louisiana Purchase, but Polk, also from the South, was most instrumental in creating a United States from sea to shining sea. Ideally, of course, the Civil War would have been the culminating factor in ending slavery and its prejudices. It wasn't, though, and politics today still are influenced by slavery's legacy.

The emigration west did little to confront the problem of slavery; the issues of pluralism, racism, and bigotry moved west with the migrants. Prior to the Civil War, much of the migration west of the Mississippi came from southern states. The Panic of 1857 prompted a number of people at the fringes of the United States, including Missouri, to migrate westward. Southerners were also the ones who first pushed into Mexican-held territory, including Texas, declaring it an independent country in 1836.

After the Civil War, those seeking a new life flooded away from the old Confederacy. The migration included both white Southerners who had nothing to go back to and recently emancipated African Americans. The Southwest and Arizona Territory in particular were heavily populated from the old South. The motivation is best described this way:

> When the weight of Southern civilization fell too heavily on Huckleberry Finn, Mark Twain offered the preferred American alternative: "I reckon I got to light out for the Territory ahead of the rest, because Aunt Sally she's going to adopt me and civilize me, and I can't stand it. I been there before."[12] The West, the theory had gone, was the place where one escaped the trials and burdens of American civilization, especially in its Southern version. Those "trials and burdens" often came in human form. Repeatedly, Americans had used the West as a mechanism for evading these "problems." Much of what went under the rubric of "Western optimism" was in fact this faith in postponement, in the deferring of problems to the distant future. Whether in Indian removal or Mormon migration, the theory was the same: the West is remote and vast; its isolation and distance will release us from conflict; this is where we can get away from each other. But the workings of history carried an opposite lesson. The West was not where we escaped each other, but where we all met.[13]

Indentured servitude was also a common feature in the New World. As these people fulfilled their contract and became "free," the opportunity of free land and a new start was compelling, and these people added to the wave of westward migration.

The earliest westward emigrations beyond the Mississippi were for extraction of natural resources. First fur trappers. Then the extractive industries, gold and other minerals to fund and fuel industrial expansion, timber for building new towns and cities, ranchers taking advantage of open grazing, and then farmers to provide food to expanding urbanization.

Events including the Louisiana Purchase, Missouri Compromise, Third Great Awakening, expansion of slavery, Texas Revolution, Panic of 1837, Mexican-American War, gold discovery in California, Gadsden Purchase, Panic of 1857, gold in Colorado, Civil War, Homestead and Morrill Acts, Reconstruction, transcontinental railroad, Panics of 1893 and 1907, and the Great Depression all motivated people to move west.

A brand-new religion called Mormonism was populated by both Americans and newly arrived immigrants from Europe. Joseph Smith, its founder born in New England, had a revelation in 1820. By 1827, the Smiths and the new co-religionists began moving west, to Pennsylvania, Ohio, Illinois, and Missouri. Its members were white, non-slaveholding, and prosperous, which they achieved partially by doing business exclusively with each other. They voted as a group and gained control of local governments. Their other white neighbors reviled them, not unlike their revulsion of African Americans, Hispanics, Native Americans, Catholics, and Jews. After massacres, extrajudicial hangings, mob activity, and the murder of their founder, Joseph Smith in 1844, the Mormons moved west to Utah, Idaho, and Nevada. Although they had their prejudices, especially against African Americans, they provided their followers with certainty, security, and community. The Mormons controlled local and state governments, only bowing to federal authority to make Utah a state in 1896.[14]

Population continued to grow in the West. This is shown in Table 1.1; for post–World War II figures, see Table 6.3. Today, California has the seventh largest economy in the world and a population approximating 39,000,000 people. That represents more than 10 percent of the United States population, which is approximately 326,000,000.

Western Law

Still one thing more, fellow citizens—a wise and frugal government,
which shall restrain men from injuring one another, which shall
leave them otherwise free to regulate their own pursuits of industry
and improvement, and shall not take from the mouth of labor
the bread it has earned. This is the sum of good government,
and this is necessary to close the circle of our felicities.

—**Thomas Jefferson**, First Inaugural
Address, March 4, 1801[15]

As Frederick Jackson Turner described in his 1893 treatise:

> So long as free land exists, the opportunity for a competency
> exists, and economic power secures political power. But the
> democracy born of free land, strong in selfishness and individ-
> ualism, intolerant of administrative experience and education,
> and pressing individual liberty beyond its proper bounds, has
> its dangers as well as its benefits. Individualism in America has
> allowed a laxity in regard to governmental affairs which has ren-
> dered possible the spoils system and all the manifest evils that
> follow from the lack of a highly developed civic spirit.[16]

And further, "…certain common traits, and these traits have, while
softening down, still persisted as survivals in the place of their origin."
These "passed down" traits were also evident in the voting patterns
in the West. In Jon Grinspan's *The Virgin Vote*, many of the so called
virgin voters of the middle and late nineteenth century followed the
practices and parties of their parents and extended families. These
young men "cast ballots without any previous experience or official
mechanisms, showing that democracy lived in their culture, not in a
state apparatus."[17]

Chapter 7 describes women in the West, but here I wish to
point out that just as from isolation necessarily developed individual responsibility, the absence of men required women to run things.
(See Chapters 7 and 9 and their associated bibliographies.) In 1869,
Wyoming passed the first women's suffrage law, followed by women's
right to serve on juries. In 1893, Colorado was the first state to adopt
an amendment granting women the right to vote, followed by Utah,
Idaho, Washington State, California, Oregon, Kansas and Arizona,

Alaska, Illinois, Montana, and Nevada. The first eastern state, New York, didn't pass women's suffrage until 1917.

Although the Nineteenth Amendment granting women universal suffrage wasn't ratified until 1921, women in the West continued to make great strides. The first woman to be elected to a local office was Susanna Salter as mayor of Argonia, Kansas, in 1887. In 1894, three women, Clara Cressingham, Carrie C. Holly, and Frances Klock, were elected to the Colorado House of Representatives. Martha Hughes Cannon was elected to the Utah State Senate in 1896, becoming the first woman state senator. In 1916, Jeanette Rankin of Montana became the first woman elected to the US Congress. In 1924, the first female governor, Nellie Tayloe Ross, was elected in Wyoming.

> The political influence of the West rose with its population, making it more and more an initiator of federal policies rather than a recipient. The West added ten U.S. Senators after 1900.... The number of westerners in the House of Representatives rose from 60 in 1900 to 127 in 1980. Theodore Roosevelt in 1901 and Herbert Hoover in 1929 were the first presidents with real western connections although Andrew Jackson (1828) and Abraham Lincoln (1860) might be considered frontier presidents. Between 1945 and 1992, genuine or honorary westerners—Truman, Eisenhower, Johnson, Nixon, Reagan, Bush—accounted for thirty-nine of the forty-seven possible years in the White House.[18]

Since 1992, Clinton from Arkansas, Bush from Texas, and Obama from Hawaii and Illinois have all been tied to the West.

It was the federal government that developed and funded most of the water reclamation in the West. The arid West needed water, and because the farmers needed it most, they supported federal activities. These were in conflict, however, with their belief that they should have unfettered access to federal lands for use and development. Westerners believed the resources belonged to them and not the nation and federal government. Interestingly, the agrarian populist movement of the late nineteenth and early twentieth centuries also included a strong element of conservation. The first national park was Yellowstone, signed into law by Ulysses S. Grant in 1872; Sequoia and Yosemite followed in 1890. The Yosemite Grant signed by Lincoln in 1864 set the stage for the national park designations.

President Theodore Roosevelt, supporting progressive programs as a Republican, was a strong advocate for conservation. In the 1880s he had lived, ranched, and hunted in the badlands of North Dakota. In his words, "We have fallen heirs to the most glorious heritage a people ever received, and each one must do his part if we wish to show that the nation is worthy of its good fortune."[19]

President Theodore Roosevelt was a strong advocate of conservation.

The Antiquities Act of 1906 was passed by the US Congress and signed into law by Theodore Roosevelt on June 8, 1906, giving the president the authority to, by presidential proclamation, create national monuments from federal lands to protect significant natural, cultural, or scientific features. The act has been used more than a hundred times since its passage and occasionally creates significant controversy.

The National Park Service Organic Act was passed in 1916. The new agency's mission as managers of national parks and monuments was clearly stated: "To conserve the scenery and the natural and historic objects and the wild life therein and to provide for the enjoyment of the same in such manner and by such means as will leave them unimpaired for the enjoyment of future generations."[20]

The military has always played a major role in the West. It was the military that helped to expand territory by removing peoples from the land; Native Americans fought a losing battle to hold on to their ancestral land. As more northern Europeans emigrated, the more pressure there was to limit Native American presence, and the military was called to do so.

The Mexican-American War resulted in the United States claiming land that is now New Mexico, Utah, Arizona, Nevada, California, and part of Colorado and Wyoming. The border was set at the Rio Grande, and Texas annexation was accepted. The Gadsden Purchase from Mexico in 1853 completed the present-day borders of

New Mexico and Arizona. (See Chapter 4 for more on the country's shifting boundaries.)

After the Civil War, the great Union general, William Tecumseh Sherman, was sent to the Southwest to solve the "Indian Problem." The army stayed to protect the emigrants and fight the Native Americans and any others who would challenge US control. A series of forts were built not just to protect but also to guide and resupply the westward migration.

At the beginning of the twentieth century, and especially up to and including World War II, the West became home both to training centers for the country's military as well as logistical support and military manufacturing. In 2010, total defense spending was 557 billion dollars, with 233.7 billion spent in the twenty-four states west of the Mississippi or 42 percent of all spending.[21]

As the west urbanized, political ideologies have sometimes been defined as rural versus urban. Cities tend to be more progressive and liberal and rural areas more conservative. Those rural areas still cling to some of the early beliefs of individualism and local control. Progressives are more supportive of federal initiatives and controls.

The line between individual rights and the common good has always shifted in politics. How to balance these two issues has been argued for all of political history and elucidated explicitly in the arguments of Utilitarianism. These arguments were also revealed during the Constitutional Convention of the late 1780s in trying to balance states' rights and federalism. Where to draw that line depends on current conditions and needs—that is what political arguments are about. Here, let's define these positions through two political giants, Barry Goldwater and George McGovern. Both men ran for president, both failed, and both were westerners; Goldwater from Arizona and McGovern from South Dakota. Both men were judged as individuals. Examples of liberal thought in conservative states include George McGovern and Tom Daschle from South Dakota, Bob Kerry from Nebraska, Lyndon Johnson from Texas, and Gary Hart from Colorado (more conservative at the time). Examples of conservatives from liberal states are Ronald Reagan from California, Barry Goldwater from Arizona (more liberal at the time), Herbert Hoover from Iowa and Oregon, and many western governors.

According to their constitutions, all Western states must balance their budgets; their expenses must be no larger than their revenue. That means that the governors and legislatures must be fiscally conservative, unlike those in the federal government who can spend what they will. In fact, the federal government has had a balanced budget in only four years since 1960, running a substantial deficit in all other years.

Justice Louis Brandeis wrote, "Those who won over independence by revolution were not cowards. They did not fear political change. They did not exalt order at the cost of liberty." *Webster's Dictionary* defines liberalism as "a political philosophy based on belief in progress, the essential goodness of man, and the autonomy of the individual and standing for the protection of political and civil liberties." Further, Reinhold Niebuhr states, "Man's capacity for justice makes democracy possible, but man's inclination to injustice makes democracy necessary." These quotes are all found in McGovern's *The Essential America*.[22] His rural, western roots are steeped in individual responsibility and rights. McGovern states, "Jefferson believed passionately in the freedom and dignity of the individual. Fearing the reach of a centralized, interventionist national government, he preferred to see the powers of government restricted to a minimum.... He believed in a largely unregulated, laissez-faire economy with minimum government involvement in economic affairs." Conservatives, he believes, are supportive of Jefferson's views with the exception of "wish for federal intervention on behalf of business and corporate interests, tax privileges for higher-income citizens and corporations, and large military contracts. One substantial category of conservatives would even favor the federal government controlling such personal or family matters as abortion, the rules of marriage, and public prayer in the schools." He goes on to say,

> The first serious challenge to this comfortable system from those who believed that government ought to be a public instrument to combat injustice and corruption came from the Populists. This largely rural-based movement sought to protect farmers from discriminatory railroad shipping rates, excessive credit costs, and unfair banking and insurance practices. The Populists also sought a graduated income tax—later to become one of the cardinal tenets of American Liberalism.

The populist movement called for direct election of senators, initiatives and referendums, primaries, non-party candidates, and women's suffrage. On the local level, they fought the political machines and corrupt mayors and other corporate monopolies, including city utilities.

Barry Goldwater (left) and George McGovern were politicians from the West.
Both ran for president and both lost.

The West was also the driving force behind Prohibition and conservation. Rural America as classified in the census of 1790 comprised 94 percent of the population; in 1900, it was 38 percent; it was 8 percent in 1965; and today it stands at 4%. Yet their political traditions have followed their relocation to some cities.

Senator Goldwater Speaks Out on the Issues, as issued by his Presidential Committee, states his belief that "federalism...—that is, a sound and effective distribution of powers between the central government and our 50 sovereign states—has the same meaning today as it did when the founders devised this revolutionary principle-of-balance. It balances the liberty of each against the needs of all. It balances diversity against unity. And it balances the interest and responsibility which is and ought to remain local against the occasional demand for national policy and the exercise of national authority.... It is there—in our states and communities—and only there that every individual citizen can still have a meaningful impact on the political process."[23] In *The Conscience of a Conservative*, Goldwater states, "People's welfare depends on individual self reliance rather than on state paternalism... maximum amount of freedom for individuals that is consistent with the maintenance of social order."[24] There is a general feeling in the West that the federal government is controlled by eastern elites who are too far away to understand their issues and are only concerned with eastern power and wealth. Goldwater states another issue of balance when he says, "We must always make a sharp distinction between civil rights guaranteed under the Constitution and those rights of association that are basically moral issues and cannot be resolved by passing unenforceable Federal laws."[25] Contrast Goldwater's stance with those statements quoted by McGovern, above.

Both men argue the same issues. The differences, if there are substantive differences, are in where to draw the line to balance conflicting priorities. Yet both men's rural backgrounds are based on liberty, justice, and an equal opportunity for all. "On the one hand, many regional conservatives often demonstrated an exaggerated individualism denoting their frontier origins and also a pronounced belief in unrestrained property rights. They saw little conflict between their dependence on federal largesse on the one hand and their condemnation of federal regulation and ownership on the other."[26]

Today's politics have moved to a different plane. As the Great Awakenings of the mid- and late nineteenth century resulted in good works for the less fortunate and non-believers, the awakening of the 1960s to the present has resulted in political action. Religious prejudices, racial and social intolerance, and rejection of diversity and pluralism and income inequality have helped to lead to a polarized electorate. The nineteenth- and early twentieth-century westerners believed in a common good achieved by non-violent means, truth and trust—especially in commerce and government—and by treating strangers and outsiders with the same truth and trust. Democracy and social stability are best achieved through peaceful diversity rather than by forcefully eradicating it. Honor and competence are more important than class or relationship. Neither Goldwater nor McGovern would support the current political positions represented in government.

No longer is the West financially dependent on the exploitation of land or resources. The technology hubs in Silicon Valley, Seattle, Portland, Denver, and Austin are financial and technology powerhouses. Quality living, cost of living, and opportunities are resulting in the movement of corporate headquarters and people to the West.

The West continues to influence political outcomes, is more favorable to mavericks, and supports women in politics. As the population continues to go westward, its influence won't stop anytime soon.

CHAPTER 9

The Rural West

by Page Lambert

Rural America and its people are integral to the national society, economy, identity, and well-being. Rural America covers more than 90 percent of our nation's land mass, comprises one-fifth of the population, and supplies our nation with food, fiber, and fuel.

—**Rural Research Brief**

HAC, Washington, D.C.

A New Tide Washes Over the Land

In the winter of 1811, ten years before Missouri would become the first territory west of the Mississippi to enter statehood, a series of terrifying earthquakes struck the low-lying country between Missouri and Arkansas. The Mississippi River "gathered her waters up like a mountain,"[1] left her banks, rose twenty feet into the air, hung suspended, then plunged to the earth. For a few terrifying moments, her roaring waters flowed backward—toward her greatest tributary and North America's longest river, the Missouri. "The earth was horribly torn to pieces," wrote eyewitness Eliza Bryan. "The inhabitants fled in every direction to the country... the earth was in continual agitation, visibly waving as a gentle sea."[2]

President James Madison in Washington, D.C., who eight years earlier had helped negotiate the Louisiana Purchase, felt the quake, as did the townsfolk of New Madrid, and the bakers, tavern owners, blacksmiths, merchants, and fur traders living in the mostly rural town of St. Louis (even then considered to be the Gateway to the West). Two more quakes struck in the ensuing weeks, sending shockwaves rippling across the land. Destructive undulations spread over 300,000 square miles, mirroring the ripples that would soon mark the country's western migration.

The land in a huge area (about 5,500 square miles or about 3.5 million acres) was also damaged or destroyed by landslides, fissures, sandblows, lateral spreads, subsidence, submergence, and uplift. Much of this land became unusable for the subsistence type agriculture of the day.[3]

One might say that the New Madrid earthquakes also marked the beginning of a migration pattern from town to country and back again, an incoming and outgoing tide of movement triggered by traders, gold rushes, weather, transcontinental railroads, economics, water, famine, technology, politics, and war, a pattern that would continue to weave itself into the American culture. After the quakes, the population of St. Louis quickly burgeoned with an influx of Irish and German immigrants, and an exodus of easterners citizens answering the call to go west. The gateway town of St. Louis grew from 2,000 folks in 1816 to more than 4,600 by 1820 (necessitating the town's first subdivision to be built, fittingly, on a hill to the west).[4]

That same year, a resolution to create a standing committee on agriculture was presented to the House of Representatives in Washington, D.C. Approved on May 3, the Committee on Agriculture was born, something George Washington had been advocating since 1799.

Crossing the Platte by emigrant train, in old overland days.

It, too, would burgeon—from the original seven committee members in 1820 to fifty-one members by 2001.[5] It is impossible to consider rural America without considering agriculture—as practiced on the land, and as manipulated by politics.

The New Madrid quakes, the most powerful earthquakes east of the Rocky Mountains in recorded history, marked the first time the federal government would grant disaster relief. Spurred into action by Missouri Territory governor William Clark (of Lewis and Clark), Congress allocated $50,000 of relief funding for the residents of New Madrid County,[6] setting a precedent for federal assistance to rural areas that would continue for at least the next 200 years. Today's Rural Development division of the Department of Agriculture supports "economic development and essential services such as housing, health care, first responder services and equipment, and water, electric and communications infrastructure" and has a loan portfolio of $216 billion,[7] a figure incomprehensible to those who experienced the New Madrid quakes.

In 1835, pioneer John Deere invented a self-cleaning plow made from an old saw and began mass producing them instead of having blacksmiths custom-make them. By 1842, House members were exploring the idea of establishing a formal Department of Agriculture. A quick look at a *House Report* published in 1856 reveals how much the nation's priorities would change by 2017.

> Agriculture is the basis of our national prosperity. It is the substratum of all other interests; and the degree of advancement which marks the progress of our country and its people in wealth, enterprise, education, and substantial independence, is measured by the prosperity of its rural interests. It is one of those arts which, from the earliest periods, have been deservedly held in the highest estimation. One of the first injunctions upon our original progenitor, after his expulsion from the Garden of Eden, was that he should "till the soil."[8]

No less than an edict, the federal government's stimulus to "till the soil" would eventually ravage the fertile topsoil of much of the country's heartland. The rural families that migrated west weren't born in the West—they had learned how to farm from fathers and grandfathers used to cultivating land made fertile by fifty inches of rain a year, not a mere ten inches. Some were displaced farmers, forced out by the large plantations in the South. Congregating in Missouri during the wet spring months, as they readied to depart and begin their journeys, certainly didn't prepare them for the arid West.

Traveling the overland trails could take months. If the goal was the Pacific Coast, the journey would unroll over the course of 2,000 rocky, perilous miles. Folklorist Barbara Allen Bogart gathered anecdotes from descendants of some of these travelers for her book *In Place: Stories of Landscape and Identity from the American West*. Here, she recounts an oral story told to her by the granddaughter of a California settler.

> My grandfather took off from Ohio in 1849, I believe. Left there, and got here in 1850. He came with a wagon train, but he had to give the captain of the train so much for the privilege of traveling with him, besides driving an ox team. So when he landed here, all he had was a rifle, and a frying pan, and a buffalo robe, besides the clothes he stood in. That's the way he got west, walked every doggone step of the way from St. Joe, Missouri, to Weaverville up here in Trinity County.[9]

The river town of St. Joe (founded in 1843 by Joseph Robidoux, a local fur trader), was filled with untethered people when her grandfather arrived there in 1850—some were opportunists following the wave of emigrants who dreamed of lush fields that would yield up a bountiful harvest, or prospectors dreaming of mountain streams glittering with gold, or old trappers looking for new careers, or businessmen dreaming of mercantiles and saloons waiting to be built. In the East, manufacturing was no longer happening on the small-scale family farms but instead had moved to the cities and large-scale factories. Many believed that their entrepreneurial dreams of rural independence could be reclaimed in the borderless and uncontained West.

Not until after the Civil War could a traveler boarding a train run by the Baltimore and Ohio Railroad journey any farther west than St. Joe. No doubt, many of the untethered travelers washed up on the shores of St. Louis, and St. Joe had certainly suffered from the financial Panic of 1837, yet few anticipated the river of people that would follow in the wake of their westward surge. As gold discoveries and land speculation continued to spur western expansion, the railways also extended their reach, but not as quickly as the restless pioneers. When the Homestead Act of 1862 opened federal lands to pioneers, within two years 1.6 million claims would be approved—enough to cover 420,000 square miles of outlying territory, far exceeding the shockwaves felt by the New Madrid quakes. The nation's population had reached an impressive 33 million when the Department of Agriculture was formed, yet the mostly rural western population comprised less than 3 percent of that total, despite an influx from the discovery of gold, silver, and copper. Even one of the West's greatest storytellers, Missouri-born Samuel L. Clemens (better known as Mark Twain), headed west to mine gold, silver, and adventure.

Rural Isolation

The history of a nation gives context to personal family stories, lending credence to oral histories and deeply rooted folklore. By examining the struggles, achievements, follies, and failures of a nation, we are able to view the lives of our ancestors through the lens of a larger history. We gain perspective, and we gain answers. Why did generations of grandparents risk the journey west? What outside forces pressed down

A bison pair out on the prairie.

upon them? What inner strengths allowed them to venture into the unknown? Examine culture, politics, economics, weather, and war at the macro level, and the micro comes into focus. A nation's history becomes your history.

In 1859, three years before President Lincoln signed the Homestead Act but after thousands of gold prospectors had poured into Colorado, a settler named John H. Craig staked a settlement claim at the junction of East and West Plum Creeks, in what would soon become the Territory of Colorado. He built a circular corral on an open expanse of prairie, and the location became known as Round Corral. In 1862, Joseph Lambert, a stonecutter by trade and disciple of William Penn, shook the Maine soil from his Quaker roots and, with his wife, Cynthia, and their asthmatic son, William, traveled west to the high, healing country air of the Rocky Mountains. When they arrived in the foothills near Round Corral, they laid the wooden bed of their wagon in a sheltered valley of high prairie, bedded down William, and declared themselves "home."

By 1873, the year the US government passed the Timber Culture Act (in response to the devastation reaped on the nation's forests by the Civil War, and in the hopes that settlers would plant 40 acres of trees for every 160 acres homesteaded), William Lambert was no longer a thin-limbed asthmatic boy. A young man of twenty-three, trained in civil engineering and already raising his own livestock during a booming cattle market, he fell in love with a young Missouri woman named Rachel. In the ensuing years, "Rachel did all the cooking for the family and up to twenty-five hired men daily. She was the real director of the ranch. They would kill two hogs a week for meat and she would cut up and dress a hog and have it in the cooler within the hour. Never a meal was served that there was not fried pork on the table. Hand-churning was done every morning—so there was plenty of butter and milk."

The Lambert family's rural life in Colorado Territory was exceptional in some ways (they planted over 28,000 apple tree saplings), but not extraordinary. Spreading across the West, thousands of homestead claims had been established under the Homestead Act. Sod houses lit with kerosene lamps dotted the Great Plains, and range wars between cattlemen and farmers were already erupting. By 1870, the nation's population had reached 38,558,371, and a third of those lived on farms. Farmers, working the land on 2,660,000 farms averaging 153 acres in size, made up 53 percent of the labor force. But in the 1870s the Lamberts weren't farmers, they were ranchers—a distinction of more than culture and economics—yet all were homesteaders. Did homesteaders consider themselves to be "rural" citizens? Without the shoulders of a nearby town to rub up against, they were as isolated as islands in a sea of grass. They measured themselves based on how they spent each hour of every day—on their relationship to a landscape, not a cityscape.

Round Corral grew into the Town of Plum, a stop along the First Territorial Road, but it was little more than a village. Eventually renamed Sedalia after a town in Missouri, when the narrow-gauge Denver & Rio Grande Railway reached the town in 1871,[10] the town became a major shipping point for lumber cut in the Pike National Forest. Businesses sprung up, including the Manhart General Merchandise Store (in-laws of the Lamberts), Marquis Victor's blacksmith shop, the Weaver House, the 25-Mile House and Saloon, and a cigar manufacturer. Largely of English descent, the town's small rural population relied heavily on the commerce of the outlying ranches, which included few other ethnicities. At the time of the 1880 US Census, only 20.5 percent of the West would be foreign born, unlike the Midwest, which was greatly impacted by a massive wave of Scandinavian immigration. Thousands of farmers left Sweden and Norway due to a depressed economy, food shortages, and farm foreclosures.

Those who came to the prairie were not simply yeoman farmers. They wanted a little more than to merely subsist on the land and be good Jeffersonian citizens. They grew wheat, a cash crop that could be raised quickly and turn a decent profit if it weren't eaten by plagues of grasshoppers (as it was for four straight summers in the early 1870s), or if the railroads didn't charge exorbitant fees for hauling grain to market, or if hail or drought didn't wreck the fields.

Investors in Europe and the eastern United States also recognized the possibilities for turning the western prairie into a giant breadbasket, and sunk money into huge "bonanza" wheat farms in the Dakotas and the western reaches of Minnesota. These forerunners to modern agribusinesses cultivated thousands of acres of wheat in fields that stretched, just as the prairie once had, as far as the eye could see.

For most of the newcomers to the western prairie, however, the farms were modest, and so were the dreams. These immigrants wanted a piece of property. They wanted to grow things. They wanted to make a little extra for a piano or a family Bible or some lace. They were glad to have left old class systems behind and hoped not to settle into new ones in this country.[11]

The term "a wave of immigration" connotes towns teeming with folks who shared common culture and language, but homesteads were often too removed for daily, or even monthly, contact. Historian Jon Gjerde (the son of Norwegian immigrants) in his book *The Minds of the West: Ethnocultural Evolution in the Rural Middle West from 1830– 1917*, discusses isolation among ethnic farmers:

> Local traditions, transplanted to the region by migrants from the East, often evolved in relative seclusion. In some cases, rural settlements remained so isolated that the contrasts between city and farm broadened over time as new values diffused more rapidly from the former. The seclusion is exemplified by the experiences of a farm youth growing up in the early twentieth century who recalled that he was eighteen years old before he saw the principal trading center near his home, only about eight miles away.[12]

As a young woman, my Missouri-born grandmother, whose grandmother was of French descent, knew both physical isolation and sensory deprivation. Tragically orphaned at the age of twelve, around 1899 she was sent by train from Bolivar, Missouri, to California to live with a distant aunt. According to family history, six years later (deafened by a careless doctor who accidentally poured acid in her ears), she was married off to the "black sheep" of two brothers who lived in the Los Angeles Basin near Compton. She found herself living as a young, deaf bride in one of the most rural and isolated places in the West—California's Mojave Desert. Barely over a thousand members of the Mojave Nation were still alive at that time, and most of them had long since been moved by the federal government to the Colorado River Indian Reservation and the Fort Mojave Indian Reservation. Spurred on by the Enlarged Homestead Act (designed to allow dry-farming claims of up to 320 acres),[13] the two Corum brothers, Ralph and Clifford, built board-and-batten cabins on 160 acres each, and, in 1910, my grandmother helped establish a post office along the tracks of the Southern Pacific rail line at the edge of a desolate expanse of a dry desert lake. The tiny settlement became known as Muroc—Corum spelled backward. The closest town was Lancaster, a town that grew out of discoveries of gold and borax. The open-pit borax mines near Lancaster became the largest in the world.

"I knew when I saw dust in the distance," my grandmother wrote, "that it was someone coming to our place, for there was no place else to go."

Eventually enough settlers moved to Muroc to start a baseball team, which kept my grandmother busy at the treadle sewing machine making uniforms and, no doubt, laundering them in borax. By 1889, the iconic twenty-mule teams had already hauled 20 million pounds of borax over a 165-mile route out of Death Valley, across the desert, and to the Mojave railyard.[14] Like Death Valley, the land around the dry lake bed of Muroc was not hospitable land, and those who came with dreams of lush alfalfa fields and irrigated cropland soon had those dreams dashed.

Jeanette Darr, a homesteader from San Diego, "thought it was the jumping off place of creation, especially when I saw that curiously flat wasteland called dry lake! The land looked worthless, which it was. Not a living thing grew on it, and its claypan was like cement. The winds blew up and down and across it carried nothing but dirt and tumbleweeds."[15]

Natural Resources, Mechanization, and Agriculture

Even as America's future was being envisioned by its citizens, the strides that moved it toward each new century did not take place without the use (and overuse) of natural resources, nor without the subjugation and annihilation of its native citizens, nor without the forced labor and importation of foreign workers. The fact that the great majority of immigrants arriving on the country's shores were themselves fleeing famine, or subjugation, or religious persecution, does not excuse or justify—but it does provide a more complete understanding. Past versions of history often told only the pioneering story, without regard to the larger truths upon which the United States of America was built. One of the intentions of this book is to shed light on the truths that make the American West unique, and the "ruralness" of the West is part of that uniqueness.

As we study the movement of our own ancestors, from rural towns to open prairies, from wooded mountains to coastal cities, the movement of the nation and the importance of its natural resources is also revealed. Lumber has always been an important national commodity, but never more so than with western expansion. Kramer Adams, in his book, *Logging Railroads of The West*, states that when logging in the West was at its prime before the Great Depression, with 300 different companies in operation, more than 7,000 miles of logging lines existed in the West. Unlike the farmers of the West who were literally rooted to the land, the rural families logging in the woodlands and forests west of the Mississippi often lived transient lifestyles.

According to the 1890 Statutes of Oklahoma,[16] four years before my paternal grandmother was born on a logging creek in the woods outside of the rural sawmill town of Fugate, Oklahoma, a person found guilty of willfully and without permission taking saw logs from a river, or nearby a river, could be imprisoned in the county jail for up to a year, and fined up to $100. More than a hundred years later, according to the Oklahoma Forestry Code of 2007, a person convicted of a similar crime could be fined up to $10,000, and imprisoned in the State Penitentiary for up to five years.[17] America needs its trees.

For every sawmill located in some small town on the edge of the woods, there were families clustered nearby. Some, like my Oklahoma

Short grass prairie.

grandparents, lived deep in heart of the woods, near a creek or river. Some lived in roving "timber camps," box houses that could be cut in half, loaded on railcars, and moved from location to location. A rural school, a church, and a company store that served only the families of the loggers might spring up.

My grandmother's birth certificate states only that she was born in 1894, on Potapo Creek, Choctaw Nation, Indian Territory. On a trip to Oklahoma several years ago, hoping to find Potapo Creek, we stopped at the Confederate Museum in Atoka. A museum staff member went into the archives and came out with a hand-drawn map labeled: "Some of the Early Sawmills that operated in Atoka County and McGee Creek Area." The map showed more than a dozen drainages feeding into McGee, which then drained into Mudd Boggy, where another dozen creeks drained—Crooked Creek, Kennedy Hollow, Little Caney, Chitwood Hollow, and there, in the midst of them all, was Potapo Creek. Scrawled in the margins of the map were the names of sixty-four small logging camps: Atchins. Markhams. Ingall. Henkley. Smith. Jenson. Miller. Beck. Newsom. Morris. Kirk. Unknown. Unknown. Houser. Fugate. Unknown. Lee. Mitchell. Fugate. Kennedy. Robinson. Unknown. Hankins. Morris. Fugate.

The woman asked if I knew the famous outlaw Belle Starr, who married into the notorious Starr clan, a group of renegade Cherokees who bootlegged whiskey, stole cattle, and thieved horses. She handed my husband a book about the outlaw and we discovered that in 1889 my great-grandfather Ancil Dan Terry was with Belle when she was murdered by a shotgun blast from a dirt farmer. He testified at her murder trial, and that same year, married my great-grandmother.

Five years and two children later, they were logging on Potapo Creek, but by June of 1900, according to the Oklahoma Census, my great-grandmother was listed as the head of the household, occupation laundress, supporting six children. Under the column for the "number of years married," there is only an X. My great-grandfather was not listed—he had followed the logging industry west to the newly formed state of Washington. Three years later, my great-grandmother died and my grandmother (after spending a few years as an indentured servant), made her way by train to Washington. She grew up to also marry a logger, and in 1925 my father was born in a logging camp deep in the woods near Trail, British Columbia. When I was a little girl, my grandmother told me stories of working in the logging camps, of cooking flapjacks for twenty men and shooting wild grouse for their dinner. In contrast to the rural lifestyle that characterized her early years, she lived much of her life as "a city girl," dying in San Francisco after working for forty years at a gift shop on Fisherman's Wharf.

According to the National Association of State Foresters, the rural towns on the West Coast (despite political pressure and environmental concerns), experienced a surge in 2012 because of improved timber economies.

> Arnold, a town of close to 4,000 people, high in the Sierra Nevada about 150 miles east of San Francisco, struggled for years from a logging slowdown. But last year, timber receipts in surrounding Calaveras County rose to $4.1 million, up from $1.8 million in 2010, according to county data. With the town's economy improving and local spending up, new businesses are finding their way into vacant storefronts on the main street.[18]

Lumber remains a highly valued natural resource, yet as the flames of global warming lick away at the earth's glaciers, it becomes clear that trees are more than sources of lumber—they are hugely important for sequestering climate-changing carbon. The good news? Trees, even the old railroad ties that stretch across the rural West, the old boardwalks and split rail fences, even the sprawling new decks wrapped around fancy country homes, still sequester carbon. Trees do not need to be rooted to sequester carbon, but like most of us, they do like to remember what it means to be rooted. Trees are gregarious and need the colonies found in forests and woodlands to thrive. Once in a while, though, the lone tree standing in a sea of tallgrass prairie will remind us of ourselves. The story of the rural West isn't just about settlement; it is equally about movement. And history, unless seen through the lives of those who have passed through her creaky corridors, has no narrative to entice us, no narrative to help us see its relevance in our modern lives. History must always be a dance between the past and the present.

The year 1910 not only ushered in Halley's Comet and marked a zenith period for the railroad companies, it also ushered in a new era of mechanized farming, drastically changing the lives of rural Americans.

An early caterpillar tractor

A farmer using a tractor could now thresh 1,000 bushels of grain a day, with relative safety. According to SodGod, a modern company selling lawn sod to homeowners in urban America,

> From 1910–1970, tractor production drastically increased from 1000 tractors to nearly 5 million. Falling prices contributed to tractor growth. Early tractors cost as much as $785 in 1920. Just two years later in 1922, a tractor could be purchased for only $395. The price dropped by nearly half in just two years, making tractors an affordable piece of agricultural machinery for almost every farmer.[19]

Tractors in the twenty-first century are no longer affordable for every farmer. By 2017, a mid-size tractor would cost between $25,000 and $50,000.

Yet for every tractor that came onto a farm in the 1920s, the workhorses left, many of them turned out on the range to become the predecessors of the estimated 60,000 wild horses roaming western rangeland today. Then the golden age of the railroad ended, and, with the onset of the Great Depression, there was no extra cash to be had for buying tractors. Ten years later, with the onset of World War II, the nation saw a migration of farmhands from the rural areas into the cities as men were drafted or enlisted, and as women volunteered to help with the war efforts. In the letter "What Are People For," esteemed author Wendell Berry wrote:

> Since World War II, the governing agricultural doctrine—in government offices, universities and corporations—has been that "there are too many people on the farm." This idea has supported, if indeed it has not caused, one of the most consequential migrations of history: millions of rural people moving from country to city in a stream that has not slackened from the war`s end until now. And the motivating force behind this migration, then as now, has been economic ruin on the farm. Today, with hundreds of farm families losing their farms every week, the economists are still saying, as they have said all along, that these deserve to fail, that they have failed because they are the "least efficient producers," and that America is better off for their failure.[20]

In the letter, after discussing weakened rural economies and urban unemployment, Berry concludes with a reminder that in the country, there is still vital work to be done:

> This is the inescapably necessary work of restoring and caring for our farms, forests and rural towns and communities—work that we have not been able to pay people to do for 40 years, and that, thanks to our 40-year "solution to the farm problem," few people any longer know how to do.[21]

As the twenty-first century began, the interior West (with less than 25 percent of the population), began growing faster than any other region in the nation.[22] If we wish to know more about the lives of modern rural citizens, then we must also understand the areas of government that impact their lives. The jurisdiction of the Department of Agriculture as defined in 1947 still exists in 2017:[23] Ask a modern rancher or farmer about any of the following jurisdictional bullet points, and you'll come away impressed by their expertise, and more aware of the complexities of raising food for the nation..

- Adulteration of seeds, insect pests, and protection of birds and animals in forest reserves

- Agriculture generally
- Agricultural and industrial chemistry
- Agricultural colleges and experiment stations
- Agricultural economics and research
- Agricultural education extension services
- Agricultural production and marketing and stabilization of prices of agricultural products, and commodities (not including distribution outside of the United States)
- Animal industry and diseases of animals
- Commodity exchanges
- Crop insurance and soil conservation
- Dairy industry
- Entomology and plant quarantine
- Extension of farm credit and farm security
- Inspection of livestock, poultry, meat products, and seafood and seafood products
- Forestry in general, and forest reserves other than those created from the public domain
- Human nutrition and home economics
- Plant industry, soils, and agricultural engineering
- Rural electrification
- Rural development
- Water conservation related to activities of the Department of Agriculture

At the heart of every one of these jurisdictions are rural families who wake to a day that might be spent planting seeds, irrigating fields, midwifing animals, gathering eggs, driving milk trucks and school buses, analyzing the market, attending noxious weed meetings, participating in land use planning sessions, or studying grazing impact on grasses, all while trying to comply with hundreds of pages of local, state, and federal regulations.

Women of the Rural West

Sometime around 1992, three writers, all women ranchers living in the rural West, decided they wanted to show the world what real rural women were like. "Strong Western women who stare down the future, eyes squinting against the glare." What better way than to ask other rural women in the West to write about their lives? They sent out a call for stories and poems to publications in six western states. They were unprepared for the hundreds of manuscripts that flooded their rural mailboxes. It took them five years to cull the submissions. The result was *Leaning into the Wind*, a 388-page anthology published in 1997 by Houghton Mifflin, a New York/Boston publisher. The rural West had come back to haunt the urban East. The rural women of the West aren't just metaphors for the heart of the West, they're also the backbone of the West. Most of these women work with husbands by their sides, but many work alone. Here are several of their abridged bios as presented in the anthology (all credit given to the editors):[24]

Sue Morrell, a South Dakota native living near the Missouri River, is reminded of her mother and grandmother each spring when she sorts the garden seeds she will soon plant. Hardy. Northern grown. Heavy bearing. The ritual expresses her hopes for her daughter's life. Jeanne Bartak, who grew up on a wheat farm in North Dakota, packed her bags when she was twenty-four, and headed to Montana to study range management. "My secretarial co-workers thought I was nuts." Dixie DeTuerk's birth town, Mason City, Nebraska, went from 250 residents to 150. Dixie started detasseling corn at the age of twelve,

A California ranch family poses in 1900 with several wild game carcasses. Typically the wife was in charge of dressing out the carcass and cooking it up for the family.

earning a dollar an hour. Penny Dye, a mixed-animal veterinarian in the Black Hills, raised 150 ewes when she was a member of the youth organization, Future Farmers of America, living in Nebraska. She was the first Nebraska girl to receive the American Farmer Degree. Genevieve Eppich was born in 1919 on a ranch in Mancos, Colorado, homesteaded by her grandparents in 1887. She farmed, ran sheep and cattle, had eight hundred laying hens, and drove a school bus for twenty-six years. June Gilman and her sister spent their teen years in Montana cutting lodgepole pines to build a ranch house, cabins, a dance hall, and a rodeo arena. She hired out as a cowgirl doing ranch work and timber work. After WAC service during WWII, she worked as a stenographer for a mining company while building and running her own ranch for forty years. Peggy Godfrey ranched for twenty-three years in the high valleys of northern New Mexico and southern Colorado. She did contract hay baling, raised cattle, sold freezer beef, made and sold jerky, sold freezer lamb and summer sausage. She welds her own machinery, serves on the school board, and has raised a foster child. Lee Helvey, born near New York City, attended Smith College and École des Sciences Politiques in Paris before spending thirty-four years on a Montana ranch. "I dislike any gasoline-powered contraption and could easily do without a telephone."

Barbara Jessing, "a reverse urban homesteader," left California to pioneer in Nebraska two generations after her great-grandmother homesteaded in eastern Colorado. Barbara was encouraged to write by the Feminist Writers Group in Omaha. Rachel Klippenstein left the paved streets of Pittsburgh for the graveled roads of South Dakota, raised Polled Hereford cattle, then, like thousands of others, lost her land and home during the 1980s farm crisis. Diane Kouris, a working cowgirl, rode the same trails as Butch Cassidy and the Wild Bunch, ranching on the Outlaw Trail near Utah, Colorado and Wyoming's "three corners."

Noreen McConnell raises elk in the same area in Colorado homesteaded by her great-grandparents. She runs a custom wheat harvest crew from Texas to Montana. She's been a well-site geologist, built a log home, and run a bed and breakfast. Nellie O'Brien was one of eight children born in a log cabin in Wyoming. Karen Obrigewitch, was born in Montana and ranch-raised on the same land as five generations of her family. "I've loved good men and rode good horses," she says. Linda Oyama's father (raised among the Cree people), taught her mountain living in Montana's Gallatin Valley—how to hunt, fish, trap, tan hide, treat fur, ride horses, snowshoe, do taxidermy. Garnet Perman grew up in a Mennonite community in South Dakota, attended college, volunteered for the library and local 4-H. Norma Plant partnered with her husband on a dairy farm until dust storms and the Great Depression drove them to Colorado. They were "driven from the good life by government regulations." Growing up on the Rosebud Sioux Indian Reservation in South Dakota, C.L. Prater found cultural richness from the people that surrounded her. The family of Ella Reichert were forced to sell their eighty-acre farm in Nebraska, then lost all their money in 1932 when the banks failed. Terry Schifferns, who lives in a cabin on the south bank of the Platte River in Nebraska, wrote, "We cohabit this space with the sandhill cranes, white-tail deer, eagles, and other assorted creatures…"

Native Coloradoan Ruth Schubarth calls herself a Renaissance Christian who believes in Jesus and the Bible, but not always in religion. Dianna Torson grew up on the back of a horse on her family's farm in Iowa. She respects the intelligence and emotions of animals and writes poetry about her love of the earth. Nellie Westerskow, born in Norway, came to America in 1905 and joined her father in Wisconsin where he sawed logs for $15 a month. At ninety-six, she retired from ranching and farming in South Dakota. Reared in California and rural Iowa, Joanne Wilke moved to Montana in 1978 on a trade scholarship.

Nancy Curtis, one of the three women who compiled and edited the anthology, when not working the Wyoming cattle ranch she and her husband own and operate, is editing the latest manuscript for her award-winning publishing company, High Plains Press. Gaydell Collier, another co-editor, owned a small ranch with her husband raising registered Morgan horses, Hereford and Jersey cattle, a few sheep, and ran Backpocket Bookshop from her ranch house in the Black Hills. Linda Hasselstrom, the third editor in the trio, dreamed of racing black stallions until she was nine. She reminds us in the anthology's introduction that today's rural Western women speak with quiet force, even when historians aren't listening. "The land is our trial, our comfort, and ultimately, our identity." Collier writes, "On the plains, in the mountains, you learn that you are as important as the beaver, the hawk, the dragonfly—but not more so. You are part of the circle."

Economic and Emotional Depression
in the Rural West

Waves of settlement continue to impact the West—but the tides that once swept over our rural shores and left homesteaders in their wake are now receding, pulling families back to the cities, replanting them on urban streets, in sprawling suburbs, and on scattered faux ranchettes. Sometimes, they leave behind only the brittle shell of a town, its residents gone to live in cities, oftentimes collecting disability checks and deeply depressed because their skills are outdated, their knowledge considered worthless.

Journalist Terrence McCoy, in an article published by *The Washington Post*, asked the reader to consider that the unprecedented increase in government disability checks going to rural residents was not because those people were truly disabled but rather because they were desperate. The article, which focused on Alabama but also included graphs showing the increase in disability in western states, concluded: "The rise in disability has emerged as yet another indicator of a widening political, cultural and economic chasm between urban and rural America."[25]

Blogger Jon Katz, who farms in upstate New York but whose sentiments seem broadly shared by displaced western residents, further explored the idea of desperation among the rural unemployed on his blog *Bedlam Farm*:

> Politically and culturally, I am now something of a refugee, I often feel schizophrenic, caught between two worlds, the urban America I grew up in and wrote about, the rural America I live in and love and write about now…. America is no longer one nation, but two nations, urban America has surged ahead on its own to join the global economy, rural America has been left behind, desperate and battered and increasingly troubled.[26]

Also left behind are the shells of towns—remnants of what were once thriving agricultural centers or thriving mining towns. Jeffrey City, Wyoming, is about as close to a ghost town as you can get. Located on a lonely rural highway not far from the historic Oregon Trail, the town's population has peaked and plummeted from its first two settlers in the 1930s, more than 4,000 during the uranium mining

Jeffrey City, Wyoming as seen from the highway in 2012. A 1957 boom town with the
discovery of uranium but went bust in 1982 when the uranium mine
shut down and 95% of the population moved away.

boom of the 1970s, about 150 in the 1990s, and, according to the 2010 Census, only 58 residents.

"During the uranium boom, the town of Jeffrey City had state-of-the-art schools and plans to create a school district based out of Jeffrey City. Today, high school students are bussed 60 miles to Lander and back to attend school."[27]

It took more than thirteen years to reclaim the defunct mining site per federal regulations, and now the town, the site of the state's first uranium mill, is almost abandoned.

I visited the town in 1994 for the rural literary project Tumblewords, scheduled as "entertainment" following the town's annual firemen's fundraising event—a wild game feed. Area ranchers flocked to town, loading the tables in the fire hall with steaming dishes of antelope lasagna, baked salmon, roasted elk, and venison meatballs. Husbands and wives came, young couples came, and the children came—the hall was packed.

When I began to read the first piece, "Deerstalking: Contemplating an Old Tradition," the audience listened with downcast eyes, slightly defensive, their stomachs full of wild meat and homegrown greens, washed down with tart lemonade and cold beer. Cowboy poetry and banjo music would soon follow, so they were patient. The banjo player's four-year-old boy ran pudgy pink fingers over the cool metal of his toy six-shooter and resisted the temptation to shoot me.

When I began to read "Home Fires," an essay about unspoken words between a husband and wife, they leaned forward in their chairs, eyes lifted, beer cans discreetly tipped. One woman placed a callused hand on her husband's denimed knee; an older man eased an arthritic arm around his wife's rounded shoulders. A pigtailed girl in cowboy boots straddled a backwards chair. A gray-haired man reached a gnarled hand to his face and dried a wayward tear.

Outlying ranchers and a few townsfolk made up the volunteer fire department. In a crisis, they had only each other to rely on. Cheyenne was more than 200 miles away, and there would certainly be no "flight for life" planes appearing quickly on the horizon. How long could the town continue to exist? Were it not for the ranchers, the town would be nothing more than a metaphor for "boom and bust." Western nuclear officials expect the reclaimed site, replanted with native grasses such as clover, Indian rice, and sagebrush, to last 1,000 years. The tracks of native pronghorns, which migrate more than 300 miles, have been found near the site. Mountain lion tracks, too, and deer and turkey vultures. These natives of the High Plains will probably be here for the next 1,000 years, too—as long as the grasses grow and the sparse rains fall. The story of Jeffrey City and the rural people I met that evening continue to haunt me.

Rural Americans— The Invisible Demographic

Dawn Wink, who lives in New Mexico but was raised on a South Dakota ranch, has reason to be wary of storms. Her parents, on the family ranch in South Dakota, suffered heartbreaking losses of horses and cattle during the devastating 2013 blizzard known as Storm Atlas. In her blog *Dewdrop*, Dawn writes:

> *The Rapid City Journal* reports, "Tens of thousands of cattle lie dead across South Dakota on Monday following a blizzard that could become one of the most costly in the history of the state's agriculture industry."
>
> The only reason I know this is because my parents' ranch, the setting for Meadowlark, lies in the storm's epicenter. Mom texted me after the storm. "No electricity. Saving power on

phone. It's really, really bad…." She turned on her phone to call me later that day. "There are no words to describe the devastation and loss. Everywhere we look there are dead cattle. I've never seen so many dead cattle. Nobody can remember anything like this." Author of several books and infinite numbers of articles, Mom said, "I can't imagine writing about this. I'm not going to take photos. These deaths are too gruesome. Nobody wants to see this."[28]

Dawn searched the national news networks for stories about the blizzard, but found nothing. Thinking it might be because of massive power outages, she checked again the next day.

Nothing. It had now been four days and no national news coverage.

Dawn's frustration exemplifies the frustrations felt by many rural American farmers and ranchers. The nation doesn't know what goes on in our lives, and worse, they don't seem to care.

When the Nelson family of South Dakota lost their entire herd of cattle in 2017 because of bovine tuberculosis, they turned to their faith, not expecting their tragedy to make the national news. Susan Nelson shared excerpts from her journal with the editor of the rural publication, *The Fencepost*.[29]

It is impossible to put into words the fear that the word tuberculosis strikes in your heart and your gut. You fear for yourself, your family, your cattle, your horses, your dogs, your cats and your neighbors. The only way we could combat it and push back the fear was to go to the Lord in prayer, trust and have faith in God that He would get us through this nightmare…. Our entire family has all put blood, sweat and tears into them to ensure they stayed content and healthy. Our kids have been helping since they could sit astride a horse. It's like a family death in many ways.

The tragic 2017 deaths in the Texas Panhandle of three young ranch hands, and the horses they were riding, who died trying to save their family's cattle from wildfires, briefly made the national news. Fuller details appeared in Jon Beilue's article, "Taken in Their Prime: Three Die Trying to Save Ranch from Texas Wildfires":

"Sloan Everett died protecting his family, the land and his way of life," said Weaver. "He was serving his family in that moment. That's important for people to know and how big a priority that was, to give his life on behalf of his family."

Protection, love, help. That fit not only Everett, but Cody Crockett and his girlfriend, Sydney Wallace. They all died Monday night while trying to move cattle away from the wildfires that were consuming the Franklin Ranch, land owned by Everett's in-laws north of McLean.

One was pronounced dead at the scene close to 10 p.m. Monday, while one died en route to Amarillo and another died shortly after arriving at Amarillo, according to Gray County office of emergency management.

"Cody was kinda like the old-time cowboy," said Thacker Haynes, minister of the McLean-Heald Methodist Church. "He did everything the right way."[30]

The western wildfires that raged across the panhandles of Texas and Oklahoma, and parts of eastern Colorado and Kansas, raged unknown to most urban Americans. The fires killed thousands of cattle and left thousands displaced and in desperate need of hay and water, yet few Americans knew. The fires left some cattle excruciatingly burned

Disasters like fire and dust storms are a hardship to those who provide crops and services to urban dwellers.

but not dead, and ranchers had to return with shotguns to humanely put down the animals that were still alive.

While most of the nation went about their daily lives, help from rural America arrived from every direction. Within forty-eight hours, ranchers (some driving as much as 800 miles) delivered hay to emergency supply drop-off locations, donating more than 5,500 large bales. Veterinarians donated supplies. Cowboys and cattlewomen donated labor and money. The rural communities of the West did what rural communities all over have always done: they helped each other. And yes, the US Department of Agriculture started by President Lincoln in 1862 provided emergency disaster assistance.

The Future of the Rural West

Patty Limerick, faculty director and board chair for the Boulder, Colorado Center of the American West, remains perplexed at the national image of the West, and at the fact that most western politicians, regardless if they have authentic rural roots, like to present themselves as ranchers and farmers (part of the mythic West) who are compelled to selflessly serve their constituents by running for public office.

> For decades, the West has been a very urbanized region, with its population concentrated in cities and suburbs. And yet its image in popular thinking—and certainly in Western movies, paintings, novels, and memoirs—remains very, very rural. Really, ultra-rural. One might call this a contradiction, a paradox, or a mystery. Whatever you call it, this curious pattern of thought has big consequences.[31]

Yet for those eking out a living on the land, "died-in-the-wool" ranchers and farmers, the rural West is not an imaginary mythic place, it is the place where they raise their families and contribute to their communities, "hanging tough" despite wind, rain, blizzards, or droughts, and despite Washington lobbyists serving only the needs of big corporate agriculture. According to the national organization Farm Aid, "A handful of corporations control our food from farm to fork. Their unbridled power grants them increasing political influence over the rules that govern our food system and allows them to manipulate the marketplace."[32]

What inner fortitude or sense of purpose keeps farmers and ranchers in the rural West committed to their rural lifestyles despite political manipulation, encroaching exurban developments that raise land taxes, radical misinformed animal rights activists, wildfires, or boarded-up main streets?

When I posed this question to the Facebook group Women in Agriculture, which has more than 69,000 members, the responses were not surprising. Here is a compilation of some of their comments:

> Simplicity ~ I like to know where my food comes from ~ Pride for my heritage and hope for our future ~ I like the smell of the country ~ Animals and work come first ~ It's a pull-together kind of thing ~ It's imperative that you work together ~ Legacy is a part of it, passing down things from one generation to the next, and improving what your family worked hard for ~ A larger sense of freedom—freedom to build another barn if we need it ~ Privacy—the freedom to relate to the natural world to domestic animals and wildlife ~ Freedom to create your own community, even if only a community for the family ~ Going to the barn and opening up feed sacks and filling buckets to feed the animals—the way they stand at the gates, no fences, and greet me ~ In the country, I know every one of my neighbors. We all stop and talk in the middle of the road. When someone drives by, they stop and visit too ~ We raised our kids

Small town America: Main Street in Russell, Kansas, 2009.

in the country and my kids are raising theirs in the country ~
The sunrises and sunsets—and the moonlit nights! ~ We always
watch out for each other and for the animals ~ Families are connected by the common bond of land stewardship and animal
husbandry ~ Helping each other—it doesn't matter if it requires
a hard day's work ~ we all pitch in.

If community and independence keep families tied to rural lives
and are vital to the future of the West, there is another demographic
that also needs to be considered—the aging population and its movement to exurban, suburban, and urban areas to be closer to quality
health care. If this segment of rural communities is not replaced by
young, rurally raised people able to return to their small towns after
college and find employment, the expansion of the West's population
will be primarily from people not raised on the land, who built close to
urban centers in desirable "fringe" areas where mountains offer scenic
values, or in fertile bottomland, encroaching even further on prime
agricultural land.

Much of the West is not habitable land. Much of the West is
public land unavailable for development. Yet if western states can
anticipate the growth that will surely come, they can develop protective and visionary land use plans that will protect the future of the
West—its scenic beauty, its agricultural families, its wildlife, and the
riparian areas so vital to life in the West.

CHAPTER 10

Education and Economic History

by Robert C. Baron and Bruce C. Paton

*The American West is just arriving at the threshold of its greatness
and growth. Where the West of yesterday is glamorized in our fiction,
the future of the American West now is both fabulous and factual.*
—Lyndon B. Johnson[1]

*The preservation of parks, wilderness, and wildlife has also aided
liberty by keeping alive the 19th century sense of adventure and
awe with which our forefathers greeted the American West.
Many laws protecting environmental quality have promoted liberty
by securing property against the destructive trespass of pollution.
In our own time, the nearly universal appreciation of these
preserved landscapes, restored waters, and cleaner air
through outdoor recreation is a modern expression
of our freedom and leisure to enjoy the wonderful life
that generations past have built for us.*
—Ronald Reagan[2]

This is a chapter about education, medicine, jobs, and the private and
public lands of the American West. It references material in other chapters and brings subjects together. This chapter is in contrast with Chapter
11, "The West in Fact and Fiction," which deals with the various images
of the West as told in books and movies—some fiction, some nonfiction.

Elementary Education and Land Grant Colleges

During a six-week period in 1862, President Abraham Lincoln
signed three pieces of legislation that influenced the settlement of
the American West.

On May 20, Lincoln signed the Homestead Act.[3] On July 1, he signed the Pacific Railroad Act to fund the Transcontinental Railroad.[4] And on July 2, he signed the Morrill Act.[5]

Education was very important to Americans. As people moved west and population increased, they established elementary schools. The states that entered the Union before the Civil War had schools in the cities and towns; because of low population density in much of the West, there might be a small elementary school or even a one-room schoolhouse in rural areas. With the increased population and the availability of school buses and good roads in the twentieth century, the education of young people increased in quality.

In 1890, less than 4 percent of Americans over the age of seventeen had graduated from high school. By 2000, the figure was more than 81 percent, and 95 percent of those aged fourteen to seventeen were in high school.[6] More than 18 million Americans are currently enrolled in college.

Under the Morrill Act, each state received 30,000 acres of federal land for each of its members of Congress. The land itself or proceeds from its sale were to be used to finance the teaching of agriculture, engineering, and the mechanical arts. Public Land Grant colleges exist

The land-grant university system is being built on behalf of the people, who have invested in these public universities their hopes, their support, and their confidence.

—Abraham Lincoln

in all of the western states, including the University of Arizona, University of Arkansas, University of California, Colorado State University, University of Illinois, Iowa State, Kansas State, Michigan State, University of Minnesota, University of Missouri, Montana State, University of Nebraska, University of Nevada, New Mexico State, Oklahoma State, Oregon State, Washington State, University of Wisconsin, and University of Wyoming.

At first, the Morrill Act was applied only to western states, but soon eastern states were given western land to sell for educational purposes. Colleges such as Auburn, University of Georgia, MIT, Rutgers, Cornell, and Ohio State are land grant colleges funded by the sale of western lands.

In the early part of the twentieth century, if you wanted a top college education and could afford it, you might go east to an Ivy League school or to one of the seven sisters such as Smith or Wellesley. But within the last century, western colleges and universities have improved, and many are world-class universities. Some graduates from these large western state universities and smaller liberal arts colleges became very successful and contributed significant amounts of money to increase the endowment of their schools. Most lists of the top American universities, by either an academic or an endowment measurement, include a number of schools in the West.[7] Today one does not have to go back East for higher education.

Medicine

The same trend applies to medicine. In the 1930s, if you had a major medical issue, you might go back to Boston, Baltimore, Philadelphia, or New York for treatment if you could afford it. That is no longer necessary or true.

Thomas Jefferson did not have a very high respect for doctors, and perhaps that is why he did not appoint one to the staff of the Lewis and Clark expedition.[8] He did, however, send Lewis to spend a couple of days with Benjamin Rush and obtain a list of drugs to take on the expedition, including a powerful laxative known as "Rush's thunderbolts." The basis for all medical care at that time was bleeding, purging, and puking. The available drugs, with the exception of quinine for malaria and cowpox for vaccination against smallpox, were mostly ineffective.

The provision of health care has always presented special problems. Early settlers had to rely on self-administered traditional and native cures. Many clergymen offered cures, and, after the founding of Yale College in 1701, many of its graduates acted as physicians and clergy. The best doctors, including Benjamin Rush, studied abroad in Edinburgh, London, Leyden, and Paris. Young men who aspired to be physicians became apprentices to the already established doctors.

Three medical schools were founded in the eighteenth century: the University of Pennsylvania (1765), Columbia (1767), and Harvard (1782). Forty-nine schools were founded in the nineteenth century in a widely scattered pattern from the east—Johns Hopkins (1893), to Stanford's predecessor in San Francisco (1858). Until the end of World War II, the University of Pennsylvania, Harvard, Johns Hopkins, Columbia, and Stanford were regarded as the elite core of American medicine.

If a tornado had not hit the city of Rochester, Minnesota, in 1883, the Mayo Clinic might not exist. There were many casualties, and Dr. William Mayo, who already practiced in the city, and Mother Alfred Moes joined forces to help the injured. It soon became obvious to them that the city needed a hospital. Mother Moes raised the money and Dr. Mayo and his two sons provided the staff. This was the beginning of the first nonprofit hospital and the first multidisciplinary clinic that is now one of the most famous in the world.

During WWII, Henry Kaiser, a major industrialist in California, wanted to provide healthcare for the 20,000 workers in his shipyards. He offered managed care that was initially opposed by the American Medical Association, a system that has since grown to be Kaiser Permanente and has been accepted nationwide.

After the war, with the return of many young, experienced physicians seeking academic careers, the western schools began to blossom. Many of those physicians had been trained in the eastern schools and installed in their new schools the same high ideals and emphasis on research they had learned back East.

Founded in 1921, the University of Colorado Medical Center[9] was modest in size and only had two full-time faculty, including James Waring, a world-recognized authority on tuberculosis. Henry Swan, a Denver native and top of his class at Harvard, had operated on more than 1,000 wounded men in Europe. He was appointed full-time chairman of surgery in 1950, and by 1953 he had done a series of open-heart operations under hypothermia before John Gibbon had done the first open-heart operation in Philadelphia, using his newly developed heart-lung machine. Swan's success with hypothermic open-heart surgery put both him and the school on the world map. Within the next two decades, Thomas Starzl had done the first successful liver transplant, and his subsequent work transformed organ transplantation. C. Henry Kempe, chairman of pediatrics, who escaped from Nazi Germany in his youth, had published the first description of the "battered child syndrome," and his keen observations had profound legal and social effects around the world. Kempe also developed a vaccinia immune globulin to offset the ill effects of the smallpox vaccination. He was nominated for the Nobel Prize for both of these achievements.

Not every important new idea in medicine deals with drugs or operations. In 1968, Henry Silver, a pediatric colleague of Henry Kempe at the University of Colorado, started the first Child Health Associate program. This program introduced the concept of specially trained physician assistants, a concept that is now widely accepted throughout the profession.

Early view of the Mayo Clinic: the exterior view of an office shared by the Mayo brothers and their father.

Heart transplantation, a dramatic operation transferring life from one patient to another, was first done in South Africa by Christiaan Barnard. But Norman Shumway at Stanford and Richard Lower at the University of Virginia did the pioneering work that made Barnard's operation possible. Shumway also performed the first adult heart transplant in the United States.

Three great plagues struck the nation and the world during the twentieth century: poliomyelitis, smallpox, and HIV/AIDS. The first two were old and were brought under control. The third was new and is still rampant in many parts of the world. Although many of the original HIV patients came from the West, most important therapy has been designed at the National Institutes of Health in Bethesda, Maryland.

The worst epidemic of poliomyelitis in the United States, with 58,000 cases, occurred in 1952, the same year that Jonas Salk of the University of Pittsburgh developed an effective vaccine against the disease. During the next three years, an enormous field trial involving 20,000 physicians and 1.8 million children demonstrated the effectiveness of the "killed polio" vaccine. Salk became a national hero and could have become a multimillionaire had he patented the vaccine.

Albert Sabin was working at the University of Cincinnati during the same period and developed a live attenuated polio oral

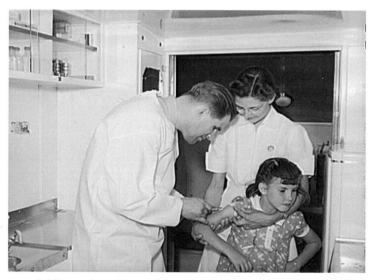

A child is vaccinated in a mobile unit at a Farm Security Administration migratory labor camp.

vaccine that could be taken on a lump of sugar. He tested the vaccine on more than 100 million people in the USSR, European countries, and Mexico. It became available in 1961 and was opposed by the March of Dimes, which was supporting Salk. It is now widely used because of its ease of administration and effectiveness. The Rotary Foundation, the World Health Organization, and UNICEF have almost eliminated poliomyelitis, and in 2015 reduced the incidence to thirty-seven cases worldwide.

Smallpox, like poliomyelitis, was another disastrous, ancient worldwide disease that was feared and caused millions of deaths. Serious attempts to eradicate it began not long after Edward Jenner discovered that cowpox could be used to immunize people in 1796. However, regional campaigns did not begin until 1950 when 50 million people died. The regional campaigns in South America extended to the rest of the world under the direction of Dr. Donald Henderson of the University of Pittsburgh. Drs. Henry Kempe and Gordon Meiklejohn of the University of Colorado also played important parts in the campaign. The last case was diagnosed in Somalia on October 26, 1977. Live virus is still being kept under deep security in the United States and Russia. Attempts to have these samples destroyed have, so far, been resisted.

Millions of people live above 8,000 feet (2438m), and some are affected by chronic altitude sickness. Roughly 25 percent of visitors from sea level to 8,000 feet or higher develop symptoms of altitude sickness that restrict their activities.

On January 1, 1960, two young men were on a cross-country ski trip near Aspen, Colorado. One of them became acutely short of breath, and his companion returned to Aspen to get help. Dr. Charles Houston, an eminent mountaineer, was one of only four doctors in the city, and he summoned the mountain rescue group and brought the man down to Aspen, a descent of about 1,000 feet. The man's symptoms disappeared quickly at the lower altitude, and Dr. Houston, because of his mountaineering experience, thought that the descent to a lower altitude was important in effecting a cure. This was the first case of high-altitude pulmonary edema published in the English language medical literature. Dr. Houston subsequently became a world-recognized expert on high-altitude diseases, making the medical world aware of the adverse effects of altitude that affect millions of people around the world.

Not only are adults affected by altitude-related illnesses. Babies conceived and born at altitude are smaller and lighter at birth than the average child. Even cattle are affected. When they are brought to the lush grass of high-altitude fields, their bodies retain fluid, resulting in brisket disease, a swelling in the neck that can result in death.

All of this knowledge has come from western scientists working in Colorado, Utah, and Tibet. In humans, there are many manifestations: altitude sickness, with symptoms of headache, shortness of breath, and difficulty in sleeping; high-altitude pulmonary edema; and the most dangerous, high-altitude cerebral edema. The economic loss from the disease is at least $50 million per year when tourists fail to spend money because they are ill.

As part of the great expansion in genetic research since the 2003 sequence of the human genome, research on this widespread affliction is now coming under the scrutiny of geneticists seeking a clue that could forecast an individual's likelihood of becoming ill with altitude sickness.

Most of the large, major studies of new drugs and procedures are now financed and run by the National Institutes of Health in Maryland, and the eastern schools still maintain their high standards and reputations. However, there are now many schools around the country that do equally good work. Stanford has published a list of seventy-seven major achievements by their faculty since 1956. Many western schools could do the same.

Had Jefferson not made the Louisiana Purchase and had we not defeated the Mexicans to obtain California, the scope of American medical achievements might have been totally different.

Job Creation

As stated earlier, for much of its history the West was a supplier of raw materials to the distant East, including beaver pelts, bison byproducts, silver and metals, petroleum, cattle, and grain. This is why Bernard DeVoto in the 1930s described the West as the "plundered provinces."[10]

During the last seventy years, however, that has not been the case. The West has led the way since World War II in job and wealth creation.

Technology Moves West

At first, most businesses were located in the East. There have been more than 1,500 auto manufacturers in the United States located in forty states, and for a variety of reasons Detroit became the automobile capital of the world.[11] Philadelphia, Cleveland, Boston, Baltimore, New York, and other eastern cities also created jobs in the nineteenth and early twentieth century.

The airplane was invented by the Wright Brothers of Dayton, Ohio, and at first the airplane manufacturers were in the East. But then William Boeing, Clyde Cessna, Donald Douglas, Howard Hughes, Walter and Olive Beech, Allan Lockheed, William Lear, and Jack Northrop founded aircraft manufacturing companies in their own names. These western companies produced planes that helped win World War II. They led the transition to commercial aviation after the War, the subsequent development of jet aircraft and growth in air travel, and they made possible the space program.

Things have changed in the past seventy years, so let's examine three industries that developed during that period: semiconductors, computers, and communications.

Generally, a change in technology results in a change in competition, even though established companies have substantial financial resources, a qualified technical staff, and good management. In 1955, vacuum tubes were used for all electronic switching and amplification in radios, television sets, and other products.[12] The leading vacuum tube manufacturers were General Electric (New York), Philco (Pennsylvania), Radio Corporation of America (New Jersey), Raytheon (Massachusetts), Sylvania (Massachusetts), and Westinghouse (Maryland). Within a dozen years, the vacuum tube was replaced by the transistor—which was invented at Bell Labs in New Jersey—in most electronic applications. Clevite and Transitron (Massachusetts) were early producers but faded from the scene. The dominant companies in the 1960s were Fairchild (California), Motorola (Arizona), National Semiconductor (California), Signetics (California), and Texas Instruments (Dallas). Not one of the vacuum tube manufacturers, all very large and strong companies with excellent marketing and strong financing, became a significant factor in the transistor industry. As transistors were impacted by integrated circuits and then microprocessors, new competitors joined the market, and these were almost all western companies.

In 1960, a list of major computer companies included Bendix, Burroughs, Control Data, General Electric, Honeywell, IBM, National Cash Register, Philco, Raytheon, RCA, Remington Rand, and Univac. Some of these companies did not continue as factors in the large computer market, none were factors in the microcomputer market, and only one was a factor in the personal computer market. Instead, newer companies, including Amdahl, Apple Computer, Commodore, Compaq Computer, Cray Research, Data General, Datapoint, Dell, Digital Equipment, Hewlett Packard, Microsoft, Oracle, Prime Computer, Seagate, Sun Microsystems, Tandem Computers, Tandy, Toshiba, Wang Laboratories, and other organizations have been founded and grown into large companies.[13] The minicomputer industry was founded in Massachusetts by DEC, Computer Control, Data General, Prime Computer, and Wang, but they have now faded from the scene. New computer-based companies such as Microsoft, eBay, Expedia, Facebook, Adobe, Amazon, Apple, Google, and others have been founded, most of which are in the West.

Denver became the hub of the communication industry starting with the cable industry and entrepreneurs like Bill Daniels, Glenn Jones, and Bill Magness, and then adding companies like Dish Network. The advances in satellite communication mentioned in Chapter 6 are because of new companies in the West.

Where once all large corporations were centered in the East, today many corporations are headquartered in the West. California

The birthplace of Silicon Valley: the garage where William Hewlett
and David Packard began developing their first product in 1938.

and Texas have more than fifty corporate headquarters in their states, and the states of Arizona, Arkansas, Colorado, Idaho, Illinois, Iowa, Kansas, Minnesota, Missouri, Nebraska, Nevada, New Mexico, Oklahoma, Oregon, South Dakota, Utah, Washington, and Wisconsin are also home to Fortune 500 companies. [14]

Not all new and growth companies are in high technology. In the 1950s, Ray Kroc started McDonald's in Illinois. In 1962, Sam Walton started a company called Wal-Mart in Arkansas, whose original purpose was to bring products to rural America. It succeeded and eventually took business away from Sears and other large corporations and is now the largest company in America. In the 1960s, the Gap, Nike, Mary Kay, Lands' End, and Humana were founded, and in the 1970s, AutoZone, Federal Express, Reebok, Toys"R"Us, Starbucks, and Southwest Airlines were founded by western entrepreneurs. Other companies started in the 1980s and 1990s include America Online, AutoNation, Charles Schwab, The Home Depot, and PetSmart, as well as numerous high-tech companies.[15]

Not all companies are large, however. Every decade thousands of companies are formed. While a few reach 100 employees, only a few become large. In 2010, there were 27.9 million small business and only 18,500 large firms in the United States. Small companies, those with fewer than twenty employees, are 89.6 percent of American companies; those with fewer than 500 employees are 99.7 percent of US firms. Small companies provide almost half of the jobs in America and are responsible for two-thirds of new employment. They may sell their products locally, to a national market, or to the world. Many of these companies are in the West; some are in rural America. With modern communication and transportation, it is possible to start and grow a company anywhere and serve an international market thanks to advances in communication and transportation. Small companies are responsible for 33 percent of US exporting value.[16]

Private and Public Ownership of the Land— Wilderness, National Parks, Forests

The American West is large. Montana is more than three times the size of Virginia but has 12 percent of its population. Colorado is almost ten times the size of Massachusetts with 80 percent of its population. Kansas is nine times the size of New Jersey and has 32 percent of its population.

While there are many large cities in the West, there are also significant areas that remain rural, as described in Chapter 6. Even the largest western states, California and Texas, have 19 percent and 47 percent, respectively, of their counties classified as rural by the Census Bureau. Chapter 9 describes some of the stories of the rural West. Farms and ranches are large. Some people prefer to live in cities, some in suburbs, and some in rural areas.

There are disagreements in many states between the needs of the urban areas and those of the rural West relative to the amounts of state money spent locally on schools, roads, medical services, water, power, and other state services. During the Constitutional Convention of 1788, the same disagreements occurred relative to whether political power was to be in the hands of the large-population states such as Massachusetts, Pennsylvania, and Virginia, or the smaller states such as Delaware, Rhode Island, and Georgia. The solution was to have a House of Representatives based on population and an upper House in which every state had two senators. Similar issues have been faced in many of the western states as they balance the needs of all citizens.

Not only is the West large and in many places sparsely populated, but the residents of the West have been mobile. The quote at the end of Chapter 6 by Alexis de Tocqueville on page 106 shows that even in 1840, westerners often moved on to another area in search of a better lifestyle or because a new place offered a new start. People move, and towns and regions gain and lose population over the decades. The stories of movement between the cities and the rural areas described in Chapter 9 are not a new phenomenon.

Throughout the West there are abandoned mining towns as well as ghost towns. There are more than 400 ghost towns in Colorado (some estimates are as high as 1,000) and more than 350 ghost towns in California. Many counties have lost population in the past half century while other regions have grown.

The West is younger than the East, and over the last century the view of preserving some land and some special places has changed.

As shown in the film *Wilderness in America: From Conquest to Conservation*,[17] for two centuries America had an almost infinite wilderness. Most European settlers clung to a small strip of land along the Atlantic Ocean. The first census in 1790 had the center of population to the east of Baltimore, Maryland. Thomas Jefferson thought that the Louisiana Purchase gave America enough land for a thousand years—a not illogical conclusion, since in the 170 years between the first settlements in New England and the 1790 Census, few Americans had moved more than 100 miles from the Atlantic Ocean. But by the 1890 Census, Americans had moved across the continent, and the Census Bureau said that the frontier was closed.

Starting in the late nineteenth century, some people believed that land should be preserved for future generations. Writers such as Henry David Thoreau, Ralph Waldo Emerson, John Muir, Edward Abbey, Aldo Leopold, Stuart Udall, and others have written about the value of open land. Every president since Theodore Roosevelt has supported national parks and national forests as well as wilderness areas. The idea was that some federal land should not be developed but rather set aside for recreation and other purposes.

The federal government established the General Land Office in 1800 to manage the public lands and to sell or give away land to settlers and later to railroads, territories, and states. The US Forest Service was established in 1905, the National Park Service was established in 1916, the Fish and Wildlife Service in 1940, and the Bureau of Land Management, the successor to the General Land Office, in 1946. This government-owned land under the auspices of these agencies is managed for all Americans, today and in the future.

Today, the federal government manages vast tracts of land. We have established national parks and forests, wilderness areas, wildlife refuges, wild and scenic rivers, and national monuments.

The amount of public lands varies across the country and is shown in Table 1.1. In most of the eastern states, little public land is available, since the land was settled in the seventeenth through nineteenth centuries. In some western states, there is also little public land. In the states settled before the Civil War, and described in Chapter 5—Arkansas, Illinois, Iowa, Kansas, Missouri, Nebraska, Texas, and Wisconsin—most land is owned by individuals, corporations, the state, or local communities. The situation is different in those states that entered the union after the Civil War (described in Chapter 6).

In the eleven western states of Arizona, California, Colorado, Idaho, Montana, Nevada, New Mexico, Oregon, Utah, Washington, and Wyoming, 660 million acres of land have been set aside to be managed by the federal government. To put it into more accessible terms, that is an area equal to 128 Massachusettses, 23 Pennsylvanias, or 6.7 Californias. Large amounts of additional land are owned by the federal government in Alaska.

Having public lands nearby offers the opportunity for hiking, camping, fishing, hunting, and all of the advantages of outdoor living. It is also good for business, and it is no coincidence that the greatest supporters of public lands are the businesses, both large and small, which support leisure activities.

Quality of Life

There is no one place or lifestyle that is preferred by all Americans. If there was, we would all live there. Some prefer large cities with the advantages of museums, concerts, theater, libraries, schools, medical facilities, sports teams, and a wide selection of restaurants and taverns. Others prefer a place less noisy, with less traffic, more reasonable housing costs, and the opportunity to spend more time outdoors.

Because of the vastness of the West and the mobility of its people, people can select where they prefer to live.

Cities need no introduction. Their excitement and noise is appealing to many. But there are advantages to rural areas.

Let's close with a quote from one of the best books on the West, *Desert Solitaire* by Edward Abbey.

> It seems to me that the strangeness and wonder of existence are emphasized here, in the desert, by the comparative sparsity of the flora and fauna: life not crowded upon life as in other places but scattered abroad in sparseness and simplicity, with a generous gift of space for each herb and bush and tree, each stem of grass, so that the living organism stands out bold and brave and vivid against the lifeless sand and barren rock. The extreme clarity of the desert light is equaled by the extreme individuation of desert life forms. Love flowers best in openness and freedom.[18]

CHAPTER 11

The West in Fact and Fiction

by Robert C. Baron

One story is good until another one is heard.
—**Thomas Fuller**[1]

I cannot tell how the truth may be,
I said the tale as 'twas told to me.
—**Walter Scott**[2]

There have been many ways the story of the American West has been told by various people. At first the story was of the special land.

Eighteenth- and Nineteenth-Century Views: Journals and Visitors

Europeans and Americans had never seen anything like the North American continent. The writings by explorers showed how different the West was from the East or Europe.

> After nine days' march, I reached some plains, so vast that I did not find their limit anywhere that I went, although I traveled over them for more than 300 leagues. And I found such a quantity of cows [bison] in these, of the kind that I wrote Your Majesty about, which they have in this country, that it is impossible to number them, for while I was journeying through these plains, until I returned to where I first found them, there was not a day that I lost sight of them.
> —Letter from **Francisco Vázquez de Coronado**
> to the king of Spain, October 20, 1541[3]

We were now about to penetrate a country at least two thousand miles in width, on which the foot of civilized man had never trodden.

　　　　　　　　　　—**Meriwether Lewis**, April 7, 1805[4]

I ascended to the top of the cutt bluff this morning, from whence I had the most delightful view of the country, the whole of which except the valley formed by the Missouri is void of timber or underbrush, exposing to the first glance of the spectator immense herds of Buffaloe, Elk, deer, & Antelopes feeding in one common and boundless pasture. We saw a number of beaver feeding on the bark of the trees along the verge of the river, several of which we shot, found them large and fat. Walking on shore that evening I met with a buffaloe calf which attached itself to me and continued to follow close at my heels until I embarked and left it.

　　　　　　　　　　—**Meriwether Lewis**, April 22, 1805[5]

In the east of the great river [Mississippi] the woods partly disappeared. In their place boundless prairies spread out. Had nature in its infinite variety refused the seeding of trees in that fertile country or had the forest that once covered them instead been destroyed by the hand of man? This is what neither tradition nor the research of science has been able to discover.

　　　　　　　　　　—**Alexis de Tocqueville**[6]

As far as the eye could reach, in every direction there was neither tree, nor shrub, nor house, nor shed visible, so that we were rolling on as it were on the bosom of a new Atlantic, but that the sea was of rich green grass and flowers, instead of the briny and bottomless deep.

　　　　　　　　　　—**James Silk Buckingham**[7]

Aside from the vast herds of bison which it contains, the country along the Platte is enlivened by great numbers of deer, badgers, hares, prairie wolves, eagles, buzzards, ravens, and owls: these, with its rare and interesting plants, in some measure relieved the uniformity of its cheerless scenery. We found a constant source of amusement in observing… the cumbrous gait, and impolitic movements of the bison; we were often delighted by the beauty and fleetness of the antelope, and the social comfort and neatness of the prairie dog.

—**Major Stephen Long**[8]

The face of the country was dotted far and wide with countless hundreds of buffalo. They trooped along in files and columns, bulls, cows and calves, on the green faces of the declivities in front. They scrambled away over the hills to the right and left; and far off, the pale blue swells in the extreme distance were dotted with innumerable specs.

—**Francis Parkman**[9]

On the nineteenth day we crossed the Great American Desert— forty memorable miles of bottomless sand.

—**Mark Twain**[10]

Our way for nearly fifty miles was through the Green River Bad Lands, a region of desolation. The rocks are sandstones and shales, gray and buff, red and brown, blue and black strata in many alternations, lying nearly horizontal, and almost always without soil or vegetation; but they are all very soft and friable, and are strangely carved by the rains and streams.

—**John Wesley Powell**[11]

Nineteenth-Century Art and Photography

After the Lewis and Clark expedition, exploration leaders took along artists and photographers to document the West. European painting had shown humans as the center of the scene, but the Hudson River School of painting, for example, showed nature in a new way. The art of Thomas Cole, Frederic Church, and Asher Durand painted the mountains of New York in full glory with a sense of awe. People, if they appeared at all, were small against the majestic landscape.

That style influenced Albert Bierstadt, Thomas Moran, Thomas Hill, Samuel Seymour, Seth Eastman, John Mix Stanley, Karl Bodmer, Richard Kern, Alfred Jacob Miller, George Bingham, and others. They documented the larger mountains and the wilderness of the American

West. Photographers such as William Henry Jackson, Timothy O'Sullivan, and Alfred Mathews also showed the true wonders of the West. Wilderness and nature took center stage.

These artists and photographers brought back images of very special places to people in both the East and Europe. Their paintings and photographs were now not only shown in galleries but were also reproduced in books through lithographs and steel engravings.

Albert Bierstadt's *A Storm in the Rocky Mountains, Mt. Rosalie*, 1866.

Thomas Hill's, *Yosemite Valley,* ca. 1861-1897.

Thomas Moran's *The Three Tetons*, 1895.

Timothy H. O'Sullivan's
photograph Ancient Ruins
in the Cañon de Chelle,
New Mexico, 1873.
Albumen silver print.

Charles Marion Russell's 1902 lithograph *Buccaroos*

Edward S. Curtis's 1905 photograph *Navaho child*

While much of the art was of landscapes, George Catlin painted pictures of the Plains Indians, John James Audubon showed the birds and animals of America, and Charley Russell painted cowboys. The West was becoming familiar through artists and photographers.

Westerners

Buffalo Bill's Wild West show, which ran from 1883 to 1913, showed attendees in the East and Europe one side of the American West—cowboys and Indians, fancy riding and shooting, colorful costumes and characters. It was a popular show, even if it did not tell the entire story.

1899 poster advertising Buffalo Bill's Wild West Show that traveled throughout the world.

In his book *The Power of Myth*, Joseph Campbell, writes, "Myth helps you to put your mind in touch with this experience of being alive."[12] He goes on in the chapter "The Hero's Adventure" to state, "A hero is someone who has given his or her life to something bigger than oneself."[13] This genre of writing goes back to the Greeks with Odysseus, the British with St. George and the Dragon, the Scandinavians with Siegfried, the Spanish with Don Quixote, and in many other cultures.

There is no type of novel where this applies more than in the western, in which a hero, usually a stranger, rides into town, takes on and

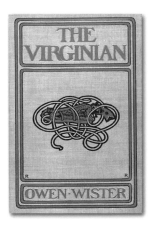

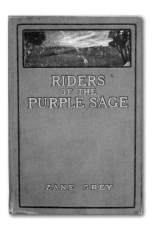

usually kills a villain, and then rides out of town to the next place where he is needed. Sometimes he helps a woman, often a school-marm or a widow, as part of the service.

Cowboy heroes were at the center of dime store novels in the nineteenth century. The first major western was *The Virginian* by Owen Wister, published in 1902. Wister, a classmate of Teddy Roosevelt at Harvard, had to leave his home and move to a Wyoming ranch for a time because of health issues. When he returned to Pennsylvania, the idea of the West stuck with him, and he wrote his first and longest-lasting novel. The Virginian uses intelligence, tact, and occasionally force to solve problems. The book sold 100,000 copies in its first year, was reprinted fifteen times, and was made into a silent film in 1914 as well as a "talkie" with the young Gary Cooper in the title role in 1929.

The concept of the stranger maintaining the forces of law and order continued in western literature. The books often had ranchers, cowboys, horses, guns, cattle, sheriffs, and outlaws and usually were a conflict between good and evil.

Zane Grey, a retired dentist, wrote sixty books of western fiction, selling 113 million copies in his lifetime. His titles have strong heroes and ruthless villains; *Riders of the Purple Sage* published in 1912 is his most popular. Many of his books were made into movies, and Grey made enough money from his novels to spend the remainder of his life fishing around the world, catching record-size fish.

Other outstanding western books include *Smoky the Cowhorse* by Will James, *Shane* by Jack Schaefer, and *True Grit* by

Charles Portis. There are many other writers of this genre as well, including Louis L'Amour, Cormac McCarthy, Walter van Tilburg Clark, Max Brand, Luke Short, and Larry McMurtry.

Western Movies, Radio, and Television

Silent films often used western stories as their basis. *The Great Train Robbery* (1903) was the first of many such films. Silent film stars such as Broncho Billy, William S. Hart, Hoot Gibson, and Tom Mix became famous; they were followed by "talkie" stars, including Gene Autry, Roy Rogers, Dale Evans, Gary Cooper, John Wayne, and Clint Eastwood. The western movies by John Ford are excellent examples of the genre, and the novels of Zane Grey as well as the novels *The Virginian, Shane, True Grit* and *Lonesome Dove* were made into outstanding movies. Among the best movies are *The Virginian, Stagecoach, The Treasure of the Sierra Madre, High Noon, Shane, True Grit, The Man Who Shot Liberty Valance, The Magnificent Seven, Butch Cassidy and the Sundance Kid, Dances with Wolves, The Alamo*, and *Broken Trail*, eight of which received Oscar nominations for Best Picture. There are thousands of Western movies; for more information on major figures, see *The Hollywood West*.[14]

Hundreds of "spaghetti Westerns" were made in Italy as well as France, Germany, Spain, the United Kingdom, Yugoslavia, and elsewhere. These films share a good story about an "exotic place," the American West, and, in most cases, the triumph of good over evil.

In addition to movies, westerns also were a major part of radio. Weekly half-hour or hour radio programs included *The Roy Rogers Show, Red Ryder, Gunsmoke, Have Gun—Will Travel, Death Valley Days, Hopalong Cassidy*, and *The Lone Ranger*. Many Americans of a certain age raced home from school to listen to their favorite western radio program.

When television came on the scene in the 1950s and 1960s, westerners became a stable of the broadcasts. Programs such as *Gunsmoke, Have Gun—Will Travel, The Rifleman, The Roy Rogers Show, Maverick, Rawhide, The Lone Ranger*, and *Bonanza* were shown weekly.

Around the world, fascination with the West was based on these stories in movies, on radio, and on television. For many viewers and readers, the American West was a place of violence, bad men, heroes, and shootings.

Novels of the West

Western novels (see page 204) are a part of the literature of the West—but only a part. If they fully represented the western story, cemeteries would be filled with bad guys, and The Lone Ranger would not have any place to go to solve problems for his weekly radio program.

Most nineteenth-century American novels were centered in Boston, New York, or Philadelphia. But in the twentieth century, as the country moved west, authors began to write novels about the people who lived in the West and their stories.

Laura Ingalls Wilder wrote about growing up in the West, including *Little House in the Big Woods, Little Town on the Prairie, Farmer Boy*, and *Little House on the Prairie*, which was the title of a popular television series. Not all western people were saved by strangers with guns. There are a variety of stories for children about western authors, artists, conservationists, and children's lives in the West.

Table 11.1 lists one outstanding novel from each of the twenty-three western states that are worth reading to get a more complete idea of the area. There are additional good novels and writers from each of the western states, and several of them are described in the book *The Best American Novels of the Twentieth Century*[15] by the late Eleanor Gehres, manager of the Denver Public Library's Western History Department. Of the 150 novels Gehres chose, 20 took place in the West.

These books show the breadth of the western experience; each of the authors had a story centered in their state. Willa Cather wrote about the Nebraska plains, Walter Clark about Nevada, and Larry McMurtry about Texas. Perhaps the most widely known is John Steinbeck's *The Grapes of Wrath*, which describes the Dust Bowl and the movement of desperate people migrating from Oklahoma to California for jobs. The book was made into an outstanding movie that won an Academy Award for Best Picture. Other western stories that were made into award-winning movies include *The Ox-Bow Incident, How the West Was Won, The Human Comedy*, and *Fargo*.

Western novelists include Maya Angelou writing about being Black in Arkansas, William Saroyan about an immigrant family in California, N. Scott Momaday about Native Americans in New Mexico, and David Guterson about being Japanese in Washington.

The novels are not only good stories but also award-winning books. The Pulitzer Prize for novels has been awarded to Willa Cather

Table 11.1

Western states and examples of their novels

State	Title	Author
Arizona	*The Monkey Wrench Gang*	Edward Abbey
Arkansas	*I Know Why the Caged Bird Sings*	Maya Angelou
California	*The Human Comedy*	William Saroyan
Colorado	*Angle of Repose*	Wallace Stegner
Idaho	*Housekeeping*	Marilynne Robinson
Illinois	*Native Son*	Richard Wright
Iowa	*A Thousand Acres*	Jane Smiley
Kansas	*The Wonderful World of Oz*	L. Frank Baum
Minnesota	*Main Street*	Sinclair Lewis
Missouri	*Tom Sawyer*	Mark Twain
Montana	*A River Runs Through It*	Norman Maclean
Nebraska	*O Pioneers!*	Willa Cather
Nevada	*The Ox-Bow Incident*	Walter Van Tilburg Clark
New Mexico	*House Made of Dawn*	N. Scott Momaday
N. Dakota	*The Round House*	Lousia Erdrich
Oklahoma	*The Grapes of Wrath*	John Steinbeck
Oregon	*The Way West*	A. B. Guthrie Jr.
S. Dakota	*Leaving the Land*	Douglas Unger
Texas	*Lonesome Dove*	Larry McMurtry
Utah	*The Executioner's Song*	Norman Mailer
Washington	*Snow Falling on Cedars*	David Guterson
Wisconsin	*The Art of Fielding*	Chad Harbach
Wyoming	*Brokeback Mountain*	Annie Proulx
Traditional Westerns	*The Virginian*	Owen Wister
	Riders of the Purple Sage	Zane Grey
	Smoky the Cowhorse	Will James
	Shane	Jack Schaefer
	True Grit	Charles Portis

(1923), John Steinbeck (1940), A. B. Guthrie Jr. (1950), N. Scott Momaday (1969), Wallace Stegner (1972), Norman MacLean (1977), Norman Mailer (1980), Larry McMurtry (1986), Jane Smiley (1992), Annie Proulx (1994), and Marilynne Robinson (2005). Other novels with western themes have been finalists for the National Book Award.

The people of the American West are varied, and their stories may be different from those of the East. Stories reflecting the lives of westerners continue to be written by excellent authors.

History, Biography, and Memoirs

Not only are novels telling the story of the West, so are works of nonfiction. As stated in the Introduction, American history is more than colonial history or southern history up to the Civil War. For a long time, the acceptable story was about European civilization moving from east to west as the frontier moved. Some believe there was no history until eastern people came west and brought it with them, and the closing of the frontier in 1890 was the end of that part of the story. The moving frontier and its influence on America is the thesis of Frederick Jackson Turner.

In the 1950s, western history began to be described in a new way and became a discipline in its own right; the bibliography lists a number of excellent books that merit reading. The work of Ray Billington, Bernard DeVoto, Bill Goetzmann, David Lavender, Patty Limerick, Wallace Stegner, Ron Tyler, Bob Utley, and Walter Prescott Webb advance the history of the American West. DeVoto, born and raised in Utah, had to move to Cambridge, Massachusetts, to be taken seriously as a historian.

Women's history, and especially western women's history, took longer to develop. Many of the history books listed in this book's bibliography have no mention of any women—as if women suddenly appeared on the scene after they had been created sometime during the 1950s. It is our hope that this book will encourage further study of the West and all its inhabitants. In addition, some books found in the bibliography are a good foundation for the study of history and biography, including women's history, Hispanic/Latino history, Native American history, Asian history, and other groups whose stories have not yet been told.

The writings of Mari Sandoz, Willa Cather, Mary Austin, Terry Tempest Williams, Frank Waters, and others are a good starting point to learn about the "real West."

Preserving the Land

The story of the West is, in part, the story of our relationship to the land. Chapter 10 introduces the public lands and the works of John Muir, Ed Abbey, Aldo Leopold, Stuart Udall, David Brower, and others. One of the factors that makes the West different from the East or the South is the amount of public lands, the vast spaces, and the rural character of many of these places. Countless writers have described the land and its impact on the western character; the bibliography lists several books that tell this part of the story.

There is distance between people, and that impacts the story of the West. While there are still many people moving to New York City, Boston, Atlanta, and other large eastern cities for their careers, there are others who want to live where there is open land nearby for relaxation and a place to recharge their batteries in an increasingly hectic world. The open lands offer opportunities for hiking, camping, skiing, climbing, biking, fishing, hunting, rafting, photography, painting, and bird-watching.

As Linda Hasselstrom wrote in her book *Land Circle: Writings Collected from the Land,*

> We are all creatures born to soil and wilderness; the outdoors, not an air-conditioned office or schoolroom with windows that can't be opened, is our natural habitat. Night or day, walk out into the grass or woods alone, sit down, and listen. Dig in the earth; plant something. Walk and watch any living thing except another human. You will find some guidance, some comfort. To find more, to become fully human, you must commit more of yourself to the search.[15]

Twentieth-Century Western Art, Sculpture, Photography, Music, Museums, and Collections

As the West has moved from settlement and survival to creativity and prosperity, there has been an increasing interest in our roots and what made us who we are. Western art is now of greater interest in museums and private collections, and the best of the artists are finding larger markets for their work.

Besides individual and corporate collectors and western galleries, there are western art museums in almost every state, and many national art museums now feature western art collections. Frederick Remington, Maynard Dixon, and Ansel Adams are important artists, as are many other artists and photographers of the nineteenth and twentieth centuries. The best way to appreciate western art is to visit to one of the many museums.

It is impossible to list all of the museums displaying western art, but a partial list would include the Tucson Museum of Art (Arizona), the Autry National Center (California), the Denver Art Museum (Colorado), the Museum of Western Art (Colorado), the Boot Hill Museum (Kansas), the C. M. Russell Museum (Montana), the Joslyn Art Museum (Nebraska), the National Cowboy & Western Heritage Museum (Oklahoma), the Gilcrease Museum (Oklahoma), the Amon Carter Museum of American Art (Texas), the Tacoma Art Museum (Washington), the Wisconsin Historical Museum (Wisconsin), the Buffalo Bill Center of the West (Wyoming), and the National Museum of Wildlife Art (Wyoming). Look online for museums near you and pay them a visit.

Western Reality and Image

The story of the West is not just that of Custer, the O.K. Corral, *The Lone Ranger*, or *Gunsmoke*. It is of a vibrant and growing part of America and the American Dream. While there are still westerners who send their children back East for an education at an Ivy League School to develop historical culture, there are many young people from the East who are moving west for their education or afterward for the quality of life and opportunity.

The Northeastern/Eurocentric story of America is no longer the only one. There is no one tale that tells the story of the West any more than there is one story that describes New England, the South, England, or Europe. There are many stories, and they all should be told.

CHAPTER 12

The American West

by Robert C. Baron

Conquest of the land was only part of pioneering. And there were
all kinds of pioneers. Some were clerks and some were storekeepers and
some were bankers, some were blacksmiths and some were printers.
They built the towns and organized the commerce and the trade
in the new land. And some were the restless folk who had to live their
lives out on the fringes ahead of the permanent settlements, moving on
as soon as towns grew up and neighbors arrived. Without their
restlessness the United States would still be a narrow band
of settlements along the Atlantic Coast.
—Hal Borland[1]

America's story is more than New England colonial and revolutionary history of the seventeenth and eighteenth centuries. It is more than southern history of the nineteenth century.

For the last century and a half, and certainly since World War II, the West has provided political, education, medical, and business leaders; created jobs; and led the way in changing roles for women.

This chapter describes how geography and other factors play a role in a country's and a region's development and character, and it describes the characteristics of the West and its people. It then discusses the relationship between the American West and the East. Finally, it raises some observations about the role of the West in the twenty-first century.

The Land

As described in Chapter 2, the land has influence on a place; there are generalizations you can make about certain countries and regions based on their geography. While these are not universal and don't apply to all people, they contain enough truth to provide useful information. Regions are influenced not only by climate and geography but also by history, culture, religion, science, literature, art, music, food, and the economy.

Each of us may have a view of New England, the Deep South, and the metropolitan New York area. But what of the West? The West is more than John Wayne, *Gunsmoke*, national parks, Midwest farms, or Hollywood, and it is my hope that this book has given you more information about the American West.

I would like first to address the characteristics of the West and westerners. Obviously, people in the West may differ individually but there are certain general observations that can be made.

The western land is very large and has a variety of features— mountains and plains, forests and grasslands, rivers and deserts. Climate varies over the region. Throughout the West, as we saw in Chapter 2, there is far less rainfall than in the East. Water management is very important.

Weather can be extreme, with temperatures ranging from 130 degrees F to 80 below zero. Wind speeds can at times be above 100 miles per hour and may be almost continuous. There is an old joke that one time the wind stopped blowing in Wyoming, and 200 people fell over. Drought, floods, rain, sleet, and hail can liven up the weather. Blizzards, thunderstorms, tornadoes, and earthquakes visit the West, and these have influenced not only westerners but also the kinds of homes they have built for themselves.

In New England, with lots of trees and fewer weather extremes, houses have been built of wood for centuries. In the West, with less wood, stone, bricks, and sod houses were often the norm.

The West was remote and vast. Distances and low population densities between 1840 and 1940 meant that much of the West was settled by people who had to stand on their own two feet. Whether on a farm in Kansas or a ranch in Idaho or Texas, there is a big sky, a horizon, and people look up and see a large landscape. Westerners, no matter where they are, look far into the distance. A Colorado friend told me when visiting the East, the tall buildings and thick forests stopped her from seeing the horizon, and she felt a sense of claustrophobia.

At first the West was explored by mountain men or people who came west for mining. But they were few, and many went home. The credo then was "get in, get rich and get out."

The People

The West was settled by people who moved west for a new beginning. They often had an independent spirit and were pioneers, adventurers, sometimes mavericks, and wanted to own land. There were farmers who developed the regions that became states before the Civil War (Chapter 5) and followed Jefferson's idea of the importance of the family farm. Then people came west to the areas where there was insufficient rainfall for farming and developed larger areas for ranching (Chapter 6).

Some did not farm or ranch but instead established towns. Hal Borland, quoted at the beginning of this chapter, was raised on a homestead in eastern Colorado. His father could not make it pay, and so he left the homestead and moved the family to a small town elsewhere in Colorado. After college, Hal Borland became a reporter for the *Denver Post* and then moved east to work for the *New York Times*; he also wrote many books on nature. Some children went east, but many stayed and raised their own families in the West. The Grant family described in the preface illustrates how a pioneer can have descendants who help build a region.

As shown earlier, population densities are low, especially in the Rocky Mountain states. Westerners are self-reliant, with a strong sense of individual responsibility. People were judged based on who they were and not who their parents were or where they went to college. Many of the settlers established family farms or family ranches, which were held by descendants for generations.

Westerners, especially in rural areas, were independent and yet interdependent, sharing with their neighbors. When a barn burned down or an illness prevented crops from being harvested, neighbors pitched in. Even today, there are western state fairs, church suppers, and shared cattle roundups or harvests. Many of the people are friendly to strangers. Throughout the West there are the deep roots of Hispanic and Indian culture, and women continue to provide leadership. Women came west to get an education in the Normal Schools (teachers' colleges) and then teach in the new elementary schools that were being opened in the expanding West. Some women were able to obtain their own land under the Homestead Act. Some Hispanic families have been in the United States for eleven generations and have contributed much to our history. The Native American story is described in Chapter 3 and is depicted in diverse Native American art and stories.

Much of the West was rural, dependent on farming and ranching for its income. As shown in Chapters 6, 9, and 10, things changed after World War II, but many westerners are only a generation or two from the land and the values and priorities of the farmers, ranchers, and small towns influenced them, and in some cases influenced new residents.

People were mobile, prepared to move on when a better place or new opportunity presented itself. As a result, there are many ghost towns in the West, and population centers have shifted over the decades. Westerners tried new things and new areas, and there was a sense of optimism, with people believing that things would get better both for themselves and their children.

There are many stories of the American West that have been told, but there are many that remain to be told by future historians, novelists, artists, and filmmakers.

Many westerners love the outdoors, the national parks and forests, and wilderness areas. They spend their spare time fishing,

The romance of the open road. Many who moved west were in search of adventure or a better life.

hunting, hiking, camping, climbing, skiing, photographing, and enjoying nature. There is a difference between earning a living and living. Cities have many advantages—jobs, museums, theaters, music, and the arts—but they can be crowded and noisy. There are advantages in being close to nature, and having a better quality of life. Much of the West can provide both.

The federal government owns much of the west, as was shown in Figure 1.1 Some western states have many wilderness areas, including Arizona (90), California (149), Colorado (43), New Mexico (28), Nevada (65), Oregon (47), Utah (35), and Washington (31). In these states, a city resident can get to wilderness easily. Some states have no wilderness areas or National Parks: Iowa, Kansas, Nebraska. Yet even here they go to state parks and special places in adjacent states for relaxation and meaning.

Government

Many westerners share Jefferson's view of limited government and can be considered anti-federalist. They believe that the state and, more importantly, their community should have control of education, roads, law and order, health care, and how to spend their tax dollars. They may be contemptuous of authority and want to get away from the control of the East, especially eastern bankers and Washington bureaucrats with their regulations. They are protective of political/civil liberties and often are anti-big business.

The Midwest and the West have been called isolationist. Yet their priorities seem to be family, neighbors, their town and state, and only later the international scene. This is not a bad set of priorities.

President Franklin Delano Roosevelt and the New Deal helped the West develop, with water projects, electric power to remote farms, and financial support for local utility companies. President Dwight David Eisenhower, with the national road-building projects of the 1950s, helped end western rural isolation and their dependence on the railroads.

The federal government was looked at mainly as being in control of water resources, forests for the storage of clean water, and electric power. The Department of Agriculture affects almost every aspect of farming. Many westerners have asked for financial subsidies while at the same time resenting government interference in their daily lives.

The disagreements between John Adams and Thomas Jefferson about the role of government and the priorities of the Federalists and Anti-Federalists are still being fought today in the legislatures of the American West.

The US West and East

The ideas presented by Bernard DeVoto in the 1930s about the West being the "plundered provinces" are no longer true. The situation is far more complicated; there is a complex relationship between the West and Washington and New York.

The states have constitutional requirements for balanced budgets, yet the federal government presents programs, rules, and regulations that may make that more difficult. This applies to almost every aspect of operating a state. At one time there were disagreements about "unfunded mandates," things that the federal government required the states to do but did not support fiscally. Today there are other federal demands.

For example, the federal government passed a law in 2001 called No Child Left Behind (NCLB), one of more than fifty laws involving education that Congress has passed in the last seventy years. And while a state can choose not to participate in NCLB, they will not get educational funds, money that has been collected in taxes from the residents of the state. So states take the money and build up bureaucracies to fill out the paperwork required by the federal government.

During the last century, there has been a creeping federalism. Amendment X to the US Constitution, a part of the Bill of Rights, states: "The powers not delegated to the United States by the Constitution, nor prohibited by it to the states are reserved to the states respectively or to the people." There is no mention in the Constitution of the federal government having power on education, or health care, local minimum salaries, or many of the other aspects of federal power. Yet even though the language seems definite, the courts have nevertheless allowed the power of the federal Government to increase, based on the commerce clause to the Constitution.

On an individual level, some westerners feel a sort of inferiority complex relative to the East. A state university is not as "good" as an Ivy League school, so they send their sons and daughters east for their education. A book is not important unless it is reviewed in the *New York Times* or *New York Review of Books*. An art exhibit is not worth seeing unless it has been at the Met in New York or Boston's Museum of Fine Arts. And news is not important unless it is reported in the eastern press. While these feelings may have been justified in the 1920s to 1940s, it is no longer the case. Western schools, medical facilities, art museums, theaters, music, and writings are comparable to those in the East.

Meanwhile the national news reports principally stories from Washington, New York, and Hollywood. The rest of the country is seldom covered unless the story involves a large-scale disaster.

Important stories, whether as current events or the base for history, are important, independent of the awareness of media people in New York or Washington. In short, the West and its people matter.

The American West
in the Twenty-First Century

In *Pioneers and Plodders: The American Entrepreneurial System*, I proposed that the history of America is the history of employment, and that job creation is to a large extent the result of new technologies and small companies. In covering the history of four industries, steel, automobiles, electronics, and computers, I showed how large companies, with extensive financial, technical, and marketing resources, often do not deal well with change. The example in Chapter 10 of the transition from vacuum tubes to transistors is but one such example; others are listed throughout this book. Aerospace, computers, communications, medical technology, alternative energy, and agricultural supplies are being developed in the West today more than in the East.

The West, due in part to factors pointed to earlier, seems to recognize innovation and entrepreneurs more than other parts of the country that instead often seem inclined to focus on older and more established ways of doing things, with more conservative investments and limited opportunities for growth in employment. We westerners hope for the future. That may mean that the West will lead the way in the future in innovation and the creation of jobs.

People vary in what they consider important in their life. But for some, new and safe cities and towns, nearby recreational areas, and more sunshine, matter. These people may choose to live in the American West rather than the crowded East.

There is no ignoring the fact that the East gets substantially more moisture from the clouds than the West, and the availability of water has been and will continue to be a major problem for the West. Demands for water will exceed supply in the future. There is an old saying: "Whiskey's for socializing, water's for fighting."

Another major problem for the West in the twenty-first century is global warming. Much of the West has always been dry, and now some of it is extremely dry, and wildfires are affecting the timberlands of many of the states. As I write this, there are more than 150 wildfires burning in the western states, and this problem may get worse. Further, warming will affect rainfall and the timing of melting of the mountain snowpack and the availably of water.

Finally, there is the question of immigration and how Congress will address the issue. Migrants from Mexico and Central America as well as the Pacific Rim are moving into the West where the jobs are. To solve this challenge by building a wall in order to create more jobs in the East seems to make no sense. Many jobs in agriculture and the service industries require immigration. In *Pioneers and Plodders*, I described four major entrepreneurs who built large companies and industries. Two were immigrants (Andrew Carnegie and David Sarnoff), and two were the sons of immigrants (Henry Ford and Ken Olsen). Today, some immigrants start companies because they see America as the land of opportunity. They wish to build a better life for themselves and their children. And that is the philosophy our ancestors had and that helped build the American West.

Throughout the book, the authors have presented histories of the American West, its people, and its places. America has changed enormously in the two centuries since Thomas Jefferson became president and purchased the Louisiana Territory from the French. Since then, the extensive public land, farms, and ranches; the independence and interdependence of the people; the experiences of Native Americans, women, and Hispanics, as well as those migrating from the East and South; the new ideas and innovation; and the belief in a better life have all become part of our past and future. In many ways, the West is America.

Notes

Introduction

1. Henry David Thoreau, *Walking* (1862).
2. Bernard DeVoto, *The Course of Empire* (Boston: Houghton Mifflin Company, 1952) xiii.
3. US Census Reports and Congressional Research Service March 3, 2017—Lands Managed by the Bureau of Land Management, Fish and Wildlife Service, National Park Service, Forest Service, and Department of Defense.

Chapter 1

1. Donald Jackson, *Thomas Jefferson & the Stony Mountains: Exploring the West from Monticello* (Urbana: University of Illinois Press, 1981), ix.
2. Merrill D. Peterson, ed., *Thomas Jefferson: Writings* (New York: The Library of America, 1984), 3.
3. Thomas Jefferson, *Notes on the State of Virginia* (London: John Stockdale, 1787), reprint ed. William Peden (Chapel Hill: University of North Carolina, 1955), 131.
4. *Report on Government for Western Territory*, Peterson, *Thomas Jefferson: Writings*, 377.
5. TJ Letter, Peterson, *Thomas Jefferson: Writings*, 783.
6. Thomas Jefferson, *The Writings of Thomas Jefferson: Containing His Autobiography, Notes on Virginia, Parliamentary Manual, Official Papers, Messages and Addresses, and Other Writings, Official and Private, Now Collected and Published in Their Entirety for the First Time Including All of the Original Manuscripts, Deposited in the Department of State and Published in 1853 by Order of the Joint Committee of Congress with Numerous Illustrations and a Comprehensive Analytical Index*, 1903TJ Letter, XI 17, ed. Andrew Adgate Lipscomb and Albert Ellery Bergh, Library ed., 20 vols. (Washington, DC: Thomas Jefferson Memorial Association, 1903).
7. E. Millicent Sowerby, *Catalogue of the Library of Thomas Jefferson*, 20 vols. (Washington, DC: Library of Congress, 1952–1959), chapter 29.
8. Jefferson, *The Writings of Thomas Jefferson*, TJ Letter to Thomas Paine, May 21, 1789, 363
9. Peterson, *Thomas Jefferson Writings*, TJ Letter, 1105.
10. Ibid., 1113.
11. Dumas Malone, *Jefferson the President, First Term* (Boston: Little, Brown, 1970), 306.
12. Peterson, Thomas Jefferson Writings, TJ Letter, 1127.

Chapter 2

1. Tacitus, *Histories*, Bk. IV, Sec. 64 (New York: E. P. Dutton, 1932).
2. Alexis de Tocqueville. *Democracy in America* (2 vols.) (Folio Society Edition

1835, 1840), reprint (New York: Library of America, 2004), 21.

3. Bernard Augustine DeVoto, *Across the Wide Missouri* (Boston: Houghton Mifflin), 43–44.

4. Maxine Benson, ed., *From Pittsburgh to the Rocky Mountains: Major Stephen Long's Expedition, 1819–1820* (Golden, CO: Fulcrum Publishing, 1988), xiv.

5. Richard A. Keen, *Skywatch East: A Weather Guide* (Golden, CO: Fulcrum Publishing, 1992).

Chapter 3

1. D. H. Lawrence, *Mornings in Mexico* (New York: Alfred A. Knopf, 1927), 103.

2. See US Park Service publication entitled *American Indians and the Civil War* (2013), an official National Park Service handbook. In this publication, in a chapter entitled, "You Cannot Remember What You Never Knew," I sketched out what one might call a spatial philosophy of history that was greatly informed by the work of Vine Deloria Jr, most noticeably his chapters on the Western notion of history and religion found in his seminal work, *God Is Red* (New York: Grosset & Dunlap, 1973). This chapter is an attempt (though not entirely successful) to put that philosophy into practice.

3. Vine Deloria Jr., *God Is Red* (New York: Grosset & Dunlap, 1973).

4. B. Fell, *Saga America* (New York: Crown, 1980); B. Fell, *America BC: Ancient Settlers in the New World* (New York: Times Books, 1976); and G. M. Gathorne-Hardy, *The Norse Discoverers of America* (Oxford, UK: Clarendon Press, 1970).

5. Vine Deloria Jr. and David Wilkins, *Legal Universe: Observations of the Foundations of American Law* (Golden, CO: Fulcrum Publishing, 2016); R. A. Williams Jr., *The American Indian in Western Legal Thought: The Discourses of Conquest* (Oxford, UK: Oxford University Press, 1992); R. A. Williams, *Savage Anxieties: The Invention of Western Civilization* (New York: Macmillan, 2012); and C. G. Calloway, *Pen and Ink Witchcraft: Treaties and Treaty Making in American Indian History* (Oxford, UK: Oxford University Press 2013).

6. Nathaniel G. Taylor et al., *Papers Relating to Talks and Councils Held with the Indians in Dakota and Montana in the Years 1866–1869* (Washington, DC: Government Printing Office, 1910). Original in the National Archives, Records of the Indian Division, Office of the Secretary of the Interior, Record Group 48.

7. P. Hämäläinen, *The Comanche Empire* (New Haven, CT: New Yale University Press, 2008).

8. George Washington to James Duane, 09/07/1783, in Francis Paul Prucha, *Documents of United States Indian Policy* (Lincoln: University of Nebraska Press, 1975), 1.

9. Ibid., 2.

10. Ibid., 15.

11. Ibid., 47.

12. Ibid., 48.

13. Ibid.

14. Ibid., 33.

15. Ibid., 73.

16. Linda F. Witmer, *The Indian Industrial School, Carlisle, Pennsylvania, 1887–1918,* 3rd ed. (Carlisle, PA: Cumberland Historical Society, 2002), 19.

17. *Official Report of the Nineteenth Annual Conference of Charities and Correction* (1892), 46–59. Reprinted in Richard H. Pratt, "The Advantages of Mingling Indians with Whites," *Americanizing the American Indians: Writings by the "Friends of the Indian" 1880–1900* (Cambridge, MA: Harvard University Press, 1973), 260–271.

18. Richard Henry Pratt and Robert M. Utley, *Battlefield and Classroom: Four Decades with the American Indian, 1867–1904* (New Haven, CT: Yale University Press, 1964), 266.

19. Theodore Roosevelt, State of the Union Message (December 3, 1901). Roosevelt's address is worth reading with respect to his attitude and expression of a growing public sentiment that tribal nations, i.e., Peoples, should be broken up, just as their homelands were dismembered by the General Allotment Act. Not surprisingly, Roosevelt oversaw the creation of the US Forest Service and the expansion of the US National Park Service to manage what only twenty-five years earlier had been the treaty-guaranteed lands of the First Peoples.

20. John Q. Smith, *Annual Report* (1876), in Prucha, *Documents of United States Indian Policy,* 148.

21. Petition left by the Indians of the Colville Reservation with the President of the United States, February 10, 1912, and forwarded to the Secretary of the Interior, February 17, 1912. Quote from p. 2 of petition.

22. Ibid., 3.

23. Response to the Colville petition by C. F. Hauke, Second Assistant Commissioner of Indian Affairs, March 17, 1912, 3-4.

24. L. Meriam, *The Problem of Indian Administration* (No. 17) (Johnson Reprint Corp., 1928),

25. Ibid., 16.

26. Ibid., 51.

27. Richard Henry Pratt, *Battlefield and Classroom: Four Decades with the American Indian, 1867–1904* (Norman, University of Oklahoma Press,1964).

28. Bob Thomas, "The Tap Roots of Peoplehood," *Getting to the Heart of the Matter: Collected Letters and Papers,* ed. Daphne J Anderson (Vancouver, BC: Native Ministries Consortium, 1990).

29. *Pawnee*: "Minutes to Meeting Held at Pawnee, Oklahoma, October 18, 1934" (Folder 78, Box 9, Subject Series, Collection of the Hon. Elmer Thomas, Carl Albert Congressional Center Archives, University of Oklahoma, Norman, Oklahoma), 32; *Miami*: "Minutes to Meeting Held at Miami, Oklahoma, October 16, 1934" (Folder 76, Box 9, Subject Series, Collection of the Hon. Elmer Thomas, Carl Albert Congressional Center Archives, University of Oklahoma, Norman, Oklahoma) 33; *Anadarko*: "Minutes to Meeting Held at Anadarko, Oklahoma, October 23, 1934" (Folder 75, Box 9, Subject Series, Collection of the Hon. Elmer Thomas, Carl Albert Congressional Center Archives, University of Oklahoma, Norman, Oklahoma), 24.

30. Although widely attributed to Twain, to date there is no record throughout his letters, speeches, or written works that Twain ever made this observation.

31. Vine Deloria, Jr. and Clifford Lytle, *The Nations Within: the Past and Future of American Indian Sovereignty* (New York: Pantheon Books, 1984).

32. Alysa Landry, "Today in Native History: Ronald Reagan Says, 'We Should Not Have Humored [Natives],'" (https://indiancountrymedianetwork.com/history/events/today-native-history-ronald-reagan-says-not-humored-natives/, May 31, 2017).

Chapter 4

1. Benjamin Franklin Letter to Josiah Quincy, September 11, 1773.

2. Franklin Delano Roosevelt Inaugural Address, March 1933 (Franklin Delano Roosevelt American Presidential Papers).

3. David J. Weber, *The Spanish Frontier in North America* (New Haven, CT: Yale University Press), 6.

4. Henry Clay, speech, November 13, 1847, Lexington, Kentucky.

5. Philip Burgess and Michael Kelly, *Profile of Western North America: Indicators of an Emerging Continental Market* (Golden, CO: North American Press, 1995), 230; US Census Bureau, 2010, https://census.gov.

6. Burgess and Kelly, *Profile of Western North America*.

Chapter 5

1. Blaise Pascal, *Pensées*, Pt. 1, Art. X, No 38.

2. Alexis de Tocqueville, *Democracy in America* (2 vols.) (Folio Society Edition 1835, 1840), reprint (New York: Library of America, 2004), 53, 21, 268, 361, 639, 487.

3. Kevin Baker, *America the Ingenious: How a Nation of Dreamers, Immigrants, and Tinkerers Changed the World* (New York: Articus Books, 2016), 9–11.

4. Library of Congress, *Primary Documents in American History.* One hundred and sixty acres to qualified individuals to build a residence and live there for five years. The only cost was a filing fee. If the settler was willing to pay $1.25 an acre, he could obtain title in six months.

5. Calculations from 1900 and 1940 US Census Reports, https://census.gov.

6. Ibid.

Chapter 6

1. Alexis de Tocqueville, *Democracy in America* (2 vols.) (Folio Society Edition 1835, 1840), reprint (New York: Library of America, 2004), 269.

2. Oscar Handlin, *The Americans* (Boston: Little, Brown, 1963).

3. Homestead Act, May 20, 1862, Documents in History (Washington, DC: Library of Congress).

4. Bernard DeVoto, "The West Against Itself," *Harper's Magazine* (January 1947).

5. R. A. Mittermeier, C. G. Mittermeier, T. M. Brooks, et al., "Wilderness and Biodiversity Conservation," *Proceedings of the National Academy of Sciences*, vol. 100, no. 18, 10309–10313 (September 2003).

6. Figures from the *Engineering News* of 1912 show how bad the road situation was. *Engineering News*, vol. 67, no. 5 (February 1, 1912): 227.

7. Robert C. Baron, *Pioneers and Plodders: The American Entrepreneurial Spirit* (Golden, CO: Fulcrum Publishing, 2004).

8. Russell Bourne, *Rivers of America: Birthplaces of Culture, Commerce, and Community* (Golden, CO: Fulcrum Publishing, 1998).

9. US Census Reports, 2010, https://census.gov.

10. Ibid.

11. Charles Caleb Colton, *Lacon*, Reflections, vol. 1, No 269 (New York: E. Bliss and W. White, 1823).

12. De Tocqueville, *Democracy in America*, 269.

13. Calculations from 1900 and 1940 US Census Reports, https://census.gov.

14. US Census Reports 1870, 1880, 1890, https://census.gov.

15. Calculations from 1940 and 2010 US Census Reports, https://census.gov.

Chapter 7

1. Laura Woodworth-Ney, *Women in the American West* (Santa Barbara, CA: ABC-CLIO, 2008), 130.

2. Bill Hosokawa, *Nisei: The Quiet Americans* (Boulder: University of Colorado Press, 1969), 90–91.

3. Virginia Scharff, "Women of the West," the Gilder Lehrman Institute of American History, https://www.gilderlehrman.org/history-by-era/development-west/essays/women-west, accessed September 2016.

4. Sandra L. Myres, *Westering Women and the Frontier Experience, 1800–1950* (Albuquerque: University of New Mexico Press, 1982), 158.

5. Quintard Taylor and Shirley Ann Wilson Moore, *African American Women Confront the West, 1600–2000* (Norman: University of Oklahoma Press), 3; Elsa Barkley Brown, "'What Has Happened Here': The Politics of Difference in Women's History and Feminist Politics," *Feminist Studies* 18 (Summer 1992): 295–312.

6. Myres, *Westering Women*, 247; Originally from Helena Gillespie, "A Dress to Make," in Sam H. Dixon, *The Poets and Poetry of Texas* (Austin, 1855, quoted in Betty Sue Flowers, "'The Crosswise Bar': Women Poets of Texas, 1836-1936," unpublished ms., Austin, TX).

7. Virginia Scharff and Carolyn Brucken, *Home Lands: How Women Made the West* Berkeley: University of California Press, 2010), 2–3.

8. Wilma Mankiller, *Every Day Is a Good Day: Reflections by Contemporary Indigenous Women* (Golden, CO: Fulcrum Publishing, 2011), 14.

9. Ibid., 8.

10. Ramona Ford, "Native American Women: Changing Statuses, Changing Interpretations," in *Writing the Range: Race, Class and Culture in the Women's West*, ed. Elizabeth Jameson and Susan Armitage (Norman: University of Oklahoma Press, 1997), 51–52.

11. Mankiller, *Every Day is a Good Day*, 117.

12. Maria Raquel Casas, "Women and the Myth of the American West," Zócalo Public Square, http://time.com/3662361/women-american-west/, accessed September 2016..

13. Ford, "Native American Women," 50 and citations in notes 19, 20, and 21.

14. Ford, "Native American Women," 58 and note 47.

15. Mankiller, *Every Day Is a Good Day*, 103.

16. "Women and the Myth of the American West," What It Means to Be American, http://www.whatitmeanstobeamerican.org/discussions/women-and-the-myth-of-the-american-west/, accessed September 2016.

17. Bonnie G. McEwan, "The Archaeology of Women in the Spanish New World," *Historical Archaeology*, 1991, vol. 25, no. 4 (1991): 33, accessed October 2016 at https://www.jstor.org/stable/25616127?seq=1#page_scan_tab_contents.

18. Ibid., 33

19. Orae Dominguez, "María Gertrudis Barceló," New Mexico History.org, newmexico history.org/people/maria-gertrudis-barcelo-dona-tules, accessed October 2016.

20. See Fray Angelico Chavez, "Dona Tules: Her Fame and Her Funeral," *El Palacio*, vol. 57 no. 8 (August 1950).

21. Era Bell Thompson, *American Daughter* (Saint Paul, MN: Historical Society, 1986).

22. Taylor and Moore, *African American Women Confront the West*, 7 and notes 13, 14.

23. Ibid., note 13.

24. Ibid., 11.

25. Ibid., 10.

26. Ibid., 3.

27. Anne M. Butler and Ona Siporin, *Uncommon Common Women: Ordinary Lives of the West* (Logan: Utah State University Press, 1996), 7.

28. Encyclopedia.com, "The Overland Trails," http://www.encyclopedia.com/history/united-states-and-canada/us-history/overland-trail.

29. Butler and Siporin, *Uncommon Common Women*, 7.

30. Susan Armitage and Elizabeth Jameson, *The Women's West* (Norman: University of Oklahoma Press, 1987), 145.

31. Ibid., 147.

32. Kathy Weiser, "Nellie Cashman—Pioneering the Mining Camps of the Old West," Legends of America, http://www.legendsofamerica.com/we-nelliecashman.html.

33. Quoted in Elizabeth Jameson, "Women as Workers, Women as Civilizers," in Armitage and Jameson, *The Women's West*, 154. The Canadian woman speaking is quoted from Linda Rasmussen, Lorna Rasmussen, Candace Savage, and Anne Wheeler, *A Harvest Yet to Reap*, interview with Hythe Anderson (Toronto: Women's Press, 1987) 142.

34. Gary Y. Okihiro, "Recentering Women," in *Margins and Mainstreams: Asians in American History and Culture* (Seattle: University of Washington Press, 2014), 77.

35. Ibid., 78.

36. "Beyond Stereotypes: Chinese Pioneer Women in the American West," in *Writing the Range: Race, Class and Culture in the Women's West*, ed. Elizabeth Jameson and Susan Armitage (Norman: University of Oklahoma Press, 1997), 259.

37. Antonia I. Casteñeda, "Women of Color and the Rewriting of Western History," in *Women and Gender in the American West*, ed. Mary Ann Irwin and James Brooks (Albuquerque: University of New Mexico Press, 2004), 85.

38. "Through Western Eyes: Discovering Chinese Women in America," in *A New Significance: Re-envisioning the History of the American West*, ed. Clyde Milner II (Cambridge, UK: Oxford University Press 1996), 165. Quote of interviewee from

Judy Yung, "The Social Awakening of Chinese American Women as Reported in Chung Sai Yat Po, 1900–1911," *Chinese America: History and Perspectives* (San Francisco, 1988).

39. Iris Chang, *The Chinese In America: a Narrative History*, reprint ed. (Penguin: 2004).

Chapter 8

1. Horace Greeley, *Dictionary of American History* (Farmington Hills, MI: The Gale Group). "Go West, Young Man, Go West" was an expression first used by John Babsone Lane Soule in the *Terre Haute Express* in 1851. It appealed to Horace Greeley, who rephrased it slightly in an editorial in the *New York Tribune* on July 13, 1865: "Go West, young man, and grow up with the country." When the phrase gained popularity, Greeley printed Soule's article to show the source of his inspiration. The phrase captured the imaginations of clerks, mechanics, and soldiers returning from the Civil War, many of whom moved west to take up a homestead.

2. Dwight D. Eisenhower, 1953–1961, 22—address recorded for the Republican Lincoln Day Dinner, January 28, 1954, http://www.presidency.ucsb.edu/ws/?pid=10008.

3. Elliott West, The *Contested Plains: Indians, Goldseekers, and the Rush to Colorado* (Lawrence: University Press of Kansas, 1998), 324.

4. Richard Hofstadter, *The American Political Tradition and the Men Who Made It* (New York: A. A. Knopf, 1948), viii.

5. Ibid., 191.

6. James Chace, *1912: Wilson, Roosevelt, Taft & Debs—the Election That Changed the Country* (New York: Simon & Schuster, 2004), 83.

7. Patricia Nelson Limerick, *The Legacy of Conquest: The Unbroken Past of the American West* (New York, W. W. Norton, 1987), 61.

8. Ibid., 152.

9. Ibid., 82

10. Clyde Milner, Carol O'Connor, and Martha Sandweiss, eds., *The Oxford History of the American West* (New York: Oxford University Press, 1994), Chapter 14, 478.

11. Ibid., 477.

12. Mark Twain, *Adventures of Huckleberry Finn*, Chapter the Last. Quote taken from Limerick, *The Legacy of Conquest*, 291.

13. Limerick, *The Legacy of Conquest*, 291.

14. Ibid., 284.

15. Thomas Jefferson, First Inaugural Address, March 4, 1801, *The Papers of Thomas Jefferson, Volume 33: 17 February to 30 April 1801* (Princeton University Press, 2006), 148–152.

16. Frederick Jackson Turner, "The Significance of the Frontier in American History," (1893), https://www.wwnorton.com/college/history/archive/reader/trial/directory/1890_1914/ch21_frontier_thesis.htm.

17. Jon Grinspan, *The Virgin Vote: How Young Americans Made Democracy Social, Politics Personal, and Voting Popular in the Nineteenth Century* (Chapel Hill: University of North Carolina Press, 2016), 74.

18. Milner, O'Connor, and Sandweiss, eds., *The Oxford History of the American West*, 505.

19. Theodore Roosevelt, National Park Service, https://www.nps.gov/thro/learn/historyculture/theodore-roosevelt-and-conservation.htm.

20. The National Park Service Organic Act (16 U.S.C. l 2 3, and 4), as set forth herein, consists of the Act of Aug. 25 1916 (39 Stat. 535) and amendments thereto, paragraph one, https://www.nps.gov/grba/learn/management/organic-act-of-1916.htm.

21. US government spending compiled by Christopher Chantrill, usgovernment spending.com/federal_spending by_state.php.

22. George McGovern, *The Essential American: Our Founders and the Liberal Tradition* (New York, Simon & Schuster, 2004), 79, 81.

23. *Senator Goldwater Speaks Out on the Issues*, pamphlet (Washington, DC: Goldwater for President Committee), 24.

24. Barry Goldwater, *The Conscience of a Conservative* (Sheperdsville, KY: Victor, 1960) reprint (Princeton, NJ: Princeton University Press, 2007), xxii.

25. *Senator Goldwater Speaks Out on the Issues*.

26. Milner, O'Connor, and Sandweiss, eds., *The Oxford History of the American West*, 505.

Chapter 9

1. "New Madrid Earthquake Eyewitness 1," *The Virtual Times*, Huntsville Edition, http://hsv.com/earthquakes/new-madrid-quake/eyewitness-1/, March 22, 1816, accessed May 23, 2017.

2. Ibid.

3. Missouri Department of Natural Resources. "Facts about the New Madrid Seismic Zone," http://dnr.mo.gov/geology/geosrv/geores/techbulletin1.htm, accessed May 16, 2017.

4. "Mound City on the Mississippi, A St. Louis History," http://stlcin.missouri.org/history/decadesummary2.cfm, accessed May 9, 2017.

5. House Committee on Agriculture, "Committee History," http://agriculture.house.gov/about/committee-history.htm, accessed May 15, 2017.

6. R. A. Williams, N. S. McCallister, and R. L. Dart. "20 Cool Facts about the New Madrid Seismic Zone—Commemorating the Bicentennial of the New Madrid Earthquake Sequence, December 1811–February 1812" [poster] (2011). U.S. Geological Survey General Information Product 134.

7. US Department of Agriculture: Rural Development, "About RD," https://www.rd.usda.gov/about-rd, accessed May 15, 2017.

8. House Committee on Agriculture, "Committee History".

9. Barbara Allen Bogart, *In Place: Stories of Landscape & Identity from the American West* (Glendo, WY: High Plains Press, 1995), 18.

10. Craig Trout, Douglas County Historical Society, Genealogy.com, "Sedalia, Colorado History," http://www.genealogy.com/forum/regional/states/topics/co/douglas/26/, accessed May 17, 2017.

11. PBS, "Homes on the Prairie," http://www.pbs.org/ktca/farmhouses/homes_farmed.html, accessed May 17, 2017.

12. Jon Gjerde. *The Minds of the West: Ethnocultural Evolution in the Rural Middle West, 1830–1917* (Durham, NC: University of North Carolina Press,1997), 229.

13. "How the West Was Settled," National Archives, https://www.archives.gov/files/publications/prologue/2012/winter/homestead.pdf, accessed May 19, 2017.

14. U.S. Borax, Inc. SCV History Station, "Borax: The Twenty Mule Team," http://www.scvhistory.com/scvhistory/borax-20muleteam.htm, accessed May 19, 2017.

15. Society for California Archeology, "Homesteading Around Muroc," https://scahome.org/publications/proceedings/Proceedings.09Hudlow.pdf, accessed May 17, 2017.

16. The Statutes of Oklahoma: 1890, 514. https://books.google.com/books?id=mdJGAQAAMAAJ&pg=PA514&lpg=PA514&dq=logging+oklahoma+1890&source=bl&ots=fsXWCb9DKn&sig=wWSMEgcoie1ikKoBWpCVLeybbGo&hl=en&sa=X&ved=0ahUKEwifn9TX6fzTAhUO0mMKHbR4CWYQ6AEIIjAA#v=onepage&q=logging%20oklahoma%201890&f=false (accessed May 19, 2017).

17. Oklahoma Department of Agriculture, Food, and Forestry, "Oklahoma Forestry Code," Oklahoma Forestry Services, 11, http://www.forestry.ok.gov/timber-theftandarson, accessed May 19, 2017.

18. National Association of State Foresters, "Western Timber Industry Shows Improvement," (August 13, 2012), http://stateforesters.org/news-events/blog/western-timber-industry-shows-improvement#sthash.W1zEPVKT.dpbs, accessed May 20, 2017.

19. SodGod, "The History of the Tractor," http://www.sodgod.com/tractor-history, accessed May 20, 2017.

20. Wendell Berry, "What Are People For?" *Chicago Tribune*, May 30, 1985.

21. Ibid.

22. William R. Travis, *New Geographies of the American West: Land Use and the Changing Patterns of Place* (Washington, DC: Island Press, 2007), 15.

23. William R. Travis, David M. Theobald, Geneva W. Mixon, Thomas W. Dickinson, Report from the Center #6, *Western Futures: A Look into the Patterns of Land Use and Future, Development in the American West* (Boulder: Center of the American West, University of Colorado at Boulder: 2005), 11.

24. Linda M. Hasselstrom, Gaydell M. Collier, and Nancy Curtis, eds., *Leaning into the Wind*: Women Write from the Heart of the West (Boston: Houghton Mifflin, 1997).

25. Terrence McCoy, "Disabled, or Just Desperate? Rural Americans Turn to Disability as Jobs Dry Up," *The Washington Post*, March 30, 2017.

26. Jon Katz, *Bedlam Farm Journal*, March 30, 2017, www.bedlamfarm.com. Accessed May 23, 2017.

27. Patricia Limerick, William Travis, Tamar Scoggin, "Boom and Bust in the American West," (Boulder: Center of the American West, University of Colorado at Boulder).

28. Dawn Wink, "The Blizzard That Never Was—and its Aftermath on Cattle and Ranchers," Dewdrop, Oct. 8, 2013, https://dawnwink.wordpress.com/category/the-ranch/page/2/, accessed May 22, 2017.

29. Carrie Stadheim, "SD Ranchers Who Lost Their Whole Herd Due to TB, Rely on Faith, Family and Friends to Move Forward," *The Fencepost*, for Tri-State Livestock

News, http://www.thefencepost.com/news/sd-ranchers-who-lost-their-whole-herd-due-to-tb-rely-on-faith-family-and-friends-to-move-forward/, accessed September 28, 2017.

30. Jon Beilue, "Taken in Their Prime: Three Die Trying to Save Ranch from Texas Wildfires." *The Amarillo Globe News*, March 7, 2017.

31. Patty Limerick, faculty director and chair of the board, "A Letter from Patty," Center of the American West, http://www.centerwest.org/news/newsletter/2007/pattyletter.html, accessed May 22, 2017.

32. Farm Aid, "Corporate Control in Agriculture," https://www.farmaid.org/issues/corporate-power/corporate-power-in-ag/, accessed May 23, 2017.

Chapter 10

1. Lyndon Baines Johnson, "Remarks, Dinner for Gale McGee," LBJ Presidential Library, Speech Collection, July 13, 1963.

2. Ronald Reagan, "Message to the Congress Transmitting the Report of the Council on Environmental Quality," October 3, 1988. In *A Shining City*, ed. D. Erik Fallen (New York: Simon & Schuster, 1998).

3. Homestead Act, 1862, Documents in History (Washington, DC: Library of Congress).

4. Pacific Railroad Act, 1862, Documents in History (Washington, DC: Library of Congress).

5. Morrill Act, 1862, Documents in History (Washington, DC: Library of Congress).

6. US Census Bureau, 2000, https://census.gov.

7. *Times Higher Education World University Rankings*, https://www.timeshigher education.com/world-university-rankings; *US News and World Report* College Ranking, https://www.usnews.com/best-colleges; *US News and World Reports* College Endowments, https://www.usnews.com/topics/subjects/college_endowments.

8. Bruce Paton. *Lewis and Clark: Doctors in the Wilderness* (Golden, CO: Fulcrum Publishing, 2001).

9. Bruce Paton. *The Anatomy of Change: Department of Surgery, University of Colorado, 1950–2015* (Golden, CO: Fulcrum Publishing, 2015).

10. Bernard DeVoto, "The West Against Itself," *Harper's Magazine* (January 1947).

11. Robert C. Baron, *Pioneers and Plodders: The American Entrepreneurial Spirit* (Golden, CO: Fulcrum Publishing), 116.

12. Ibid., 6.

13. Ibid., 232–245.

14. Fortune 500 Companies, 2010 (*Fortune Magazine*, July 2010).

15. Baron, *Pioneers and Plodders*, 12.

16. US Census Bureau, 2010, https://census.gov.

17. Robert C. Baron, *Wilderness in America: From Conquest to Conservation* (Golden, CO: Films by Fulcrum, 2015), DVD, 54:11 minutes.

18. Edward Abbey, *Desert Solitaire*, chapters 4, 5 (New York: McGraw Hill), reprint (New York: Ballantine Books,1971).

Chapter 11

1. Thomas Fuller, *History of the Worthies* (London: T. Teig, 1840), ii, 125.
2. Walter Scott, *The Lay of the Last Minstrel*, Canto II, st. 22.
3. George Parker Winship, ed. and trans., *The Journey of Coronado, 1540–1542* (Golden, CO: Fulcrum Publishing, 1990), 200.
4. Bernard DeVoto, *The Journals of Lewis and Clark* (Boston: Houghton Mifflin, 1953), 92.
5. Ibid., 98.
6. Alexis de Tocqueville, *Democracy in America* (2 vols.) (Folio Society Edition 1835, 1840), reprint (New York: Library of America, 2004), 5.
7. James Silk Buckingham, *America Historical Statues and Description* (Harper & Brothers, 1841).
8. Maxine Benson, ed., *From Pittsburgh to the Rocky Mountains: Major Stephen Long's Expedition, 1819–1820* (Golden, CO: Fulcrum Publishing, 1988), 183.
9. Francis Parkman, *The Oregon Trail: Sketches of Prairie and Rocky-Mountain Life*, illustrated by Thomas Hart Benton (New York: Doubleday, 1946), 67.
10. Mark Twain, *Roughing It* (Hartford, CT: American Publishing Company), Chapter XX, 1.
11. John Wesley Powell, *Scribner's Magazine* (January, February, March 1845).
12. Joseph Campbell and Bill D. Moyers, *The Power of Myth* (New York: Anchor Books, 1988), 5.
13. Ibid., 151.
14. Richard Etulain and Glenda Murphy, *The Hollywood West: Lives of Film Legends Who Shaped It* (Golden, CO: Fulcrum, 2001).
15. Eleanor Gehres, *The Best American Novels of the Twentieth Century: Still Readable Today* (Golden, CO: Fulcrum 2001).

Chapter 12

1. Hal Borland, *High, Wide and Lonesome: Growing Up on the Colorado Frontier* (Philadelphia: Lippincott, 1956).

Illustration
Acknowledgments

cover   Moran, Thomas. *The Grand Canyon of the Yellowstone*. From 1893–1901. Smithsonian American Art Museum, Gift of George D. Pratt, Washington, D.C. https://commons.wikimedia.org/wiki/File:Thomas_Moran_-_Grand_Canyon_of_the_Yellowstone_-_Smithsonian.jpg.

2   Peale, Rembrandt. *Thomas Jefferson*. 1800. White House Historical Association, Washington, D.C. https://commons.wikimedia.org/wiki/File:Thomas_Jefferson_by_Rembrandt_Peale,_1800.jpg.

4   Waud, Alfred R. *Three Miles Above La Crosse*. In *Picturesque America, or The Land We Live In*, Vol. II. New York: D. Appleton and Co., 1874, p. 337.

11   Peale, Charles Willson. *Meriweather Lewis and William Clark, Side by Side*. Ca. 1807. https://commons.wikimedia.org/wiki/File:Lewis_and_Clark,_side_by_side.jpg.

17   Moran, Thomas. *Vernal Falls, Yosemite*. In *The Pacific Tourist: Adams and Bishop's Illustrated Trans-Continental Guide of Travel, from the Atlantic to the Pacific Ocean*. New York: Adams & Bishop, 1881. https://commons.wikimedia.org/wiki/File:The_Pacific_tourist_-_Adams_and_Bishop%27s_illustrated_trans-continental_guide_of_travel,_from_the_Atlantic_to_the_Pacific_Ocean_-_a_complete_traveler%27s_guide_of_the_Union_and_Central_Pacific_railroads_(14738425706).jpg.

21   Kirsh, Michael. *Pawnee Buttes Storm Clouds*. May 21, 2011. https://commons.wikimedia.org/wiki/File:Pawnee_Buttes_Storm_Clouds.jpg.

22   Smillie, James D. *Yosemite Fall*. In *Picturesque America, or The Land We Live In*, Vol. I. New York: D. Appleton and Co., 1874, p. 485.

23   Kurz, Louis, lithographer. *Buffaloes at Rest*. Ca. 1911. Library of Congress Prints and Photographs Division, Washington D.C. http://www.loc.gov/pictures/item/93506232/.

24   uxyso/Wikimedia Commons/CC-BY–SA-3.0. *Mesquite Flat Sand Dunes in the Morning, Death Valley*. September 14, 2013. https://commons.wikimedia.org/wiki/File:Mesquite_Flat_Sand_Dunes_Panorama_Morning_2013.jpg.

26   Wolcott, Marion Post. *Grazing Land and Grass on King Ranch. Laramie, Wyoming*. September 1941. Farm Security Administration/Office of War Information Black-and-White Negatives, Library of Congress Prints and Photographs Division, Washington, D.C. http://www.loc.gov/pictures/item/fsa2000040030/PP/.

27   Smillie, James D. *Big Trees—Mariposa Grove*. In *Picturesque America, or The Land We Live In*, Vol. I. New York: D. Appleton and Co., 1874, p. 466.

30   Longtin, Matt. *Vine DeLoria, Jr*. N.d. Courtesy of Fulcrum Publishing, Inc.

31   *Chief Ten Bears of the Tamparika Comanche.* Taken before 1872. https://commons.wikimedia.org/wiki/File:Ten_bears.jpg.

35   *John Ross of the Cherokee.* Nineteenth-century photograph. https://commons.wikimedia.org/wiki/File:John_Ross_of_the_Cherokee.jpg.

38   Grabill, John C. H. *U.S. School for Indians at Pine Ridge, S.D.* 1891. Grabill Collection, Library of Congress Prints and Photographs Division, Washington, D.C. http://www.loc.gov/pictures/item/99613795/.

40   Choate, J. N. *Tom Torlino, Navajo, Before and After.* Ca. 1882. Image courtesy of Richard Henry Pratt Papers, Beinecke Rare Book & Manuscript Library, Yale University, New Haven, Connecticut. https://commons.wikimedia.org/wiki/File:Tom_Torlino_Navajo_before_and_after_circa_1882.jpg.

48   *John Collier (May 4, 1884–May 8, 1968), Commissioner for the Bureau of Indian Affairs 1933-1945.* N.d. https://commons.wikimedia.org/wiki/File:John_Collier.png.

53   Menominee Tribal member, Ada Deer, 2007. Morris K. Udall Foundation. https://commons.wikimedia.org/wiki/file:Ada_Deer_1.jpg.

77   Johnston, Frances Benjamin. *Toll Gate on Winchester Pike, Virginia.* Ca. 1900 or 1901. Johnston (Frances Benjamin) Collection, Library of Congress Prints and Photographs Division, Washington, D.C. http://www.loc.gov/pictures/item/2008675925/.

80   Waud, Alfred R. *Red River, Dakota.* In *Picturesque America, or The Land We Live In, Vol. II.* New York: D. Appleton and Co., 1874, p. 538.

82   *Three Women and One Man Hoeing in Field.* Collection of W. E. B. DuBois. 1899 or 1900. African American Photographs Assembled for 1900 Paris Exposition, Library of Congress Prints and Photographs Division, Washington, D.C. http://www.loc.gov/pictures/item/91785649/.

84   *Evolution of the Sickle and Flail, 33-Horse Team Combined Harvester, Walla Walla, Washington.* 1902. Robert N. Dennis Collection of Stereoscopic Views, New York Public Library, New York, New York. https://commons.wikimedia.org/wiki/File:Evolution_of_the_sickle_and_flail,_33-horse_team_combined_harvester,_Walla_Walla,_Washington,_from_Robert_N._Dennis_collection_of_stereoscopic_views.png.

85   Kinsey, Darius. *Horses Hauling Spruce Log 30 Feet in Circumference.* 1905. Library of Congress Prints and Photographs Division, Washington, D.C. http://www.loc.gov/pictures/item/2004680475/.

87   Beard, Frank. *"Does not such a meeting make amends?"* May 29, 1869. Library of Congress Prints and Photographs Division, Washington, D.C. http://www.loc.gov/pictures/item/2002720304/.

90   Grabill, John C. H. *Giant Bluff. Elk Canyon on Black Hills and Ft. P. R.R.* 1890. Grabill Collection, Library of Congress Prints and Photographs Division, Washington, D.C. http://www.loc.gov/pictures/item/99613829/.

93   US Population density in 2006. NASA image by Robert Simmon, based on data archived by the Socioeconomic Data and Applications Center.

96   Grabill, John C. H. *Gold Dust. Placer Mining at Rockerville, Dak. Old Timers, Spriggs, Lamb and Dillon at Work.* 1889. Grabill Collection, Library of Con-

gress Prints and Photographs Division, Washington, D.C. http://www.loc. gov/pictures/item/99613953/.

99 Griffith and Turner Company. *1905 Griffith & Turner Co: Farm and Garden Supplies, (Page 149).* 1905. Henry G. Gilbert Nursery and Seed Trade Catalog Collection. https://commons.wikimedia.org/wiki/File:1905_Griffith_ and_Turner_Co_(Page_149)_BHL43830456.jpg.

103 U.S. Department of Agriculture. *Rural Electrification Administration (REA) Erects Telephone Lines in Rural Areas.* December 14, 2011. Photo courtesy of National Archives and Records Administration, Washington, D.C. https:// commons.wikimedia.org/wiki/File:20111110-OC-AMW-0030_-_Flickr_-_ USDAgov.jpg.

115 *Portrait of Biddy Mason (1818–1891), an African-American Los Angeles Pioneer Leader.* N.d. https://commons.wikimedia.org/wiki/File:Biddy_ Mason_(00026783).jpg.

115 *Esther Hobart Morris, the First Female Justice of the Peace in the United States.* Ca. 1902. Library of Congress Prints and Photographs Division, Washington, D.C. http://www.loc.gov/pictures/item/2002736583/.

115 *Susanna M. Salter (March 2, 1860–March 17, 1961), Mayor of Argonia, Kansas, and the First Woman Elected to Any Political Office in the United States.* 1887. Kansas Historical Society, Topeka, Kansas. https://commons.wikimedia. org/wiki/File:Susanna_Madora_Salter.jpg.

115 *Dr. Justina Ford.* Ca. 1910. https://commons.wikimedia.org/wiki/File: Justina_Ford.jpg.

115 *Jeanette Rankin, 1880–1973.* Ca. 1917. Library of Congress Prints and Photographs Division, Washington, D.C. http://www.loc.gov/pictures/ item/2003688488/.

115 Bain News Service. *Gov. Nellie T. Ross.* Ca. 1915–ca. 1920. Bain Collection, Library of Congress Prints and Photographs Division, Washington, D.C. http://www.loc.gov/pictures/item/ggb2006004938/.

115 *Hattie Caraway, First Elected Female U.S. Senator.* Before 1945. https://commons. wikimedia.org/wiki/File:Senator_hcaraway.jpg.

120 Curtis, Edward S. *A Navaho Smile.* Ca. 1904. Curtis (Edward S.) Collection, Library of Congress Prints and Photographs Division, Washington, D.C. http://www.loc.gov/pictures/item/97505182/.

124 *Portrait of a Californio Woman During the Gold Rush.* August 1, 1850. https:// commons.wikimedia.org/wiki/File:Californio_woman,_Gold_Rush.jpg.

128 *Mary Fields (c. 1832–1914), the First African-American Woman Employed as a Mail Carrier in the United States.* Ca. 1895. https://commons.wikimedia. org/wiki/File:Mary_Fields.jpg.

131 Ames, E. A. *Mormons at Mormon Dairy.* 1887–1889. National Archives and Records Administration, College Park, MD. https://commons.wikimedia. org/wiki/File:%22Mormons_at_Mormon_Dairy.%22_DESCR%3D_Two_ women_and_their_small_children_pose_before_a_building_at_what_is_ now_known_as_Morm_-_NARA_-_523552.jpg.

137 *Polly Bemis in Her Wedding Dress, 1894, Idaho.* 1894. https://commons. wikimedia.org/wiki/File:PollyBemis1894.jpg.

145   *William Jennings Bryan, Democratic Party Presidential Candidate.* Ca. October 3, 1896. Library of Congress Prints and Photographs Division, Washington, D.C. http://www.loc.gov/pictures/item/2001697076/.

152   Pach Brothers. *Theodore Roosevelt, Bust Portrait, Facing Front.* Ca. 1915. Library of Congress Prints and Photographs Division, Washington, D.C. http://www.loc.gov/pictures/item/2001696037/.

155   Trikosko, Marion S. *Interviews: Berry (i.e., Barry) Goldwater/MST.* September 25, 1962. Library of Congress Prints and Photographs Division, Washington, D.C. http://www.loc.gov/pictures/item/2009632121/.

155   *George McGovern.* Author photo. Courtesy of Fulcrum Publishing, Inc.

158   *Crossing the Platte, by Emigrant Train, in Old Overland Days.* In *The Pacific Tourist: Illustrated Trans-Continental Guide of Travel from the Atlantic to the Pacific Ocean.* New York: H. T. Williams, 1879. 40. https://commons. wikimedia.org/wiki/File:The_Pacific_tourist_(1879)_(14574624209).jpg.

161   Norton, Boyd E. *A Bison Pair Graze in the Short Grass Prairie.* Photo © and courtesy of Boyd Norton.

166   Norton, Boyd E. *Short Grass Prairie.* Photo © and courtesy of Boyd Norton.

169   Lange, Dorothea. *West Side of San Joaquin Valley, California. Caterpillar Diesel Type Tractor Is Common in California. Only Very Large-Scale Operations Can Afford This Type. Cultivating Potato-Fields.* February 1939. Farm Security Administration/Office of War Information Black-and-White Negatives, Library of Congress Prints and Photographs Division, Washington, D.C. http://www.loc.gov/pictures/item/2017771414/.

172   Alfred B. Campbell Art Co. *Ranch Family in 1900.* Ca. 1900. Library of Congress Prints and Photographs Division, Washington, D.C. http://www.loc. gov/pictures/item/2012649610/.

176   Chevsapher. *A Portion of Jeffrey City, Wyoming.* May 24, 2012. https:// commons.wikimedia.org/wiki/File:Jeffrey_City,_Wyoming_1.JPG.

179   NOAA George E. Marsh Album. *Dust Storm Approaching Stratford, Texas. Dust Bowl Surveying in Texas.* April 18, 1935. https://commons.wikimedia. org/wiki/File:Dust-storm-Texas-1935.png.

181   Grey, C. G. P. (http://www.cgpgrey.com). *Main Street America: Russell, Kansas.* August 7, 2009. https://commons.wikimedia.org/wiki/File:Main_ Street_America_Russell,_Kansas_4891612609.jpg.

184   Baker, Joseph E. *Abraham Lincoln.* Ca. 1865. Popular Graphic Arts Collection, Library of Congress Prints and Photographs Division, Washington, D.C. http://www.loc.gov/pictures/item/2006677686/.

187   Mayo Clinic and Foundation. *Exterior View of Early Office Shared by Mayo Brothers and Their Father.* N.d. https://commons.wikimedia.org/wiki/File: Mayo_Clinic_(2).jpg.

188   Lee, Russell. *Doctor and Nurse with Little Girl in Trailer-Clinic at the FSA (Farm Security Administration) Migratory Labor Camp Mobile Unit, Wilder, Idaho.* Farm Security Administration/Office of War Information Black-and-White Negatives, Library of Congress Prints and Photographs Division, Washington, D.C. http://www.loc.gov/pictures/item/2017789428/.

192 Calrosl. *The HP Garage in Palo Alto Where William Hewlett and David Pack-ard Started the Hewlett Packard Company.* April 11, 2009. https://commons. wikimedia.org/wiki/File:The_HP_garage_in_Palo_Alto,_California,_ April_2009.jpg.

200 Bierstadt, Albert. *A Storm in the Rocky Mountains, Mt. Rosalie.* 1866. Brooklyn Museum, New York, New York. https://commons.wikimedia.org/ wiki/File:Albert_Bierstadt_-_A_Storm_in_the_Rocky_Mountains,_Mt._ Rosalie_-_Google_Art_Project.jpg.

200 Hill, Thomas. *Yosemite Valley.* Ca. 1861–ca. 1897. Boston Public Library, Boston, Massachusetts. https://commons.wikimedia.org/wiki/File: Yosemite_Valley_by_Boston_Public_Library.jpg.

201 Moran, Thomas. *The Three Tetons.* 1895. The White House, Washington, D.C. https://commons.wikimedia.org/wiki/File:Thomas_Moran_-_The Three_ Tetons.jpg.

201 O'Sullivan, Timothy H. *Ancient Ruins in the Cañon de Chelle, New Mexico.* 1873. Getty Center, Los Angeles, California. https://commons.wikimedia. org/wiki/File:Timothy_H._O%27Sullivan_(American_-_Ancient_Ruins_ in_the_Ca%C3%B1on_de_Chelle,_New_Mexico_-_Google_Art_Project.jpg.

202 Russell, Charles Marion. *Buccaroos.* 1902. Library of Congress, Washington, D.C. https://commons.wikimedia.org/wiki/File:Charles_Marion_ Russell_-_Buccaroos_(1902).png.

202 Curtis, Edward S. *Navaho Child.* Ca. 1905. Curtis (Edward S.) Collection, Library of Congress Prints and Photographs Division, Washington, D.C. http://www.loc.gov/pictures/item/94514093/.

203 *Buffalo Bill's Wild West Show and Congress of Rough Riders of the World.* Ca. 1899. Library of Congress Prints and Photographs Division, Washington, D.C. http://www.loc.gov/pictures/item/97503242/.

204 *The Virginian, by Owen Wister, Book Cover.* 1902. https://commons.wikimedia. org/wiki/File:The_Virginian_1902.jpg.

204 *Riders of the Purple Sage, by Zane Grey, Book Cover.* 1912. https://commons. wikimedia.org/wiki/File:Riders_of_the_Purple_Sage_by_Zane_Grey,_ Harper_and_Brothers_publisher,_1912,_book_cover_-_Harry_Ransom_ Center_-_University_of_Texas_at_Austin_-_DSC08536.jpg.

204 *My Antonia, by Willa Cather, Book Cover.* 1918. https://commons. wikimedia.org/wiki/File:My_Antonia_by_Willa_Cather,_Houghton-Mifflin_ publisher,_1918,_book_cover_-_Harry_Ransom_Center_-_University_of_ Texas_at_Austin_-_DSC08529.jpg.

214 Highsmith, Carol. *Road to Distant Mountains in Jackson County, Colorado.* May 14, 2016. Highsmith (Carol M.) Archive, Library of Congress Prints and Photographs Division, Washington, D.C. http://www.loc.gov/pictures/ item/2017687478/.

Bibliography

Chapter 1. Thomas Jefferson and the West

By Jefferson

Gilreath, James, and Douglas L. Wilson, eds. *Thomas Jefferson's Library: A Catalog with the Entries in His Own Order*. Washington, DC: Library of Congress, 1989.

Jefferson, Thomas. *The Papers of Thomas Jefferson*. Edited by Julian P. Boyd et al. (42 vols. to date). Princeton, NJ: Princeton University Press, 1950.

Jefferson, Thomas. *The Papers of Thomas Jefferson: Retirement Series*. Edited by J. Jefferson Looney (13 vols. to date). Princeton, NJ: Princeton University Press, 2004.

Jefferson, Thomas. *The Family Letters of Thomas Jefferson*. Edited by Edwin Morris Betts and James A. Bear, Jr. Columbia: University of Missouri Press, 1966.

Jefferson, Thomas. *Writings*. Edited by Merrill D. Peterson. The Library of America Series, Book 17. New York: Library of America, 1984.

Jefferson, Thomas. *Notes on the State of Virginia*. London: John Stockdale, 1787. Reprint. Edited by William Peden. Chapel Hill: University of North Carolina Press, 1955.

Jefferson, Thomas. *Jefferson's Memorandum Books: Accounts, with Legal Records and Miscellany, 1767–1826*. Edited by James A. Bear and Lucia C. Stanton. The Papers of Thomas Jefferson. Second Series. Princeton, NJ: Princeton University Press, 1997.

Jefferson, Thomas. *Thomas Jefferson: The Garden and Farm Books*. Edited by Robert C. Baron. Golden, CO: Fulcrum Publishing, 1987.

Jefferson, Thomas, John Adams, and Abigail Adams. *The Adams–Jefferson Letters: The Complete Correspondence between Thomas Jefferson and Abigail and John Adams*. Edited by Lester J. Cappon. Chapel Hill: Published for the Institute of Early American History and Culture at Williamsburg, Virginia, by the University of North Carolina Press, 1988.

Jefferson, Thomas. *The Writings of Thomas Jefferson: Containing His Autobiography, Notes on Virginia, Parliamentary Manual, Official Papers, Messages and Addresses, and Other Writings, Official and Private, Now Collected and Published in Their Entirety for the First Time Including All of the*

Original Manuscripts, Deposited in the Department of State and Published in 1853 by Order of the Joint Committee of Congress with Numerous Illustrations and a Comprehensive Analytical Index. Edited by Andrew Adgate Lipscomb and Albert Ellery Bergh. Library ed. (20 vols.). Washington, DC: Thomas Jefferson Memorial Association, 1903.

Lewis and Clark Expedition. *Letters of the Lewis and Clark Expedition, with Related Documents, 1783–1854.* Edited by Donald Jackson. Urbana: University of Illinois Press, 1962.

Madison, James, and Thomas Jefferson. *The Tour to the Northern Lakes of James Madison & Thomas Jefferson, May–June 1791: A Facsimile Edition of Their Travel Journals.* Edited by J. Robert Maguire. Ticonderoga, NY: Fort Ticonderoga, 1995.

Sowerby, E. Millicent, ed. *Catalogue of the Library of Thomas Jefferson* (5 vols.). Washington, DC: Library of Congress, 1952–1959.

Books about Jefferson

Ambrose, Stephen. *Undaunted Courage: Meriwether Lewis, Thomas Jefferson, and the Opening of the American West.* New York: Simon & Schuster, 1996.

Ambrose, Stephen E., and Sam Abell. *Lewis & Clark: Voyage of Discovery.* Washington, DC: National Geographic Society, 1998.

Baron, Robert C., and Conrad Edrick Wright, eds. *The Libraries, Leadership and Legacy of John Adams and Thomas Jefferson.* Golden, CO: Fulcrum Publishing, and Boston: Massachusetts Historical Society, 2010.

Benson, Maxine, ed. *From Pittsburgh to the Rocky Mountains: Major Stephen Long's Expedition, 1819–1820.* Golden, CO: Fulcrum Publishing, 1988.

Cogliano, Francis D. *Emperor of Liberty: Thomas Jefferson's Foreign Policy.* New Haven, CT: Yale University Press, 2014.

Conant, James B. *Thomas Jefferson and the Development of American Public Education.* Berkeley: University of California Press, 1962.

Fenster, Julie M. *Jefferson's America: The President, the Purchase, and the Explorers Who Transformed a Nation.* New York: Crown, 2016.

Gordon Reed, Annette, and Peter S. Onuf. *"Most Blessed of the Patriarchs": Thomas Jefferson and the Empire of the Imagination.* New York: Liveright, 2016.

Hatch, Peter J. *A Rich Spot of Earth: Thomas Jefferson's Revolutionary Garden at Monticello.* New Haven, CT: Yale University Press, 2012.

Honeywell, Roy J. *The Educational Work of Thomas Jefferson.* Cambridge, MA: Harvard University Press, 1931.

Jackson, Donald. *Thomas Jefferson & the Stony Mountains: Exploring the West from Monticello*. Urbana: University of Illinois Press, 1981.

Jefferson, Thomas. *Thomas Jefferson in His Own Words*. Edited by Robert C. Baron. Published with the Library of Congress. Golden, CO: Fulcrum Publishing, 2009.

Kukla, Jon. *A Wilderness So Immense: The Louisiana Purchase and the Destiny of America*. New York: A. A. Knopf, 2003.

Lavender, David. *The Way to the Western Sea: Lewis & Clark across the Continent*. New York: Harper & Row, 1988.

Malone, Dumas. *Jefferson and His Time* (6 vols.). Boston: Little, Brown, 1948–1981.

Onuf, Peter S. *Jeffersonian Legacies*. Charlottesville: University of Virginia Press, 1993.

Peterson, Merrill D. "The American Scholar: Emerson and Jefferson." In *Thomas Jefferson and the World of Books: A Symposium Held at the Library of Congress, September 21, 1976*. Washington, DC: Library of Congress, 1977.

Peterson, Merrill D. *Thomas Jefferson and the New Nation: A Biography*. New York: Oxford University Press, 1970.

Reveal, James L. *Gentle Conquest: The Botanical Discovery of North America*. Washington, DC, and Golden, CO: Starwood/Fulcrum Publishing, 1992.

Ronda, James P., and Missouri Historical Society. *Thomas Jefferson and the Changing West: From Conquest to Conservation*. Albuquerque: University of New Mexico Press, 1997.

Van der Linden, Frank. *The Turning Point: Jefferson's Battle for the Presidency*. Golden, CO: Fulcrum Publishing, 2000.

Chapter 2. The Land

Abbey, Edward. *Desert Solitaire: A Season in the Wilderness*. New York: McGraw-Hill, 1968.

Baron, Robert C. *Wilderness in America: From Conquest to Conservation*. Golden, CO: Films by Fulcrum, 2015. DVD, 54:11 minutes.

Barsness, Larry. "Buffalo." *American Heritage* 30, no. 6 (October/November 1979): 22–27.

Bartram, William, and James Trenchard. *Travels through North & South Carolina, Georgia, East & West Florida, the Cherokee Country, the Extensive Territories of the Muscogulges, or Creek Confederacy, and the Country of the Chactaws: Containing, an Account of the Soil and Natural Productions* of Those Regions, Together with Observations on the Manners of the Indians: Embellished with Copper-Plates. Philadelphia: Printed by James & Johnson, 1791.

Bourne, Russell. Rivers of America: Birthplaces of Culture, Commerce, and Community. Golden, CO: Fulcrum Publishing, 1998.

Bryant, William Cullen, and Oliver Bell Bunce. Picturesque America, or, the Land We Live in: A Delineation by Pen and Pencil of the Mountains, Rivers, Lakes, Forests, Water-Falls, Shores, Cañons, Valleys, Cities, and Other Picturesque Features of Our Country (2 vols.) New York: D. Appleton, 1872–1874.

Ehrlich, Gretel. The Solace of Open Spaces. New York: Viking, 1985.

Green, Daniel. To Colonize Eden: Land and Jeffersonian Democracy. London: Gordon & Cremonest, 1977.

Lavender, David Sievert. The American Heritage History of the Great West. New York: American Heritage, 1965.

Muir, John. The Mountains of California. New York: Century, 1894.

Murray, William Cotter. "Grass." American Heritage 19, no. 2 (April 1968): 30–47.

Nobles, Gregory H. John Jacob Audubon: The Nature of the American Woodsman. Philadelphia: University of Pennsylvania Press. 2017.

Reveal, James L. Gentle Conquest: The Botanical Discovery of North America. Washington, DC, and Golden, CO: Starwood/Fulcrum Publishing. 1992.

Russell, Howard S. A Long, Deep Furrow: Three Centuries of Farming in New England. Hanover, NH: University Press of New England, 1976.

Stegner, Wallace. "By Chaos Out of Dream." American Heritage 32, no. 2 (February/March 1981): 4–13.

Utley, Robert M. A Life Wild and Perilous: Mountain Men and the Paths to the Pacific. New York: Henry Holt, 1997.

Williams, Terry Tempest. Refuge: An Unnatural History of Family and Place. New York: Pantheon Books, 1991.

Chapter 3. Native Americans

Akwe:kon Press and National Museum of the American Indian. Native American Expressive Culture. Originally published as Vol. XI, nos. 3–4, of Akwe:kon Journal. Golden, CO: Fulcrum Publishing, 1994.

Barreiro, José, and Tim Johnson. America Is Indian Country: Opinions and Perspectives from Indian Country Today. Golden, CO: Fulcrum Publishing, 2005.

Borland, Hall. *Where the Legends Die*. Philadelphia: Lippincott, 1963.

Brown, Dee. *Bury My Heart at Wounded Knee*. New York: Holt, Rinehart and Winston, 1971.

Bruchac, Joseph. *Our Stories Remember: American Indian History, Culture, and Values through Storytelling*. Golden, CO: Fulcrum Publishing, 2003.

Catlin, George. *Native American Indian Portfolio*. New York: James Ackerman, 1845.

Cutter, Donald. *The Protector de Indios in Colonial New Mexico*. Albuquerque: University of New Mexico Press, 1986.

Dejong, David H. *Promises of the Past: History of Indian Education*. Golden, CO: North American Press, 1993.

Deloria, Vine, Jr. *Custer Died for Your Sins*. Norman: University of Oklahoma Press, 1988.

Deloria, Vine, Jr. *God Is Red: A Native View of Religion*, 30th anniversary ed. Golden, CO: Fulcrum Publishing, 2003.

Deloria, Vine, Jr., and Clifford M. Lytle. *The Nations Within: The Past and Future of American Indian Sovereignty*. New York: Pantheon Books, 1984.

Deloria, Vine, Jr., and Daniel R. Wildcat. *Power and Place: Indian Education in America*. Golden, CO: Fulcrum Publishing, 2001.

Deloria, Vine Jr. *Indians of the Americas*. New York: Doubleday. Reprint. Golden, CO: Fulcrum Publishing, 2013.

Echo-Hawk, Walter R. *In the Courts of the Conqueror*. Golden, CO: Fulcrum Publishing, 2010.

Echo-Hawk, Walter R. *In the Light of Justice: The Rise of Human Rights in Native America and the United Nations Declaration on the Rights of Indigenous Peoples*. Golden, CO: Fulcrum Publishing, 2013.

Etulain, Richard W., and Glenda Riley, eds. *Chiefs & Generals: Nine Men Who Shaped the American West*. Notable Westerners Series. Golden, CO: Fulcrum Publishing, 2004.

Harvey, Karen D., and Lisa D. Harjo. *A History of Native People in America*. Golden, CO: North American Press, 1994.

Hill, Norbert. *Words of Power*. Golden, CO: Fulcrum Publishing, 1994.

Josephy, Alvin M. *The Indian Heritage of America*. New York: Knopf, 1968.

Mankiller, Wilma. *Every Day Is a Good Day: Reflections by Contemporary Indigenous Women*. Golden, CO: Fulcrum Publishing, 2004.

Marshall, Joseph. *Crazy Horse Weeps*. Golden, CO: Fulcrum Publishing, in press.

Matheson, Peter. *In the Spirit of Crazy Horse*. New York: Viking Press, 1963.

Momaday, N. Scott. *House Made of Dawn*. New York: Harper & Row, 1968.

Prucha, Francis Paul, ed. *Documents of United States Indian Policy*. Lincoln: University of Nebraska Press, 1975.

Ratterson, Kathleen, and Norbert Hill, eds. *The Great Vanishing Act: Blood Quantum and the Future of Native Nations*. Golden, CO: Fulcrum Publishing, 2017.

Standing Bear, Luther. *Land of the Spotted Eagle*. Lincoln: University of Nebraska Press, 1978.

Utley, Robert M. *The Indian Frontier of the American West 1846–1890*. Albuquerque: University of New Mexico Press, 1984.

Viola, Herman J. *After Columbus: The Smithsonian Chronicle of the North American Indians*. Washington, DC: Smithsonian Books, 1990.

Waters, Frank, and Oswald White Bear Fredericks. *Book of the Hopi*. New York: Viking Press. 1965.

Chapter 4. Changing Boundaries

Anderson, Fred, and Andrew R. L Cayton. "Santa Ana's Honor." In *The Dominion of War: Empire and Liberty in North America, 1500–2000* (chapter 6). New York: Viking, 2005.

Bogart, Barbara Allen. *In Place: Stories of Landscape and Identity from the American West*. Glendo, WY: High Plains Press, 1995.

Bolton, Herbert Eugene. *The Spanish Borderlands: A Chronicle of Old Florida and the Southwest*. New Haven, CT: Yale University Press, 1921.

Brown, Robert Craig, ed. *The Illustrated History of Canada*, rev. ed. Toronto: Key Porter Books, 2000.

Burgess, Philip M., and Michael Kelly. *Profile of Western North America: Indicators of an Emerging Continental Market*. Golden, CO: North American Press, 1995.

Carter, Hodding. *Doomed Road of Empire: The Spanish Trail of Conquest*. New York: McGraw-Hill, 1963.

Chapman, Donald E. *Spanish Texas, 1519–1821*. Austin: University of Texas Press, 1992.

Chavez, Thomas E. *An Illustrated History of New Mexico*. Boulder: University Press of Colorado, 1992.

Eagle, John A. *The Canadian Pacific Railway and the Development of Western Canada, 1896–1914*. Kingston, ON: McGill-Queen's University Press, 1989.

Eisenhower, John S. D. *So Far from God: The U.S. War with Mexico, 1846–1848*. New York: Anchor, 1990.

Foster, Lynn V. *A Brief History of Mexico*, rev. ed. New York: Checkmark Books, 2004.

García, Mario T. *Mexican Americans: Leadership, Ideology, & Identity, 1930–1960*. Yale Western Americana Series, 36. New Haven, CT: Yale University Press, 1989.

Goetzmann, William H., and William N. Goetzmann. *The West of the Imagination*. New York: W. W. Norton, 1986.

Friesen, Gerald. *The Canadian Prairies: A History*. Toronto: University of Toronto Press, 1984.

Hall, Basil. *Travels in North America, in the Years 1827 and 1828*. Vol. 1–2. Philadelphia: Carey, Lea and Carey, 1829.

Hanbury-Tenison, Robin. *The Great Explorers*. London: Thames & Hudson, 2010.

Kanellos, Nicolás. *Thirty Million Strong: Reclaiming the Hispanic Image in American Culture*. Golden, CO: Fulcrum Publishing, 1998.

Krauze, Enrique. *Mexico: Biography of Power: A History of Modern Mexico, 1810–1996*. New York: HarperCollins, 1998.

Lavender, David Sievert. *Bent's Fort: A Historical Account of the Adobe Empire That Shaped the Destiny of the American Southwest*. Garden City, NY: Doubleday, 1954.

Lopez, Enrique Hank. "Mexico." *American Heritage* 20, no. 3 (April 1969): 4–8.

Maclennan, Hugh. "Canada." *American Heritage* 17, no. 1 (December 1965): 6–45.

Parkman, Francis. *A Half-Century of Conflict: France and England in North America*, Part Sixth. Boston: Little, Brown, 1910.

Parkman, Francis. *The Oregon Trail: Sketches of Prairie and Rocky-Mountain Life*, 4th ed., rev. Boston: Little, Brown, 1872.

Paton, Bruce C. *Adventuring with Boldness: The Triumph of the Explorers*. Golden, CO: Fulcrum Publishing, 2006.

Ronda, James P. *Astoria & Empire*. Lincoln: University of Nebraska Press, 1990.

Ruiz, Ramón Eduardo. *Triumphs and Tragedies: A History of the Mexican People*. New York: W. W. Norton, 1992.

Smith, James K. *Wilderness of Fortune: The Story of Western Canada*. Vancouver, BC: Douglas & McIntyre, 1983.

Utley, Robert M. *A Life Wild and Perilous: Mountain Men and the Paths to the Pacific*. New York: Henry Holt, 1997.

Viola, Herman J. *Exploring the West*. Washington, DC: Smithsonian Books, 1987.

Weber, David J. *Myth and the History of the Spanish Southwest*. Albuquerque: University of New Mexico Press, 1988.

Weber, David J. *The Spanish Frontier in North America*. Yale Western Americana Series. New Haven, CT: Yale University Press, 1992.

Western Canadian Studies Conference, University of Calgary, and Anthony W. Rasporich. *Western Canada: Past and Present*. Calgary, AB: University of Calgary, 1975.

Chapter 5. Migration from the East

Act of May 20, 1862 (Homestead Act), Public Law 37-64, 05/20/1862; Record Group 11; General Records of the United States Government; National Archives. (Signed into law by President Abraham Lincoln.)

Andrist, Ralph K., and David Plowden. "The Erie Canal Passed This Way." *American Heritage* 19, no. 6 (October 1968): 22–31, 77–80.

Apps, Jerry. "From Wheat to Dairy Farming and More," *Wisconsin Magazine of History* 100, no. 4 (Summer 2017): 4–9.

Benson, Maxine, ed. *From Pittsburgh to the Rocky Mountains: Major Stephen Long's Expedition, 1819–1820*. Golden, CO: Fulcrum Publishing, 1988.

Billington, Ray Allen. *Westward Expansion: A History of the American Frontier*, 4th ed. New York: Macmillan, 1974.

Bogue, Allan G. *From Prairie to Corn Belt: Farming in the Illinois and Iowa Prairies in the Nineteenth Century*. Chicago: University of Chicago Press, 1963.

Bowles, Samuel, and Schuyler Colfax. *Across the Continent: A Summer's Journey to the Rocky Mountains, the Mormons, and the Pacific States, with Speaker Colfax*. Springfield, MA: S. Bowles & Co., 1866.

Catton, Bruce, and William B. Catton. *The Bold and Magnificent Dream: America's Founding Years, 1492–1815*. The Doubleday Basic History of the United States. Garden City, NY: Doubleday, 1978.

Churchill, Winston. *A History of the English-Speaking Peoples*, 4th ed. Vol. 4. The Great Democracies. London: Cassell, 1967.

Danborn, David. *Sod Busting: How Families Made Farms on the 19th-Century Plains*. Baltimore, MD: Johns Hopkins University Press, 2014.

DeVoto, Bernard Augustine. *Across the Wide Missouri*. Boston: Houghton Mifflin, 1947.

DeVoto, Bernard Augustine. *The Course of Empire*. Boston: Houghton Mifflin, 1952.

DeVoto, Bernard Augustine. *The Year of Decision, 1846*. Boston: Little, Brown, 1943.

Durham, Michael S. *Desert between the Mountains: Mormons, Miners, Padres, Mountain Men, and the Opening of the Great Basin, 1772–1869*. New York: Henry Holt, 1997.

Goetzmann, William H. *The Mountain Man*. Cody, WY: Buffalo Bill Historic Center, 1978.

Goetzmann, William H., and Glyndwr Williams. *The Atlas of North American Exploration: From the Norse Voyages to the Race to the Pole.* New York: Prentice Hall, 1992.

Handlin, Oscar. *The Americans: A New History of the People of the United States.* Boston: Little, Brown, 1963.

Hayden, F. V., Thomas Moran, and William Henry Jackson. *The Yellowstone National Park, and the Mountain Regions of Portions of Idaho, Nevada, Colorado and Utah.* Boston: L. Prang, 1876.

Heat-Moon, William Least. *PrairyErth: (a deep map).* Boston: Houghton Mifflin, 1991.

Jackson, Donald, ed. *The Journals of Zebulon Montgomery Pike.* Norman: University of Oklahoma Press, 1966.

Kaplan, Robert D. *Earning the Rockies: How Geography Shapes America's Role in the World.* New York: Random House, 2017.

Kirkpatrick, Frederick Alexander. *The Spanish Conquistadores.* London: Adam and Charles Black, 1946.

Kraenzel, Carl Frederick. *The Great Plains in Transition.* Norman: University of Oklahoma Press, 1955.

Lavender, David. *Westward Vision: The Story of the Oregon Trail.* New York: McGraw-Hill, 1963.

Limerick, Patricia Nelson. *The Legacy of Conquest: The Unbroken Past of the American West.* New York: W. W. Norton, 1987.

Merk, Frederick. *History of the Westward Movement.* New York: Knopf, 1978.

Morgan, Robert. *Lions of the West: Heroes and Villains of the Westward Expansion.* Chapel Hill, NC: Algonquin Books, 2011.

Morison, Samuel Eliot. *The Oxford History of the American People.* New York: Oxford University Press, 1965.

Neuberger, Richard L. "Bloody Trek to Empire." *American Heritage* 9, no. 5 (August 1958): 58–61.

Parkman, Francis. *The Oregon Trail: Sketches of Prairie and Rocky-Mountain Life*, 8th ed., rev. Boston: Little, Brown, 1892.

Remington, Frederic. *Western Types.* New York: Charles Scribner's, 1902.

Remini, Robert V. "Texas Must Be Ours." *American Heritage* 37, no. 2 (February/March 1986): 42–47.

Ronda, James P. *Beyond Lewis & Clark: The Army Explores the West.* Tacoma: Washington State Historical Society, 2003.

Roosevelt, Theodore. *Ranch Life and the Hunting Trail.* New York: Century, 1888.

Sandoz, Mari. *Love Song to the Plains.* New York: Harper & Row, 1961.

Stegner, Wallace. *Beyond the Hundredth Meridian: John Wesley Powell and the Second Opening of the West.* Boston: Houghton Mifflin, 1953.

Turner, Frederick Jackson. "The Significance of the Frontier in American History." Presentation to a special meeting of the American Historical Association in Chicago, IL, 1893.

Twain, Mark (Samuel L. Clemens). *Roughing It.* Hartford, CT: American Publishing Company, 1872.

Webb, Walter Prescott. *The Great Frontier.* Austin: University of Texas Press, 1964.

Webb, Walter Prescott. *The Great Plains.* Lincoln: University of Nebraska Press, 1981.

Weisberger, Bernard. "A Nation of Immigrants." *American Heritage* 45, no. 1 (February/March 1994): 75–91.

West, Elliott. *The Contested Plains: Indians, Goldseekers, and the Rush to Colorado.* Lawrence: University Press of Kansas, 1998.

Chapter 6. The Country Moves West

Ambrose, Stephen E. *Nothing Like It in the World: The Men Who Built the Transcontinental Railroad, 1863–1869.* New York: Simon & Schuster, 2000.

American Telephone and Telegraph Company. *1904 Annual Report of the Directors.* Boston: Alfred Mudge and Son, 1905.

Andrist, Ralph K., and David Plowden. "The Erie Canal Passed This Way." *American Heritage* 19, no. 6 (October 1968): 22–31, 77–80.

Bain, David Haward. *Empire Express: Building the First Transcontinental Railroad.* New York: Viking, 1999.

Baldwin, Leland D, and Western Pennsylvania Historical Survey. *The Keelboat Age on Western Waters.* Pittsburgh, PA: University of Pittsburgh Press, 1980.

Banta, Richard Elwell. *The Ohio.* Illustrated by Edward Shenton. The Rivers of America. New York: Rinehart, 1949.

Baron, Robert C. *America: One Land, One People: Noted Historians Look at America.* Golden, CO: Fulcrum Publishing. 1987.

Baron, Robert C. *Pioneers and Plodders: The American Entrepreneurial Spirit.* Golden, CO: Fulcrum Publishing, 2004.

Boorstin, Daniel J. *The Americans: The Democratic Experience.* New York: Random House, 1973.

Bourne, Russell. *Americans on the Move: A History of Waterways, Railways, and Highways.* With Illustrations from the Library of Congress. Golden, CO: Fulcrum Publishing, 1995.

Brooks, John. *Telephone: The First Hundred Years.* New York: Harper & Row, 1975.

Carter, Hodding. *Lower Mississippi*. Illustrated by John McCrady. The Rivers of America. New York: Farrar & Rinehart, 1942.

Chandler, Alfred D. *The Railroads: The Nation's First Big Business*. New York: Harcourt, Brace & World, 1965.

Commager, Henry Steele. *The Empire of Reason: How Europe Imagined and America Realized the Enlightenment*. New York: Oxford University Press, 1982.

Damon, Allan L. "A Look at the Record: The Facts Behind the Current Controversy Over Immigration." *American Heritage* 33, no. 1 (December 1981): 50–56.

Greeley, Horace. *An Overland Journey, from New York to San Francisco in the Summer of 1859*. New York: C. M. Saxton, Barker, 1860.

Havighurst, Walter, and Constance Lindsay Skinner. Illustrated by David and Lolita Granahan. *Upper Mississippi: A Wilderness Saga*. The Rivers of America. New York: Farrar & Rinehart, 1937.

Hawke, David Freeman. *Nuts and Bolts of the Past: A History of American Technology, 1776–1860*. New York: Harper & Row, 1988.

Hornung, Clarence P. *The Way It Was in the USA: The West*. New York: Abbeville Press, 1978.

Jensen, Oliver. *Railroads in America*. New York: American Heritage, 1975.

Kreck, Dick. *Hell on Wheels*. Golden, CO: Fulcrum Publishing, 2015.

Lamm, Richard D., and Michael McCarthy. *The Angry West: A Vulnerable Land and Its Future*. Boston: Houghton Mifflin, 1982.

Martin, Albro. *Railroads Triumphant: The Growth, Rejection, and Rebirth of a Vital American Force*. New York: Oxford University Press, 1992.

McCarthy, Joe. "The Lincoln Highway." *American Heritage* 25, no. 4 (June 1974): 32–37, 89.

Perry, John Curtis. *Facing West: Americans and the Opening of the Pacific*. Westport, CT: Praeger, 1994.

Reck, Franklin M. *The Romance of American Transportation*, rev. ed. New York: Thomas Y. Crowell, 1962.

Riegel, Robert Edgar. *The Story of the Western Railroads*. New York: Macmillan, 1926.

Sale, Kirkpatrick. *The Fire of His Greatness: Robert Fulton and the American Dream*. New York: Free Press, 2001.

Smith, Duane. *Rocky Mountain Mining Camps: The Urban Frontier*. Bloomington: Indiana University Press, 1967.

Smithsonian Institution. *The Smithsonian Book of Invention*. Washington, DC: Smithsonian Exposition Books, 1978.

Taylor, George Rogers. *The Transportation Revolution, 1815–1860*. The Economic History of the United States. Vol. 4. New York: Rinehart, 1951.

Tyler, Ron. *Prints of the West*. A Library of Congress Classic. Golden, CO: Fulcrum Publishing, 1994.

West, Elliott. *The Contested Plains: Indians, Goldseekers, and the Rush to Colorado*. Lawrence, University Press of Kansas, 1998.

White, John H. *Wet Britches and Muddy Boots: A History of Travel in Victorian America*. Railroads Past & Present. Bloomington: Indiana University Press, 2013.

White, Richard. *Railroaded: The Transcontinentals and the Making of Modern America*. New York: W. W. Norton, 2011.

Vestal, Stanley. *The Missouri*. Illustrated by Getlar Smith. The Rivers of America. New York: Farrar & Rinehart, 1945.

Chapter 7. Women of the West

Amer, Mildred L. *Women in Congress, 1917–2007*. New York: Novo Science, 2008.

Barkley Brown, Elsa. "'What Has Happened Here': The Politics of Difference in Women's History and Feminist Politics." *Feminist Studies* 18 (Summer 1992): 295–312.

Butler, Anne M., and Ona Siporin. *Uncommon Common Women: Ordinary Lives of the West*. Logan: Utah State University Press, 1996.

Cooper, Ilene. *A Woman in the House (and Senate): How Women Came to the United States Congress, Broke Down Barriers, and Changed the Country*. New York: Abrams Books for Young Readers, 2014.

Danneberg, Julie. *Women Icons of the West: Five Women Who Forged the American Frontier*. Golden, CO: Fulcrum Publishing, 2011.

Dichamp, Christiane Fischer. *Let Them Speak for Themselves: Women in the American West, 1849–1900*. New York: Dutton, 1978.

DuBois, Ellen Carol. *Women's Suffrage and Women's Rights*. New York: New York University Press, 1998.

Gallagher, Robert S. "'me For Ma—and I Ain't Got a Dern Thing Againts Pa.'" *American Heritage* 17, no. 6 (October 1966): 46–47, 104–105.

Hasselstrom, Linda M., Gaydell M. Collier, and Nancy Curtis, eds. *Leaning into the Wind: Women Write from the Heart of the West*. Boston: Houghton Mifflin, 1997.

Hollihan, Kerrie Logan. *Rightfully Ours: How Women Won the Vote, 21 Activities*. Chicago: Chicago Review Press, 2012.

Jameson, Elizabeth, and Susan H. Armitage. *Writing the Range: Race, Class, and Culture in the Women's West*. Norman: University of Oklahoma Press, 1997.

Leonard, Stephen J. "'Bristling for Their Rights'": Colorado's Women and the Mandate of 1893." *Colorado Heritage* (Spring 1993), 7–15.

Mankiller, Wilma. *Every Day Is a Good Day*. Memorial Edition. Golden, CO: Fulcrum Publishing, 2011.

Milner, Clyde A., and Allan G. Bogue. *A New Significance: Re-Envisioning the History of the American West*. New York: Oxford University Press, 1996.

Mulford, Karen. *Trailblazers: Twenty Amazing Western Women*. Great American Women Series. Flagstaff, AZ: Northland, 2001.

Myres, Sandra L. *Westering Women and the Frontier Experience, 1800–1915*. Histories of the American Frontier. Albuquerque: University of New Mexico Press, 1982.

Porter, Lavinia Honeyman. "By Ox Team to California". *In Westward Journeys: Memoirs of Jesse A. Applegate and Lavinia Honeyman Porter Who Traveled the Overland Trail*. The Lakeside Classics, 87. Chicago: Lakeside Press, 1989. Riley, Glenda. *Confronting Race: Women and Indians on the Frontier, 1815–1915*. Albuquerque: University of New Mexico Press. 2004.

Riley, Glenda, and Richard W. Etulain, eds. *Wild Women of the Old West*. Notable Westerners. Golden, CO: Fulcrum Publishing, 2003.

Scharff, Virginia. "Women of the West." The Gilder Lehrman Institute of American History, https://www.gilderlehrman.org/history-by-era/development-west/essays/women-west.

Scheer, Teva J. *Governor Lady: The Life and Times of Nellie Tayloe Ross*. Missouri Biography Series. Columbia: University of Missouri Press, 2005.

Smith, Norma. *Jeanette Rankin: America's Conscience*. Helena: Montana Historical Society Press, 2002.

Taylor, Quintard, and Shirley Ann Wilson Moore. *African American Women Confront the West: 1600–2000*. Norman: University of Oklahoma Press, 2003.

Travis, William R., David M. Theobald, Geneva W. Mixon, and Thomas W. Dickinson. Report from the Center #6, *Western Futures: A Look into the Patterns of Land Use and Future, Development in the American West*. Boulder: Center of the American West, University of Colorado at Boulder, 2005.

Woodworth-Ney, Laura. *Women in the American West*. Cultures in the American West. Santa Barbara, CA: ABC-CLIO, 2008.

Chapter 8. Political Leadership

Birzer, Bradley J. *Russell Kirk, American Conservative*. Lexington: University Press of Kentucky, 2015.

Chace, James. *1912: Wilson, Roosevelt, Taft & Debs—the Election That Changed the Country*. New York: Simon & Schuster, 2004.

Cross, Coy F. *Go West, Young Man! Horace Greeley's Vision for America*. Albuquerque: University of New Mexico Press, 1995.

Fenster, Julie M. *Jefferson's America: The President, the Purchase, and the Explorers Who Transformed a Nation*. New York: Crown, 2016.

Goldwater, Barry. *The Conscience of a Conservative*. Shepherdsville, KY: Victor, 1960. Reprint. Princeton, NJ: Princeton University Press 2007.

Grinspan, Jon. *The Virgin Vote: How Young Americans Made Democracy Social, Politics Personal, and Voting Popular in the Nineteenth Century*. Chapel Hill: University of North Carolina Press, 2016.

Hofstadter, Richard. *The American Political Tradition and the Men Who Made It*. Vintage Books. New York: A. A. Knopf, 1948.

Kirk, Russell. *The Conservative Mind, from Burke to Eliot*. Chicago: H. Regnery, 1960.

Koenig, Louis William. *Bryan: A Political Biography of William Jennings Bryan*. New York: Putnam, 1971.

Limerick, Patricia Nelson. *The Legacy of Conquest: The Unbroken Past of the American West*. New York: W. W. Norton, 1987.

McCarthy, Eugene J. *Parting Shots from My Brittle Bow: Reflections on American Politics and Life*. Speaker's Corner Books. Golden, CO: Fulcrum Publishing. 2004.

McGovern, George S. *The Essential America: Our Founders and the Liberal Tradition*. New York: Simon & Schuster, 2004.

Milner, Clyde, Carol O'Connor, and Martha Sandweiss, eds. *The Oxford History of the American West*. New York: Oxford University Press, 1994.

Nevins, Allan. *The Origins of the Land-Grant Colleges and State Universities: A Brief Account of the Morrill Act of 1862 and Its Results*. Washington, DC: Civil War Centennial Commission, 1962.

Norris, George William. *Fighting Liberal: The Autobiography of George W. Norris*. New York: Macmillan, 1945.

Reagan, Ronald. *Reagan, in His Own Hand: The Writings of Ronald Reagan That Reveal His Revolutionary Vision for America*. Edited by Kiron K. Skinner, Annelise Graebner Anderson, and Martin Anderson. New York: Free Press, 2001.

Thelen, David P. *Robert M. La Follette and the Insurgent Tradition*. Boston: Little, Brown, 1976.

West, Elliott. *Contested Plains: Indians, Goldseekers and the Rush to Colorado*. Lawrence: University Press of Kansas, 1998.

Chapter 9. The Rural West

Billington, Ray Allen. *America's Frontier Heritage.* New York: Holt, Rinehart and Winston, 1966.

Billington, Ray Allen. "How the Frontier Shaped the American Character." *American Heritage* 9, no. 3 (April 1958): 4, 7–9, 86–89.

Bogart, Barbara Allen. *In Place: Stories of Landscape & Identity from the American West.* Glendo, WY: High Plains Press, 1995.

Gjerde, Jon. *The Minds of the West: Ethnocultural Evolution in the Rural Middle West from 1830–1917.* Chapel Hill: The University of North Carolina Press, 1997.

Grinstead, Steve, and Ben Fogelberg, eds. *Western Voices: 125 Years of Western Writing.* Golden, CO: Fulcrum Publishing, 2004.

Hasselstrom, Linda. *Land Circle: Writings Collected from the Land.* Golden, CO: Fulcrum Publishing, 1991.

Hasselstrom, Linda, Gaydell Collier, and Nancy Curtis, eds. *Leaning into the Wind.* Boston: Houghton Mifflin, 1997.

"How the West Was Settled." National Archives, https://www.archives.gov/files/publications/prologue/2012/winter/homestead.pdf.

Lambert, Page. *In Search of Kinship: Modern Pioneering on the Western Landscape.* Golden, CO: Fulcrum Publishing. 1996.

Limerick, Patricia, William Travis, and Tamar Scroggin. *Boom and Bust in the American West.* Boulder: Center of American West, University of Colorado, 2002.

Travis, William R. *New Geographies of the American West: Land Use and the Changing Patterns of Place.* Washington, DC: Island Press, 2007.

Chapter 10. Education and Economic History

Abbey, Edward. *Desert Solitaire: A Season in the Wilderness.* New York: McGraw-Hill, 1968.

Act of July 2, 1862 (Morrill Act), Public Law 37-108, which established land grant colleges. Record Group 11; General Records of the United States Government; National Archives. (Signed into law by President Abraham Lincoln.)

Anschutz, Philip F., William Joseph Convery, and Thomas J. Noel. *Out Where the West Begins: Profiles, Visions, and Strategies of Early Western Business Leaders.* Denver, CO: Cloud Camp Press, 2015.

Baron, Robert C. *Pioneers and Plodders: The American Entrepreneurial System.* Golden, CO: Fulcrum Publishing, 2004.

Bolles, Albert Sidney. *Industrial History of the United States: From the Earliest*

Settlements to the Present Time: Being a Complete Survey of American Industries, Embracing Agriculture and Horticulture; Including the Cultivation of Cotton, Tobacco, Wheat; the Raising of Horses, Neat-Cattle, Etc.; Also a History of the Coal-Miners and the Molly Maguires; Banks, Insurance, and Commerce; Trade-Unions, Strikes, and Eight-Hour Movement; Together with a Description of Canadian Industries, 3rd ed. 1878. Norwich, CT: Henry Hill. Reprint of Economic Classics. New York: Augustus M. Kelley, 1966.

Boorstin, Daniel J. *The Discoverers*. New York: Random House, 1983.

Breeden, Robert L., ed. *Those Inventive Americans*. Washington, D.C.: National Geographic, 1971.

Brinkley, Douglas. *The Wilderness Warrior: Theodore Roosevelt and the Crusade for America*. New York: HarperCollins, 2009.

Brower, David, and Steve Chapple. *Let the Mountains Talk, Let the Rivers Run: A Call to Those Who Would Save the Earth*. San Francisco: HarperCollins West, 1995.

De Tocqueville, Alexis. *Democracy in America* (2 vols.). 1835, 1840. Reprint. New York: Library of America, 2004.

Groner, Alex. *The American Heritage History of American Business & Industry*. New York: American Heritage, 1972.

Lamm, Richard D, and Michael McCarthy. *The Angry West: A Vulnerable Land and Its Future*. Boston: Houghton Mifflin, 1982.

Leopold, Aldo, and Charles Walsh Schwartz. *A Sand County Almanac, and Sketches Here and There*. New York: Oxford University Press, 1949.

Locker, Thomas. *Thomas Locker's Visual Biographies*. Stories from *Walking with Henry, John Muir, Rachel Carson* and *Rembrandt and Titus*. Read by Judy Volc. Golden, CO: Films by Fulcrum, 2015. DVD, 22 minutes.

Mcclay, Wilfred M. "A Tent on the Porch." *American Heritage* 44, no. 4 (July/August 1993): 88–93.

McPhee, John. *Encounters with the Archdruid*. New York: Farrar, Straus and Giroux, 1971.

Morgan, Jane. *Electronics in the West: The First Fifty Years*. Palo Alto, CA: National Press Books, 1967.

Muir, John. *The Mountains of California*. New York: Century, 1894.

Nash, Roderick. *Wilderness and the American Mind*. New Haven, CT: Yale University Press, 1967.

Nevins, Allan. *The Origins of the Land-Grant Colleges and State Universities: A Brief Account of the Morrill Act of 1862 and Its Results*. Washington, DC: Civil War Centennial Commission, 1962.

Noel, Thomas J. *Riding High: Colorado Ranches and 100 Years of the Western Stock Show.* Golden, CO: Fulcrum Publishing, 2005.

Packard, David. *The HP Way: How Bill Hewlett and I Built Our Company.* Edited by David Kirby and Karen Lewis. Collins Business Essentials. New York: HarperCollins, 1995.

Paton, Bruce. *The Anatomy of Change: Department of Surgery, University of Colorado, 1950–2015.* Golden, CO: Fulcrum Publishing, 2015.

Paton, Bruce. *Lewis and Clark: Doctors to the Wilderness.* Golden, CO: Fulcrum Publishing, 2001.

Reisner, Marc. *Cadillac Desert: The American West and Its Disappearing Water.* New York: Viking, 1986.

Scott, Doug. *The Enduring Wilderness.* Golden, CO: Fulcrum Publishing, 2004.

Scott, Doug. *Our Wilderness: America's Common Ground.* Golden, CO: Fulcrum Publishing, 2014.

Sullivan, Mark. *Our Times* (6 vols.). New York: Scribner's, 1926–1935.

Turner, Frederick Jackson. *The Frontier in American History.* New York: Holt, Rinehart and Winston, 1920.

Udall, Stewart L. *The National Parks of America.* New York: Putnam, 1966.

Wallace, James, and Jim Erickson. *Hard Drive: Bill Gates and the Making of the Microsoft Empire.* New York: Wiley, 1992.

Webb, Walter Prescott. *The Great Frontier.* Austin: University of Texas Press, 1964.

Williams, Terry Tempest. *Refuge: An Unnatural History of Family and Place.* New York: Pantheon Books, 1991.

Chapter 11. The West in Fact and Fiction

Abbey, Edward. *The Monkey Wrench Gang.* Philadelphia: Lippincott, 1975.

Anderson, Nancy K., and Linda S. Ferber. *Albert Bierstadt: Art & Enterprise.* New York: Hudson Hills Press in association with the Brooklyn Museum, 1990.

Athearn, Robert G. Foreword by Elliott West. *The Mythic West in Twentieth Century America.* Lawrence, KS: University Press of Kansas, 1986.

Berger, Thomas. *Little Big Man.* New York: Dial Press, 1964.

Borland, Hal. *High, Wide, and Lonesome.* Boston: G. K. Hall, 1984.

Bradford, Richard. *Red Sky at Morning.* Philadelphia: Lippincott, 1968.

Campbell, Joseph, and Bill D. Moyers. *The Power of Myth.* New York: Anchor Books, 1988.

Cather, Willa. *Death Comes for the Archbishop.* New York: A. A. Knopf, 1927.

Clark, Carol. *Thomas Moran: Watercolors of the American West: Text and Catalogue Raisonné*. Austin: University of Texas Press, 1980.

Clark, Walter Van Tilburg. *The Ox-Bow Incident*. New York: Random House, 1940.

Danneberg, Julie. *Women Artists of the West: Five Portraits in Creativity and Courage*. Golden, CO: Fulcrum Publishing, 2002.

Davidson, Levette Jay, and Prudence Bostwick, eds. *The Literature of the Rocky Mountain West, 1803–1903*. Caldwell, ID: Caxton Printers, 1939.

Etulain, Richard W., and Glenda Riley. *The Hollywood West: Lives of Film Legends Who Shaped It*. Notable Westerners. Golden, CO: Fulcrum Publishing. 2001.

Fisher, Vardis. *Mountain Man*. New York: Morrow, 1965.

Friesen, Steve. *Buffalo Bill: Scout, Showman, Visionary*. Golden, CO: Fulcrum Publishing, 2010.

Gehres, Eleanor M. *The Best American Novels of the Twentieth Century: Still Readable Today*. Golden, CO: Fulcrum Publishing, 2001.

Geoffrion, Alan. *Broken Trail*. Golden, CO: Fulcrum Publishing, 2006.

Grey, Zane. *Riders of the Purple Sage: A Novel*. New York: Harper Brothers, 1912.

Guterson, David. *Snow Falling on Cedars*. New York: Harcourt Brace, 1994.

Guthrie, A. B. *The Big Sky*. New York: William Sloane Associates, 1947.

Jackson, William Henry. *Time Exposure: The Autobiography of William Henry Jackson*. New York: G. P. Putnam's Sons, 1940.

James, William. *Smoky the Cowhorse*. New York: Scribner's, 1926.

Locke, Harvey, ed. *Yellowstone to Yukon: The Journey of Wildlife and Art*. Golden, CO: Fulcrum Publishing, 2012.

Lukas, John. "From Camelot to Abilene." *American Heritage* 32, no. 2 (February/March 1981): 52–57.

Malone, Michael, ed. *Historians and the American West*. Lincoln: University of Nebraska Press, 1983.

McMurtry, Larry. *Lonesome Dove*. New York: Simon & Schuster, 1985.

Muir, John. *Picturesque California and the Region West of the Rocky Mountains from Alaska to Mexico*. San Francisco: J. Dewing, 1888.

Nichols, John Treadwell. *The Milagro Beanfield War*. New York: Holt, Rinehart and Winston, 1974.

Paton, Dr. Bruce. *Wilderness and Art*. Golden, CO. Films by Fulcrum, 2017. DVD, 44.52 minutes.

Portis, Charles. *True Grit: A Novel*. New York: Simon & Schuster, 1968.

Saroyan, William, and Don Freeman. *The Human Comedy*. New York: Harcourt, Brace and Company, 1943.

Schaefer, Jack. *Shane*. Boston: Houghton Mifflin, 1949.

Shapiro, Michael Edward, and Peter H. Hassrick. *Frederic Remington: The Masterworks*. New York: Harry N. Abrams, 1988.

Stegner, Wallace Earle. *Angle of Repose*. Garden City, NY: Doubleday, 1971.

Steinbeck, John. *The Grapes of Wrath*. New York: Viking, 1939.

Tyler, Ron. *Prints of the West*. A Library of Congress Classic. Golden, CO: Fulcrum Publishing, 1994.

Tyler, Ron C., and Fred Erisman. *Visions of America: Pioneer Artists in a New Land*. London: Thames & Hudson, 1983.

Waters, Frank. *The Man Who Killed the Deer*. American Fiction Library. Chicago: Sage Books, 1942.

Wilder, Laura Ingalls, and Garth Williams. *Little House on the Prairie*. New York: HarperCollins, 1994.

Winship, George Parker, ed. and trans. *The Journey of Coronado, 1540–1542*. Introduction by Donald Cutter. Golden, CO: Fulcrum Publishing, 1990.

Wister, Owen. *The Virginian*. New York: Macmillan, 1902.

Chapter 12. The American West

Baron, Robert C. *High Technology and America in the Twenty-First Century*. Concord, MA: Meeting of Latin American Fulbright Scholars, 1988.

Gardner, John W. *Self-Renewal: The Individual and the Innovative Society*. New York: Harper & Row, 1965.

McCarthy, Eugene J. *America Revisited: 150 Years after Tocqueville*. Garden City, NY: Doubleday, 1978.

Platt, Corinne, and Meredith Ogilby. *Voices of the American West*. Golden, CO: Fulcrum Publishing, 2009.

Index

About the Authors

Robert C. Baron was program manager for the onboard computers that flew on *Mariner 2* (Venus) and *Mariner 4* (Mars), and founder and president of Prime Computer. He then founded Fulcrum, a book publishing company that has published about 1,000 titles. He is the author or contributor to twenty-five books, including *Pioneers and Plodders: The American Entrepreneurial Spirit*. Baron was chair of the American Antiquarian Society for ten years, and is a fellow of the Massachusetts Historical Society. He organized a John Adams and Thomas Jefferson conference in Boston and Charlottesville. Baron started the International League of Conservation Writers, and produced *Conversations on Conservation* as well as *Wilderness in America*, a film about America's relationship to the land during the past four centuries.

Elizabeth Darby is an award-winning international journalist, editor, and author of several books on conservation, public lands, and memoir. She is a former correspondent for *Newsweek*, for whom she opened the Rocky Mountain Bureau in the 1980s, and was subsequently managing editor of *Buzzworm: The Environmental Journal*. Darby covered regional, national, and international issues of environment, conservation, and politics. A third-generation native of Colorado, her family arrived in the 1880s seeking the dreams of the open spaces of the West; her latest project is a memoir of her great-grandmother's voyage to the state in 1882 entitled *Return Voyage*.

Page Lambert has been writing about the western landscape and leading nature retreats in the West for twenty years. A founding member of Women Writing the West and author of the memoir *In Search of Kinship: Modern Pioneering on the Western Landscape*, Lambert's widely anthologized writing is found inside monumental sculptures at the Denver Art Museum, online at the *Huffington Post*, and inside the pages of *Sojourns*, official publication of the Peaks, Plateaus and Canyons Association. She writes the award-winning blog *All Things Literary/All Things Natural*, and teaches graduate classes for the University of Denver.

Dr. Bruce Paton, born in India and educated in Scotland, served in World War II as a lieutenant in the 41st Royal Marine Commando. A retired cardiac surgeon and wilderness medicine expert, he has accomplished expeditions as a trip doctor to Alaska, South America, Africa, and Nepal. He is the author of *Lewis and Clark: Doctors in the Wilderness, Adventuring with Boldness: The Triumph of the Explorers,* and *The Anatomy of Change: Department of Surgery, University of Colorado, 1950–2015.*

Daniel Wildcat is the director of the American Indian Studies Program and the Haskell Environmental Research Studies Center at Haskell Indian Nations University in Lawrence, Kansas. He is the author of *Red Alert: Saving the Planet with Indigenous Knowledge* and co-author of *Power and Place: Indian Education in America* and *Destroying Dogma: Vine Deloria Jr. and His Influence on American Society.*

Donald A. Yale practiced as a certified public accountant for eighteen years before leading a retail jewelry store resulting in its sale to Berkshire Hathaway. After a lifetime of professional, civic, and charitable involvement, he currently serves on the Executive Steering Committee of the Council for Western History and Genealogy at the Denver Public Library and as a trustee of the Friends Foundation for the Denver Public Library. He is also a board member of I. M. Education, whose mission is to teach critical thinking, writing skills, and civic education.